THE
GARDENER'S
GUIDE
TO BRITAIN

THE
GARDENER'S
GUIDE
TO BRITAIN

PATRICK TAYLOR

PAVILION

First published 1992 by
PAVILION BOOKS LIMITED
196 Shaftesbury Avenue, London WC2H 8JL

This book was produced by
Open Books Publishing Ltd, Beaumont House,
Wells BA5 2LD, Somerset, UK

Designer: Andrew Barron

Maps: John Gilkes

Computer Consultant: Mike Mepham

A CIP catalogue record for this book is available
from the British Library

ISBN: 1 85145 739 9

Printed and Bound in Hong Kong
produced by Mandarin Offset

CONTENTS

——— ❦ ———

Dedication

For Laura, with much love

INTRODUCTION &
ACKNOWLEDGEMENTS

The Gardener's Guide to Britain makes the
assumption that gardeners visiting unfamiliar parts of
the country are interested in nurseries, botanic
gardens and arboreta as well as outstanding gardens.
The book is arranged by region and within that
alphabetically. Each section is preceded by a map
showing the location of the places. If you know the
name of a garden but are not sure where it is, the
index will help you to find it. If you are interested in
a particular type of garden – say one with especially
good borders – there is an appendix which groups
gardens in this way. There are also lists of gardens
under the name of their designers; of kinds of plants
(e.g. Alpines) with the names of nurseries which have
particularly good collections; and of National
Collections of groups of plants.

The purpose of this book is to provide a guide
that will direct gardeners to the best places of interest
in each area. It reflects the taste of the author, and
the viewpoint is mine alone, but major places that
open for more than a handful of occasions during the
year have all been listed and described. It is certainly
not the intention of this book to wag fingers and lay
down criteria. There is no attempt to grade gardens
according to some invidious scale of excellence. The
point is to try and show what their distinctive virtues
are and to explain why they are worth visiting.

Opening times, and other practical details, are given and have been checked to the last possible moment. However, these, like all human arrangements, are subject to last minute changes and if you are setting out on a long journey to visit some particular garden or nursery, it is worth checking opening times by phone. This is especially true of the smaller nurseries whose owners are sometimes absent attending shows. It should also be remembered that most gardens will admit visitors to about one hour before closing time. I mention if a house is open as well as the garden but opening times very often differ. Dates shown are inclusive – Apr to Sept means from the 1st of April to the 30th of September.

Only those gardens that open regularly are included. I have not listed gardens such as those that open for only one or two days a year in aid of the National Gardens Scheme. These are shown in the admirable 'Yellow Book' (*Gardens of England and Wales Open to the Public*) which is published annually. Nursery gardens that open by appointment only are not included. Since some of the privately owned gardens allow groups to make special visits outside normal visiting hours, I give the name of the owner and the full postal address of each place.

I should like to thank The National Trust, and The National Trust for Scotland, both of which have given me much help. Many private owners have given me access – and cups of coffee – at odd hours and I am extremely grateful to them. My wife Caroline has once again edited my text with great skill and patience, and my daughter Annabel did some valuable research on opening details: I am most grateful to them both. Michael Walter very generously gave me a great deal of precious advice about computer systems for which I thank him most warmly. It has been a particular pleasure to work with the designer, Andrew Barron, who took so much trouble with the layout.

All the photographs were taken by myself.

Patrick Taylor
Wells, Somerset

SOUTH-EAST ENGLAND

——— ❧ ———

Kent, London, Surrey, Sussex

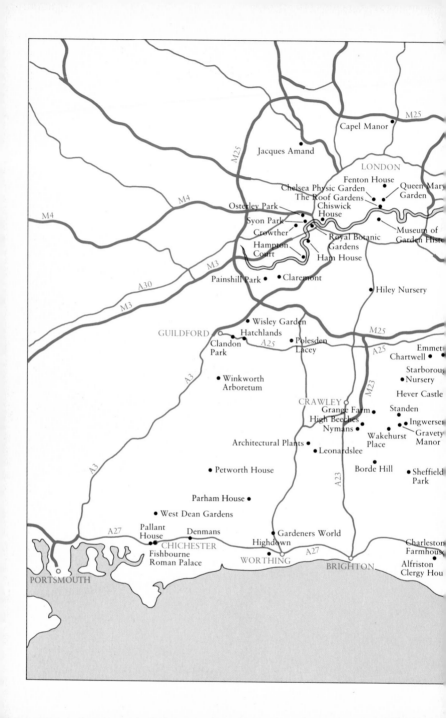

ALFRISTON CLERGY HOUSE
East Sussex

The Tye, Alfriston,
Polegate BN26 5TL
4m NE of Seaford by
B2108
Tel: 0323 870001

Owner:
The National Trust

Open: Apr to Oct, daily
11-6 or sunset if earlier. 1/2
acre. House open

ALTHOUGH THE garden surrounding the beautiful medieval hall house is quite small it has all sorts of virtues and many ideas for owners of small gardens. It has a wide range of different styles – from brick-edged borders of cottage-garden exuberance to a charmingly austere parterre of standard box trees clipped into umbrellas underplanted with pinks. A herb garden has square beds with low hedges of santolina and there is a proper kitchen garden. A trickling stream runs along one side of the garden and beyond there are views of the countryside and the downs.

JACQUES AMAND LTD
Middlesex

The Nurseries, 145 Clamp
Hill, Stanmore HA7 3JS
NW of London off the
Uxbridge Road (A410)
Tel: 081 954 8138

Open: Mon to Fri 9–5,
Sat 9–1, Sun 9–1.30

JACQUES AMAND specialises in bulbs of which he sells one of the best selections in the country, and regularly wins medals at R.H.S. shows and elsewhere. Although he also carries a few shrubs such as dwarf rhododendrons and lace-cap hydrangeas and some herbaceous perennials, especially those that are suitable for woodland gardens like *Jeffersonia diphylla* and *Mertensia virginica*, it is the bulbs that are the great glory of

Illustration: Erythronium
'*White Beauty*'

the place – very many fritillaries, narcissi, alliums and lilies are stocked, and less usual plants such as trilliums of which an exceptional range is listed. Well illustrated catalogues are produced in spring and autumn, full of useful advice on cultivation, from which orders by post may be made.

ARCHITECTURAL PLANTS

West Sussex

Cooks Farm, Nuthurst,
Horsham RH13 6LH
2m S of Horsham by A281
and minor roads
Tel: 0403 891772

Open: Mon to Sat 9–5 but
phone before to make sure

ARCHITECTURAL PLANTS has a completely distinctive house style. It sells plants that have strong architectural shapes and contribute to the structure of the garden. Angus White, the founder, described his garden in winter as being as fascinating to look at as 'a wet breeze block'; he wanted to find exotic, preferably evergreen plants to give winter liveliness. This nursery is his answer. His elegantly produced list is colour coded – green means that a plant is perfectly hardy, orange that a plant will survive in the right site in the southern counties, and red that a plant will survive only on the Atlantic coast or the privileged islands. The list is full of rarities – like Himalayan box (*Buxus wallichiana*) or the Mexican strawberry tree (*Arbutus glandulosa*) – and packed with information. A mail order service is provided but it is much better to go to Cooks Farm and see the exotics in splendid action.

BATEMAN'S
East Sussex

Burwash,
Etchingham TN19 7DS
1/2 m S of Burwash by
A265
Tel: 0435 882302

Owner:
The National Trust

Open: Apr to Oct, daily
except Thur and Fri (open
Good Fri) 11–5.30. 10
acres. House open

RUDYARD KIPLING lived here, in the handsome early 17th-century house, from 1902 to 1936 and himself designed many of the existing features of the elegant garden. The site is flat but it is animated by attractive decorative ingredients and a strongly designed layout. Above the house a beautiful tunnel of pears and clematis trained over broad arches is underplanted with bergenias, spring bulbs, geraniums and Corsican hellebores. A path leads down one side of the house and occasional 'windows' cut in a yew hedge give glimpses of the country beyond. In the formal garden a curved seat in a bower of clipped yew overlooks a long rectangular pool. At the end of the pool there is a rose garden with flagged paths and beds of floribunda roses, and to one side of it a shady double pleached lime walk.

BEDGEBURY NATIONAL PINETUM
Kent

nr Goudhurst,
Kent TN17 2SL
4 1/2 m S of Goudhurst by
B2079
Tel: 0580 211044

Owner: The Forestry
Commission

Open: Daily 10–dusk. 160
acres

BEDGEBURY PINETUM lies in a splendid site in a broad and deep valley. An ornamental lake at the bottom provides the right conditions for moisture-loving plants such as swamp cypresses, of which there are some handsome specimens and on the slopes of the valley conifers are grouped either by kind – spruces, junipers, cypresses and so on – or by place of origin – the Chinese glade, the American glade or the Japanese glade. Conifers are obviously the main meal here but the menu is varied with some deciduous trees and many rhododendrons. The appearance of evergreens varies subtly through the growing year – the changing colour of foliage and fruit – and a visit is rewarding in any season. At the visitors' centre there is a marvellous display of different cones. Bedgebury holds National Collections of junipers and of Lawson cypresses. In the autumn an added interest is the outstanding range of mushrooms that flourishes here.

BORDE HILL
West Sussex

Haywards Heath
RH16 1XP
1 1/2m N of Haywards
Heath by minor roads
Tel: 0444 450326

Owner: Borde Hill
Gardens Ltd

Open: 28 Mar to 25 Oct,
daily 10–6. 300 acres

Borde hill is famous for trees and shrubs but near the house there are handsome flower gardens and formal planting: a pair of ebullient borders leading towards the house and, on the west terrace, a mysterious marble statue of a veiled lady emerging from clumps of euphorbia. That is all very decorative but the serious matter at Borde Hill is the splendid collection of ornamental woody plants. It was started in 1892 by Colonel Stephenson Clark who was one of the financers of the great plant-hunting expeditions to the Chinese Himalayas between the wars. Thus, the garden is wonderfully rich in magnolias and rhododendrons (particularly species) which relish the light, slightly acid soil. But the collection is wide-ranging and there are also very good conifers in Warren Wood and rare deciduous trees, particularly American species, in Little Bentley Wood. The site is agreeably undulating and this is one of the most attractive places in which to see some marvellous plants.

BRICKWALL HOUSE
East Sussex

Northiam, Rye TN31 6NL
11m N of Hastings by the
A28
Tel: 0797 252494

Owner: Frewen
Educational Trust

Open: Apr to Sept, Sat and
Bank Hol 2–5. 1 1/2 acres.
House open

THE VERY FINE brick house is Jacobean with many later additions and the garden has some of the formal character of the 17th century. Its chief attraction is a modern one – a splendid giant game of chess made of topiary yew (common and golden, to distinguish the sides) designed by William Mount and made since 1981. The pieces are set in squares of contrasting black and white gravel, in a setting of old clipped yews. An avenue of tall pyramids of yew leads towards the house with, on the left, a decorative screen of clipped beech.

CAPEL MANOR
Middlesex

Bullsmoor Lane,
Enfield EN1 4RQ
14m N of Central London
by A10. Off M25 by
Jnct 25
Tel: 0992 763849

Owner: London Borough
of Enfield

Open: Apr to Oct, daily
10–4.30 (5.30 weekends);
Nov to Mar, Mon to Sat
10–4.30. 30 acres

DISPLAY GARDENS such as this can be both entertaining and instructive. On this substantial site surrounding the 18th-century manor house are many different thematic and demonstration gardens. A series of historical gardens includes a Tudor-style knot, a formal 17th-century garden and a recently planted prickly maze of holly taken from William Nesfield's design for the great exhibition in 1851. A garden for the physically disabled is full of ideas and a 'Sensory Garden' rich with the scent of herbs and the sounds of water is designed for the visually impaired. Demonstration gardens – woodland, water and courtyard – give ideas for design and planting. The magazine 'Gardening from Which?' has sponsored a trial garden and the National Gardening Centre has a permanent exhibition of horticultural equipment. This is a satisfying mixture of both useful practical information and inspiration.

CHARLESTON FARMHOUSE
East Sussex

nr Firle, Lewes BN8 6LL
6m E of Lewes by A27
Tel: 0323 811265

Owner:
The Charleston Trust

Open: Apr to Oct, Wed, Thur, Sun and Bank Hol 2–6. 1 acre. House open

CHARLESTON FARMHOUSE may fairly be described as the country seat of the Bloomsbury set. Vanessa and Clive Bell lived here, and later Duncan Grant, and the whole place, now most sympathetically restored, is full of their atmosphere. The 17th-century house has a south-facing garden walled in brick and flint. Gravel paths and narrow borders run round the walls and the planting is cheerfully colourful – the horticultural equivalent of Omega workshop textiles. Old apple trees erupt from borders and a long box hedge has been clipped into undulating waves, echoing the smooth surface of the downs that rise above the house. Everywhere there are decorative touches – a pottery mask overlooking a little pool, mosaics of broken china (Bloomsbury and older) on a terrace, amusing busts dotted along a wall. Outside the walled garden, by a wild orchard, Ophelia floats on the edge of a pool and Venus lurks in a grove of cow parsley. All this gives a vivid picture of one of the most attractive aspects of Bloomsbury life.

CHARTWELL
Kent

Westerham TN16 1PS
2m S of Westerham by
A2026
Tel: 0732 866368

Owner:
The National Trust

Open: Apr to Oct, Tue,
Wed and Thur 12–5.30,
Sat, Sun and Bank Hol
11–5.30. 22 acres. House
open

SIR WINSTON CHURCHILL went to live at Chartwell in 1924 and the place is still full of his character. The house lies on one side of a gentle valley with good views down to a lake. By the house a formal rose garden is enclosed by a brick wall built by Sir Winston in his brick-laying days, with flagged paths and beds of Hybrid Tea roses. Terraces look down over lawns towards a vine-covered pergola leading to an elegant corner pavilion. Farther along the slope is Churchill's garden studio, still set up with easels and paints, and hung with his paintings. In an old walled kitchen garden a rose walk was planted with golden roses to celebrate Sir Winston and Lady Churchill's golden wedding in 1953.

CHELSEA PHYSIC GARDEN
London

66 Royal Hospital Road,
SW3 4HS
Tube: Sloane Square
Tel: 071 352 5646

Owner: Trustees of Chelsea
Physic Garden

Open: 25 Mar to 21 Oct,
Sun and Wed 2–5; also
during Chelsea Flower
Show week. 4 acres

WHEN ONE HAS got over the astonishment of finding a 4-acre walled garden – with full Secret Garden character – in the middle of London there is still plenty to marvel at. It was founded as a garden of medicinal herbs in 1673 and, especially under the directorship of Philip Miller in the 18th century, became an important botanic garden. That tradition is continued with a large collection of herbs, a range of 'order' beds – containing plants grouped by

botanic families – and a research area. But there are magnificent trees – a superb *Koelreuteria paniculata*, gnarled like an oak and probably the biggest in Britain, a splendid olive tree (which in fine years produces big crops) and all sorts of other tender things relishing the protection of the old walls. There is a fern house and an excellent range of hothouses. The garden holds the National Collection of cistus and has some good plants for sale. It is also the home of a well-attended gardening school.

CHILHAM CASTLE
Kent

Chilham, nr Canterbury
CT4 8DB
6m SW of Canterbury off
A28
Tel: 0227 730319

Owner: Viscount
Massereene and Ferrard

Open: 12 Apr to 18 Oct,
daily 11–5. 25 acres. Castle
open for guided tours only

A RED-BRICK JACOBEAN house took the place of the stone and flint medieval castle on this fine site on the chalk downs with views of the river Stour. It was built by Sir Dudley Digges for whom John Tradescant the Elder almost certainly laid out the terraces which still form part of the garden, and ancient trees, sweet chestnuts and a holm oak could date from this time. The walls of the house are decorated with climbing plants and below them are disposed formal gardens – an enclosed box parterre with a central pool, a rose garden and old yew topiary. To one side lawns give way to a ha-ha, beyond which lies the park and lake designed by 'Capability' Brown in 1777.

CHILSTONE GARDEN ORNAMENTS
Kent

Sprivers Estate,
Lamberhurst Road,
Horsmonden TN12 8DR
On the southern edge of
Horsmonden village
Tel: 0892 723553

Open: Daily except Sat 10–5

Illustration opposite:
Chilstone Roman bust

CHILSTONE, founded in 1957, make high-quality composition stone garden ornaments and architectural pieces. Many are meticulous copies of fine originals. At Sprivers, an elegant mid-18th-century house, urns, statues and temples may be seen effectively displayed in the context of yew hedges, distant vistas and herbaceous borders. In the display garden to one side a large selection from their stock is arranged in lovely profusion – colonnades, sprinkling fountains, impassive sphinxes, stately urns and the busts of emperors.

CHISWICK HOUSE
London

Burlington Lane, Chiswick
W4 2RP
4m SW of Central London
by A4 and A316
Tel: 081 995 0508

Owner: English Heritage

Open: Daily dawn–dusk.
62 acres. House open

LORD BURLINGTON built Chiswick House in 1723-9 as a pleasure dome and surrounded it with appropriate gardens. The house itself, domed and portico'd, dominates the formal garden with its avenue of cypresses interspersed with grand urns. To one side, slightly hidden, a circular sunken pool is surrounded by orange trees in pots and overlooked by a temple. At a little distance from the house a Victorian garden has a dazzling conservatory and a parterre of arabesques of clipped box, lush bedding schemes and an avenue of mop-headed acacias.

CHURCH HILL COTTAGE GARDENS
Kent

Charing Heath, Ashford
TN27 0BU
8m NW of Ashford by A20
Tel: 0233 712522

Open: Feb, Jun to Nov,
Wed to Sun (closed Bank
Hol Sun)10–5; Mar to
May, daily 10–5

AN ATTRACTIVE development in recent years is that of the small nursery alongside the owners' private garden where the plants can be seen in cultivation. The nursery here specialises in herbaceous perennials with excellent collections of penstemons, named varieties of pinks, herbaceous sages, unusual verbenas and violas. The garden next door to the nursery permits the distinctive virtues of these and other plants to be seen and savoured. A winding stream allows waterside plants, and herbaceous beds are given an occasional note of emphasis by some well-placed ornamental tree – a golden acacia or a variegated maple, for example. An immense number of plants is grown, some of them very unfamiliar.

CLANDON PARK
Surrey

West Clandon GU4 7RQ
3m E of Guildford off A25
Tel: 0483 222482

Owner:
The National Trust

Open: Apr to Oct, daily
except Thur and Fri (open
Good Fri) 1.30–5.30; Bank
Hol and preceding Sun
11–5.30. 8 acres.

THE MANSION at Clandon Park, built of brick and stone in about 1730, dominates the garden. Under its south façade a neat parterre of box hedges, clipped box cones and summer bedding is flanked by raised hedges of clipped hornbeam. Across the lawn, a damp and ferny flint grotto houses a cluster of shivering nymphs, almost certainly dating from the late 18th-century landscaping of the garden. To one side of this, in the shade of an immense oak, there is a charming oddity, a carved and painted Maori house brought here in the 1890s by the 4th Earl of Onslow who had served as Governor of New Zealand.

Half-way up the drive, rather tucked away and easy to miss, is a Dutch garden enclosed in tall yew hedges and laid out in a geometric pattern of hedges of box, lavender and variegated euonymus, above which rise pyramids of white roses.

CLAREMONT LANDSCAPE GARDEN

Surrey

Portsmouth Road, Esher
KT10 9JG
14m SW of Central London
by A3
Tel: None

Owner:
The National Trust

Open: Apr to Oct, daily
9–7 (15–19 Jul closes 4);
Nov to March, daily 9–5
or sunset if earlier (closed
25 Dec, 1 Jan). 49 acres

THE LANDSCAPE GARDEN at Claremont had virtually disappeared from view, drowned in a sea of rhododendrons and laurels, until the National Trust took it in hand in 1975. Some of the greatest figures in landscape design worked here from 1720 onwards – Sir John Vanbrugh, Charles Bridgeman, William Kent and 'Capability' Brown. What has now been restored is chiefly the work of the first three and what the visitor may see, never mind garden history, is an enchanting garden of woodland, beech alleys rising steeply uphill, a vast turf amphitheatre which looks down on a lake with an island temple designed by Kent, and beautiful stands of sweet chestnuts. This is not a garden for those who love only flower power but at summer weekends it fills with people picnicking and savouring the delights of this Elysian oasis threatened on all sides by suburbia.

COGHURST NURSERY
East Sussex

Ivy House Lane, nr Three
Oaks, Hastings TN35 4NP
3 1/2m NE of Hastings by
A259 and minor roads
Tel: 0424 437657

Open: Mon to Fri 2–4.30;
Sun 10–4.30

CAMELLIAS ARE the main thing at Coghurst and they have one of the best collections in the country, including many that are available commercially nowhere else. They have well over 300 varieties including a particularly choice range of cultivars of the autumn-flowering *C. sasanqua* and the tender *C. reticulata*. Despite the prominence of the camellia list Coghurst also sell a good range of rhododendrons, mostly cultivars but with a choice handful of species. Catalogues are issued and a postal service is provided for smaller specimens.

CROWTHER OF SYON LODGE
Middlesex

London Road, Isleworth
TW7 5BH
3 1/2m SW of central
London by A315
Tel: 081 560 7978

Open: Mon to Fri 9–5; Sat
to Sun 10.30–4.30 and at
other times by appointment

CROWTHER PIONEERED dealing in antique garden ornaments and architectural fragments and their premises at Syon Lodge are a treasure trove of wonderful things. Here, displayed in a crowded garden is a bewildering and constantly changing profusion of temples, seats, statues, urns and fountains. All are decorative and some are distinguished – and expensive – works of art. Many of them have grand provenances and are the sort of thing about which a new garden may be designed. There are very few places anywhere in the world where such a range of garden ornaments of this quality may be found for sale.

DENMANS
West Sussex

Fontwell,
nr Arundel BN18 0SU
4 1/2m E of Chichester on
A27
Tel: 0243 542808

Owner: Mrs J.H. Robinson

Open: Mid-Mar to
mid-Dec, daily 9–5.
3 1/2 acres

MRS ROBINSON came here in 1946 and started to make the unusual garden that visitors may see today. The entrance is through a huge glasshouse, once used to raise tomatoes commercially and now the home of a very large collection of tender plants. Gravel paths meander across a walled garden in which profuse herbaceous planting is given structure by huge clipped mounds of variegated box, a handsome strawberry tree and the bold foliage of rhus and rheum. Beyond, in the main garden, sweeping beds have mixed plantings and there is repeated use of yellow foliage, particularly of golden yew and *Robinia pseudoacacia* 'Frisia'. There are many unusual plants here, and an attractively bold sense of design. A small nursery sells some good plants, mostly herbaceous but with a carefully chosen selection of shrub roses. An excellent catalogue is produced but there is no mail order. The potential of most the plants may be seen displayed very effectively in the adjacent garden so a visit will be doubly rewarded.

EMMETTS GARDEN
Kent

Ide Hill,
Sevenoaks TN14 6AY
1 1/2m N of Ide Hill by
B2042
Tel: 073 275429

Owner:
The National Trust

Open: Apr to Oct, Wed to
Sun and Bank Hol 2–6. 6
acres

Illustration opposite:
Emmetts in the spring

THIS IS THE highest point in Kent and the garden has splendid views of the North Downs. Many of the best plants date from the sale of stock from Veitch's famous nursery in 1907 when Frederick Lubbock, a friend of William Robinson, lived here. He put into practice Robinson's idea of arranging hardy exotic plants in a naturalistic setting. A formal rose garden hedged in thuja, and a rock garden added by a later owner, are the only tamed parts of what is essentially an informal garden of wild character which merges almost imperceptibly with the surrounding woodland and scrub. The soil is acid and there are many azaleas, camellias, eucryphias rhododendrons, stewartias and other ericaceous plants. Excellent trees and shrubs are visible everywhere – *Kalmia latifolia*, magnolias, maples, dogwoods – and there are also real rarities, such as the charming fringe tree, *Chionanthus virginicus*. The slopes of the densely wooded valley are carpeted with bluebells. The two best seasons are spring for the profusion of flowering shrubs and bulbs, and autumn when there is a wonderful display of colour from azaleas, cercidiphyllums, maples and other deciduous trees and shrubs.

FENTON HOUSE
London

Windmill Hill,
Hampstead NW3 6RT
In Hampstead village.
Tube: Hampstead
Tel: 071 435 3471

Owner:
The National Trust

Open: Mar, Sat and Sun
2–6; Apr to Oct, Sat, Sun
and Bank Hol 11–6, Mon,
Tue and Wed 1–7. 1 acre.
House open

A COMPLETE COUNTRY garden in the middle of Hampstead village reminds the visitor of the former rural character of this part of London. Fenton House, a suave Georgian house of brick, looks out over a formal garden in which a gravel path is edged with standard-trained Portugal laurels in tubs, and borders are given formality with rhythmic plantings of clipped lavender or Irish yews. At the far end, yew hedges conceal hidden borders and elegant benches. At a lower level, parallel to this, an orchard bursts into life in spring, with fruit blossom and many bulbs naturalised in the long grass – anemones, narcissi and snake's head fritillaries.

FISHBOURNE ROMAN PALACE GARDEN
West Sussex

Salthill Road,
Fishbourne PO19 3QR
1 1/2m W of Chichester by
A259
Tel: 0243 785859

Owner: Sussex
Archaeological Society

Open: Mar, Apr, Oct, daily
10–5; May to Sept, daily
10–6; Nov, daily 10–4; Dec
to Feb, Sun 10–4. 2 acres

THIS IS AN unusual attempt to show what an aristocratic Roman garden would have looked like, using information from a careful archaeological examination of the site, together with background knowledge of Roman gardening practice. The garden was originally entirely surrounded by a verandah with a colonnade; in this area a low box hedge is shaped into a geometric pattern and some of the characteristic Roman plants (such as acanthus) are used. The original irrigation system – which also supplied water for fountains – has been excavated. In the adjoining museum are mosaics of exquisite beauty and a detailed model of the palace and the garden, showing how it appeared in its original state.

GARDENERS WORLD AND ENGLISH WATER GARDENS
West Sussex

London Road,
Washington RH20 3BL
6m N of Worthing by A24
Tel: 0903 892006

Open: Daily 9–5.30

THIS NURSERY describes itself as 'a real garden centre for plantsmen' which may certainly be true but does not do justice to this extraordinary place. The thing for which it is remarkable is mature trees of many kinds at prices that may take your breath away. Not everything is in stock but the nursery can often track down a mature specimen to order. Its other speciality is everything to do with water gardens – plants, ponds and equipment. There is a list of plants from which orders are sent by mail.

GRANGE FARM
West Sussex

Turners Hill Road,
Crawley Down RH10 4EY
On the southern edge of
the village of Crawley
Down, 5m E of Crawley by
A264 and B2028
Tel: 0342 71493

Open: Mon to Fri 2–6, Sat
and Sun 10–6

MOST GARDEN POTS are mass produced to fairly commonplace designs but Grange Farm sells a unique range of hand-made Cretan pots in many different designs and sizes. They are fired at a very high temperature and are therefore frost-proof. The great attraction is their beautiful patina and the liveliness of their design and decoration, with patterns that are either incised or applied in delicate ribbons of clay. These are the kind of pots that, without being in the slightest pretentious, can have tremendous presence in a garden. A well illustrated catalogue is produced but there is no mail order. However the place is an attractive one to visit – a real farm with the whiff of the farmyard and the clucking of chickens.

GRAVETYE MANOR
West Sussex

nr East Grinstead
RH19 4LJ
4m SW of East Grinstead
by B2110
Tel: 0342 810567

Owner: Peter Herbert

Open: Tue and Fri 10–5;
private garden by house,
for visitors not using the
hotel or restaurant, on Fri
by appointment only. 20
acres

THIS WAS the house and garden of William Robinson, the greatest and most influential of late-Victorian gardeners. Thanks to a brilliant restoration carried out by the present owner, visitors may now see a properly Robinsonian garden in all its splendour. The gabled 17th-century manor house, now an unashamedly comfortable hotel with one of the best restaurants in England, looks south across a valley. South and west of the house are formal gardens with many of the plants that Robinson loved. On the northern wooded slopes things become wilder, with azaleas, camellias and magnolias planted among the trees. South of the house, sweeping down to a lake made by Robinson, is a meadow dazzling in spring with naturalised bulbs where in summer the grass is allowed to grow long. Although in a densely populated part of England, Gravetye is at the heart of a large Forestry Commission wood and has preserved to a remarkable degree the authentically wild atmosphere that Robinson cherished.

GREAT COMP
Kent

nr Borough Green
TN15 8QS
7m E of Sevenoaks off A25
Tel: 0732 882669

Owner: Great Comp
Charitable Trust

Open: Apr to Oct, daily
11–6. 7 acres

THERE IS something enticing about the design of the garden at Great Comp – paths lead the visitor on, curving out of sight round bold plantings. The atmosphere is essentially informal, an impression which is only sharpened by the occasional straight line and touch of formality. Against a background of old deciduous woodland a very wide range of ornamental trees and shrubs relishes the acid loam. Spreading out south of the house a generous apron of impeccable lawn is fringed with tall conifers, oaks and willows and, as it reaches the woodland, bordered with beds of heathers. Paths lead off into the wilder woodland (and a temple lost in the woods) and thence back towards the house. Everywhere there are excellent trees and shrubs set off by well chosen underplanting – the larger campanulas, geraniums, hostas, lilies, and violas. This is not a garden which depends on superficial fripperies – but capitalises on the very skilful use of carefully chosen ornaments and plants; and, although very densely planted, it has managed to preserve a air of spacious repose.

GREAT DIXTER
East Sussex

Northiam, Rye TN31 6PH
11m N of Hastings off A28
Tel: 0797 43160

Owner: Quentin Lloyd

Open: Apr to mid-Oct,
daily except Mon 2–5.
House open

THE DISTINGUISHED gardener-writer Christopher Lloyd is the genius of this place, with its timbered 15th-century house restored by Edwin Lutyens who also planned the garden upon which Mr Lloyd has put his lively stamp. Billowing yew topiary dates from Lutyens's time but most of the planting is of more recent date. Here is Christopher Lloyd's virtuoso mixed border which he constantly improves; sheets of spring flowers in the orchard; a meadow garden; and, wherever you look, fastidiously chosen plants of all kinds. No gardener could visit Great Dixter without making discoveries and rekindling the zest for gardening. There are good plants for sale, especially clematis, of which there is a catalogue and they are sold by mail order.

HAM HOUSE
Surrey

Ham, Richmond
TW10 7RS
Off A307 at Petersham,
SW of Central London
Tel: 081 940 1950

Owner:
The National Trust

Open: Daily except Mon
(open bank Hol) 10.30–6 or
dusk if earlier. 18 acres.
House open (but closed
1992/3 for major
restoration)

THE EARLY 17th-century brick house was modernised in the smartest taste in the 1670s by the Duke and Duchess of Lauderdale who took as much interest in the garden as they did in the house. The garden decayed until in 1976 work was started by the National Trust on its restoration. This was helped by the survival of late 17th-century documentation – plans and plant lists – which enabled an authentic reconstruction. The formal walled garden south of the house is divided into spacious grass plats with a maze-like wilderness of hornbeam, winding paths and hidden pavilions. To one side a further walled garden has a large orangery (now a tea-room) with, sprawling in front of it, a vast *Paliurus spina-christi*, the thorned tree from which Christ's crown of thorns was supposed to have been made. In the east court on the other side of the house a parterre of gravel paths and box hedges is arranged in racy lozenges of lavender and santolina and overlooked by shady tunnels of yew and pleached hornbeam.

HAMPTON COURT

Surrey

East Molesey KT8 9AU
At Hampton Wick where
A308 and A309 meet,
6m SW of Central London
Tel: 081 977 8441

Owner: Historic Royal
Palaces

Open: Daily, dawn–dusk.
30 acres. Palace open

THIS IS ONE of the most famous places in England and has much to interest the gardener. It was started by Thomas Wolsey in the early 16th century and became a royal palace, which it remains. In the late 17th century Sir Christopher Wren added grandiose extensions to the Tudor palace and was involved in the design of a new garden of which part of his 'wilderness' survives, a maddening maze of yew and the earliest known hedge maze in England. South of the palace the original royal privy garden, now a 19th-century shrubbery, has views of the Thames through Jean Tijou's exquisite late 17th-century wrought-iron screen. Nearer the palace there is a colourful sunken pond garden and a reconstructed Tudor knot. In the vinery is a 'Black Hamburgh' grape-vine planted in 1796 and still productive. To the east of the palace old topiary of yew and holly rise above spring and summer bedding schemes, and three grandiose lime avenues radiate from a semi-circle of clipped yew and holly.

HATCHLANDS

Surrey

East Clandon, Guildford
GU4 7RT
3m E of Guildford by A25
and A246
Tel: 0483 222787

Owner:
The National Trust

Open: Apr to Oct, Tue,
Wed, Thur, Sun and Bank
Hol 2–5.30; Aug, also Sat
2–5.30. 12 acres. House
open

THE GARDEN at Hatchlands is undergoing restoration but it is worth a visit to see how work of this sort is carried out. South of the brick 18th-century mansion a formal garden of geometric box-edged beds is being modified to take into account Gertrude Jekyll's suggestions, and to the west a fussy Victorian parterre is being changed to resemble Humphry Repton's early 19th-century design. The park, with its decorative pillared temple, was also designed by Repton and that, too, is to be restored.

HAZELDENE NURSERY

Kent

Dean Street, East Farleigh,
Maidstone ME15 0PS
3m SW of Maidstone by
B2010
Tel: 0622 726248

Open: Mar to Sept, daily
except Mon 10–3; rest of
year by appointment

Illustration: Viola
'Princesse de Galles'

PANSIES AND VIOLAS are the speciality of this nursery which has won Gold Medals at Chelsea for its excellent plants. An immense range is sold of winter- and summer-flowering pansies, violas, violettas and species violets. Many varieties are propagated by cuttings to preserve their identity. A particularly informative list is produced, with valuable information on cultivation, and a mail order service is provided both for growing plants and for seeds of those varieties that come true from seed.

HEVER CASTLE

Kent

nr Edenbridge TN8 7NG
3m SE of Edenbridge by
minor roads
Tel: 0732 865224

Owner: Broadland
Properties Ltd

Open: Mid-Mar to
beginning Nov, daily 11–6.
50 acres. Castle open

HEVER HAS everything a castle should have – a romantic moat, whimsical topiary, an infuriating maze and a garden full of all sorts of interesting things. The setting of old woodland is very fine and in spring there are some excellent rhododendrons and azaleas. The enormous Italian garden was designed chiefly to show off the collection of classical statuary collected by William Waldorf Astor who bought the estate in 1903 and made the garden as it is today. Much of the statuary is artfully arranged in enclosures running along the Pompeian Wall which is planted to great decorative effect. Facing it, on the shady north-facing side, is an immense pergola draped with vines, clematis and roses and behind which there is a series of grotto-like niches, dripping with water, where ferns, hostas and other moisture-loving plants thrive. Much of the garden is flamboyantly grand – like the swashbuckling Italianate loggia with fountains and naked nymphs overlooking the lake – but there are more intimate moments and much attractive planting.

The High Beeches

West Sussex

Handcross RH17 6HQ
1m E of Handcross off
B2110
Tel: 0444 400589

Owner: The High Beeches
Gardens Conservation
Trust

Open: Easter Mon to Jun,
Sept to Oct, daily except
Wed and Sun 1–5, Bank
Hol 10–5. 20 acres

AFTER WALKING round this exquisite woodland garden it is hard to believe that it is only 20 acres in area. Winding paths, shifting views and the subtle lie of the gently undulating land give such a rich diversity of scenery. The High Beeches formerly belonged to the Loder family of Leonardslee and Wakehurst; the Hon. Edward and Mrs Boscawen came here in 1966 and have added immensely to it. Unlike some other fine collections of plants, the emphasis here is as much on the quality of the landscape as on the distinction of the planting. There are, of course, marvellous camellias, magnolias, maples and rhododendrons and many other groups of woody plants, including National Collections of pieris and stewartias. But there are many herbaceous plants – including splendid drifts of naturalised willow gentian, irises and primulas – and a 4-acre meadow, unploughed in living memory, which has 24 species of grass, cowslips and orchids.

35

HIGHDOWN
West Sussex

Littlehampton Road,
Goring-by-Sea BN12 6NY
3m W of Worthing by A259
Tel: 0903 48067

Owner: Worthing Borough
Council

Open: Mon to Fri 10–4.30,
Sat, Sun and Bank Hol
10–8. 5 acres

SIR FREDERICK STERN, who died in 1967, was a
banker whose passionate hobby was gardening.
He lived at Highdown and the making of the garden
here is vividly described in his book *A Chalk
Garden*, a 20th-century gardening classic. On his
death it was left to Worthing Borough Council and
there is still much to admire; the site is a steep,
south-facing slope and the layout is informal with
occasional formality such as the avenue of *Prunus
serrula*, with its glistening, peeling bark, at the
entrance. The garden is of particular interest to
gardeners who want to know more about the
splendours and miseries of gardening on chalk. Stern
was able to discover here exactly what flourished in
chalk; for example, maples from China and Europe
did very well but those from Japan and the U.S.A.
did not. Although the garden is particularly rich in
woody plants there are marvellous groups of
herbaceous perennials and bulbs – agapanthus,
anemones, hellebores, irises, narcissi and peonies.

HILEY NURSERY
Surrey

25 Little Woodcote Estate,
Wallington SM5 4AU
In central Wallington, off
Woodmansterne Lane
Tel: 081 647 9679

Open: Wed to Sat 9–5

Illustration: Bidens
ferulifolia

BRIAN HILEY specialises in rare perennials, some of them non-hardy, with some particularly good collections of penstemons, species and cultivars, and an exceptional list of sages. But throughout his list there are unusual and well chosen things, not all of them herbaceous. He sells the tender yellow *Bidens ferulifolia*, felicias, the creeping loosestrife *Lysimachia henryi*, several kinds of phygelius and four different species of polemonium. A catalogue is issued and there is a mail order service but plants are often propagated in numbers too small to allow them to be listed. Brian Hiley's own 1-acre garden next door, stuffed with excellent plants, is open once or twice a month and by appointment.

IDEN CROFT HERBS
Kent

Frittenden Road,
Staplehurst TN12 0DH
In the village of Staplehurst
8m S of Maidstone by
A229
Tel: 0580 891432

Open: May to Sept, Mon
to Sat 9–5, Sun 11–5; Oct
to Apr, daily except Sun
9–5

IDEN CROFT supplies culinary herbs on a massive scale to the catering trade and this is a full-scale working herb farm. There are also well planted herbaceous beds showing the decorative use of herbs in the garden, a garden specially designed for the blind, partially sighted or disabled – with plenty to feel and smell – and a walled garden that is gradually being restored and at present is planted with a sea of rosemary. Iden Croft holds a National Collection of thymes. The nursery department sells culinary herbs as well as a selection of other herbaceous perennials.

W.E.Th. INGWERSEN LTD
West Sussex

Birch Farm Nursery,
Gravetye,
East Grinstead RH19 4LE
2 1/2m SW of East
Grinstead by B2110 and
minor roads
Tel: 0342 810236

Open: Mar to Oct, daily
9–1, 1.30–4; Nov to Feb,
Mon to Fri 9–1, 1.30–4

ANYONE WHO HAS not heard of Ingwersen has probably not heard of alpine plants either. The late Will Ingwersen, who died in 1990, was one of the great plantsmen and nurserymen of his time. His sons carry on the business and here you will find 1,800 different plants for sale, with a strong alpine emphasis, all carefully chosen, grown to exemplary standards and often rare. The elegantly produced list has wonderful groups of plants – alliums, campanulas, dianthus, primulas, dwarf rhododendrons, an immense range of saxifrages, sempervivums and violas. Bulbs are listed separately and there is plenty of interest there, too, with excellent colchicums, crocuses, fritillaries, narcissi, and marvellous species tulips. By no means everything available is listed in the catalogue so although there is a mail order service, a personal visit is all the more worthwhile. The nursery presents a mouth-watering sight, with endless neat rows of plants. It is on sacred ground, too, for this was formerly part of William Robinson's Gravetye estate.

LEEDS CASTLE
Kent

nr Maidstone ME17 1PL
4m E of Maidstone by A20
and B2163. Jnct 8 of M20
Tel: 0622 765400

Owner: Leeds Castle
Foundation

Open: Mid-Mar to Oct,
daily 11–5; Nov to Mar,
Sat, Sun 11–4. 15 acres.
Castle open

DISTANT VIEWS of Leeds Castle are enchanting – the silvery 12th-century castle wildly romantic, apparently floating on its vast moat. The gardens are modern and there are two features of special interest. The Culpeper Garden, designed by Russell Page, is a series of box-edged beds overflowing with herbaceous plants underplanted among shrub roses. Farther from the castle a yew maze finished in 1988 was designed by Randall Cote and Adrian Fisher, its shape echoing the medieval architecture of the castle. The elusive goal at its centre is the entrance to an extraordinary grotto designed by Vernon Gibberd, lined with tufa and richly ornamented with statues, rare stones and shells, the cave-like gloom occasionally pierced by circular skylights.

LEONARDSLEE GARDENS

West Sussex

Lower Beeding,
nr Horsham RH13 6PP
5m SE of Horsham by
A281
Tel: 0403 891212

Owner: The Loder Family

Open: Mid-Apr to
mid-Jun, daily 10–6; Jul to
Sept, Sat, Sun 12–6; Oct,
Sat, Sun 10–5. 200 acres

SIR EDMUND LODER bought the estate of
Leonardslee in 1889 and started to make his great
woodland garden. It is a spectacular site, a steep
valley with a series of linked pools running along the
bottom. This is a superb place to grow ornamental
trees and shrubs. The soil is a slightly acid
moisture-retentive silt; the densely clothed sides of
the valley give protection from the wind and there is
excellent frost drainage. Rhododendrons were Sir
Edmund's first love and he raised the hybrid *R.*
'Loderi' which has produced some of the best garden
varieties. But there are also especially choice
collections of camellias and magnolias of which there
are some of the largest specimens in the country.
Large numbers of evergreens – wellingtonias,
Douglas firs, deodars and spruce – make a fine
background for the brilliant spring flowering and the
explosion of autumn colour. It is, I believe, the only
garden in Britain in which wallabies are used to keep
the grass in control.

MUSEUM OF GARDEN HISTORY
London

St-Mary-at-Lambeth,
Lambeth Palace Road,
SE1 7JU
Immediately S of Lambeth
Bridge
Tel: 071 261 1891

Owner: The Tradescant
Trust

Open: Mon to Fri 11–3,
Sun 10.30–5

JOHN TRADESCANT, father and son, were immensely influential gardeners and plant collectors in the 17th century and lived and died in Lambeth where a splendid gravestone commemorates them. In the disused church an excellent museum of garden history has been formed, containing a small permanent collection (including Gertrude Jekyll's desk) and housing temporary exhibitions from time to time. In the old churchyard a charming garden has been made with a knot of box hedges designed by the Marchioness of Salisbury and containing plants of a Tradescantian flavour.

NYMANS GARDEN
West Sussex

Handcross, nr Haywards
Heath RH17 6EB
7m NW of Haywards
Heath by A272 and B2114
Tel: 0444 400321

Owner:
The National Trust

Open: Apr to Oct, daily
except Mon and Fri (open
Bank Hol and Good Fri)
11–7 or sunset if earlier.
30 acres

THERE ARE FEW gardens anywhere in England where rare and beautiful plants are grown in such an attractive setting, in which formality and informality are subtly interwoven. Nymans was acquired by Leonard Messel in 1890 and he began introducing a wide range of plants. He made a woodland garden in which magnificent trees and flowering shrubs – particularly camellias, eucryphias, magnolias and rhododendrons – are seen to great advantage. One of the best hybrid eucryphias, *E.* x *nymansensis*, had its origins here. In an irregularly shaped walled garden Leonard Messel laid out a pair of spectacular herbaceous borders, whose design was influenced by William Robinson. These are wonderful today and in late summer their flowering season is prolonged by the subtle use of annuals. Surrounding the borders are choice ornamental trees, such as dogwoods, *Koelreuteria paniculata* and styrax. There is much topiary of yew and box – geometric shapes and plump birds – and romantic ruins. A great number of trees were lost in the great storm of October 1987 but the rose garden containing many old roses – in whose use Mrs Messel was a pioneer – has been restored.

OSTERLEY PARK
Middlesex

Isleworth TW7 4RB
5m W of Central London
by A4.
Tube: Osterley
Tel: 081 560 3918

Owner:
The National Trust

Open: Daily 9–7.30 or
sunset if earlier. 140 acres.
House open

THE PARK AT Osterley survives only in part but there are some good remaining garden buildings and some marvellous trees decorating the landscape; if one can block one's ears to the roar of the Great West Road something of the Elysian atmosphere of the past can be brought to life. The late Elizabethan mansion was rebuilt after 1761 by Robert Adam who also designed the semi-circular conservatory against the old kitchen garden wall. A series of lakes to the south and east of the house glitter among splendid trees – old cedars of Lebanon, oaks, limes and London planes. The lake nearest the house has an octagonal Chinese pavilion on an island.

PAINSHILL PARK

Surrey

Portsmouth Road,
Cobham KT11 1JE
1m W of Cobham by
A245
Tel: 0932 68113

Owner: Painshill Park
Trust

Open: Mid-Apr to
mid-Oct, Sun 2–6.
158 acres

THIS EXTRAORDINARY landscape garden is being
restored by a private trust and it is one of the
most worthwhile of all recent garden restorations.
The garden was made by the Hon. Charles Hamilton
between 1738 and 1773 when he ran out of money.
It is an intensely original example of the large-scale
creation of ornamental landscape. At the heart of the
garden a long curvaceous lake with islands is
overlooked by decorative buildings – an airy
ten-sided gothic pavilion, a fake ruined abbey and a
ruined Roman arch. One of the islands has the
remains of a dazzling grotto and is linked to the
mainland by an elegant Chinese bridge. Paths wind
through woods and across meadows about the shores
of the lake. In the westernmost part of the park a
huge water wheel is revealed and on the wooded
slopes high above, a castellated gothic tower
commanding immense views over the landscape and
the country beyond. A visit to Painshill is a great
adventure, with its exotic and picturesque ingredients
giving constant surprises. Everywhere the landscape
composes itself into delicious views and the place has
an unforgettable exhilaration.

PALLANT HOUSE

West Sussex

9 North Pallant,
Chichester PO19 1TJ
In the centre of Chichester
Tel: 0243 774557

Open: Tue to Sat 10–5.30

THERE ARE NOT many very small town gardens that can be visited by the public and this must be the smallest. It is designed to be in keeping with the beautiful Queen Anne house and a neat formality prevails. Gravel paths run round square beds edged in box with standard honeysuckles at the centre. Trellis is shaped into gothic curves and a mask spouts water into a lead cistern. The walls are draped with vines, roses and an unusual honeysuckle with scarlet flowers, *Lonicera sempervirens.*

PARHAM HOUSE

West Sussex

Pulborough RH20 4HS
4m S of Pulborough by
A283
Tel: 0903 742021

Owner: Parham Park Ltd

Open: Easter Sun to 1st
Sun in Oct, Sun, Wed,
Thur and Bank Hol 1–6.
11 acres. House open

PARHAM IS a grand Tudor house and is splendidly situated in an atmospheric old deer park dotted with ancient oaks. The chief ornamental part of the garden lies in the walled former kitchen garden, divided by gravel paths. Here are some very effective herbaceous borders with carefully controlled colour schemes: a pair of blue borders enlivened with dashes of magenta (*Lychnis coronaria*), pink diascias and purple penstemons; a gold border, given structure by repeated plantings of yellow potentilla, golden elder and juniper, yellow loosestrife and achilleas; and a cool white border against an east-facing wall. Part of the walled garden is still devoted to fruit trees, many of which are espaliered on the walls. To the west, a lake is overlooked by a pavilion and, to one side, a fiendish new turf maze with infuriatingly complicated rules.

PENSHURST PLACE
Kent

nr Tonbridge TN11 8DG
In Penshurst village
Tel: 0892 870304/307

Owner: The Rt Hon.
Viscount De L'Isle

Open: Apr to Sept, daily
except Mon (open Bank
Hol) 12.30–6. 10 acres.
House open

THE SIDNEY FAMILY have been here since the 16th century but the house is much older and magnificently dominates the huge walled gardens that surround it. Although the planting is modern in this enclosure, with its lovely Tudor bricks, the present pattern of beds, pools and walks closely resembles that shown in Kip's engraving of around 1700. Very few gardens preserve their essential layout from such an early time as Penshurst does. The entrance leads straight down a pair of herbaceous borders, on either side of which all sorts of ornamental schemes spread out: a charming orchard of apples and Kentish cobs; a garden of magnolias and golden Irish yews; a parterre planted as a dazzling Union Jack with the colours picked out in spring and summer bedding; a rose garden; a spring garden; and a pair of handsome borders designed by Lanning Roper. Below the south-facing walls of the house a vast parterre, laid out in the middle of the 19th century, has box-edged beds planted with scarlet 'Karen Poulsen' roses surrounding a stately circular pool. On one side, a raised terrace shows that in the remote past this had been the site of a pleasure garden.

PETWORTH HOUSE
West Sussex

Petworth GU28 0AE
In Petworth village
Tel: 0798 42207

Owner:
The National Trust

Open: Garden: Apr to Oct,
daily except Mon and Fri
(open Good Fri and Bank
Hol, closed Tue following)
12.30–6; Park: daily
8–sunset. 700 acres. House
open

PETWORTH HAS an ancient gardening history: formal Elizabethan gardens had a fountain and roses; and in the late 17th century George London, the greatest garden designer of the day, made new gardens for the newly built house. But today the park is the thing at Petworth and it is best appreciated by taking a long walk in it (for this, go to the Park, rather than the House, car park). It was laid out for the 2nd Earl of Egremont by 'Capability' Brown and is one of the best of all his surviving landscapes. It is big enough to reduce the very large mansion, seen from a distance framed in trees, to the stature of a garden ornament. Brown started in 1752 by damming

a stream to make a curving lake and planting clumps of trees to animate the undulating land. He placed the Doric temple to the north of the house and the Ionic rotunda beyond it on an eminence. Many wonderful trees survive from Brown's time – marvellous limes, oaks, sweet chestnuts and planes. The artist Turner was a frequent visitor to Petworth and loved the house and park which inspired some of his finest paintings.

PICKARD'S MAGNOLIA GARDENS
Kent

Stodmarsh Road,
Canterbury CT3 4AG
E of the city centre by
A257, near golf course
Tel: 0227 463951

Open: Feb to Christmas
Eve, daily except Mon;
Wed, Fri 12–dusk, other
days 10–dusk (5 in winter)

IT IS QUITE clear what the speciality of this unusual establishment is. Unique hybrids of magnolia, with seductive names like 'Firefly', 'Garnet' or 'Cornelian', are bred by the Pickards. They also carry various soulangeana hybrids, rare forms of *Magnolia stellata*, the unusual *M.* x *watsonii* and other interesting kinds. In addition to these there are collections of yakushimanum rhododendrons, camellias, deciduous azaleas and various cultivars of pieris. Almost all the plants are raised from cuttings and grown on their own roots. A brief list is issued but plants are sold on a cash and carry basis only. The fact that several are unique to Pickards is another reason for visiting.

45

PLAXTOL NURSERIES
Kent

The Spoute, Plaxtol,
Sevenoaks TN15 0QR
5 1/2m N of Tonbridge by
A227 and minor roads
Tel: 0732 810550

Open: Daily 10–5; closed
24 Dec for two weeks

Illustration:
Mesembryanthemums

TESSA AND DONALD Forbes's nursery is best known for supplying plants of special interest to flower arrangers. In fact they carry a very wide general range with something of interest in all departments – many heathers, conifers, plants that thrive in shade, some good herbaceous perennials and flowering shrubs. The nursery continues enticingly up the hill and is well worth foraging around in because, although a catalogue is produced, there are always things that have escaped its pages. A mail order service is provided.

POLESDEN LACEY
Surrey

nr Dorking RH5 6BD
5m NW of Dorking by
A246
Tel: 0372 458203

Owner:
The National Trust

Open: Daily 11–6.
30 acres. House open

THE DAPPER early 19th-century house was owned by the great Edwardian political hostess the Hon. Mrs Ronald Greville and the garden has much of the blowsy charm of the age. A beech avenue leads up the hill and wonderful views of the valley are revealed from the house at the top. Beyond the house a very large formal rose garden, with such distinctive Edwardian varieties as 'Dorothy Perkins' and 'American Pillar', has at its centre a white marble well-head. Although there are about 2,000 rose plants

only a relatively small number of varieties is used in a colour scheme of pink and white with occasional sharper tones of red. South of the rose garden is a magnificent herbaceous border which is an object lesson in bold but disciplined planting.

PORT LYMPNE GARDENS
Kent

Lympne, Hythe CT21 4PD
3m W of Hythe by A26
and B2067
Tel: 0303 264646

Owner: John Aspinall

Open: Daily 10–5 (or 1
hour before dusk in
winter). 15 acres

HIGH ABOVE Romney Marsh the gabled brick house was built by Sir Philip Sassoon to designs by Sir Herbert Baker before World War I and completed after the war by Philip Tilden who, in collaboration with his patron, laid out the garden. Sassoon died in 1939 and subsequently the place deteriorated until John Aspinall bought it in 1973 and commissioned a complete restoration with advice from Russell Page. The garden is formal in spirit and decorative in execution, making full use of the lovely position. Compartments are hedged in yew or Leyland cypress and the chess-board garden and the striped garden present dazzling geometric patterns in bedding schemes. Beautiful herbaceous borders, a fig garden, vineyard, and terraces of roses and dahlias decorate the slopes. Within its carefully designed architectural setting the garden at Port Lympne has a brilliantly festive air.

QUEEN MARY'S GARDEN
London

Inner Circle, Regents Park
NW1
In S part of Regents Park.
Tube: Regents Park
Tel: 071 486 7905

Owner: Department of the
Environment

Open: Daily, dawn–dusk

O FTEN MISLEADINGLY referred to as Queen Mary's rose garden this charming piece of miniature picturesque landscaping has much more to offer. There are indeed ramparts of roses in season, and a famous rosy rondel with swags of flowers trained on ropes. To one side, however, there is a little lake overhung with weeping willows and a fern-bedecked rocky waterfall. An arched bridge leads to an island with winding gravel paths, ornamental shrubs and a rock garden. Good trees – oaks, acacias and purple beeches – provide a handsome background and mute the roar of London traffic.

G. REUTHE LTD
Kent

Crown Point Nursery,
Sevenoaks Road, Ightham,
nr Sevenoaks TN15 0HB
4m E of Sevenoaks by A25
Tel: 0732 810694

Open: Mon to Sat 9–4.30

Illustration: Rhododendron
campylocarpum

R EUTHE IS FAMOUS for rhododendrons which it exhibits at the Chelsea Flower Show where it has won Gold Medals with relentless success. Here is an exceptionally wide range of species and hybrids and a choice collection of evergreen and deciduous azaleas. The nursery sells other things, particularly woody plants, but its real distinction is in its rhododendrons of which it publishes an especially good list from which orders are fulfilled by mail.

THE ROOF GARDENS
London

99 Kensington High Street,
W8 5ED
Central London.
Tube: High Street,
Kensington
Tel: 071 937 7994

Open: Daily 9–5 but
telephone beforehand as
sometimes closed for
private functions. 1/4 acre

THESE ARE THE largest roof gardens open to the
public in London. On the top of the old Derry &
Toms department store they are one of the most
unexpected horticultural sights that the capital has to
offer. Once one has got over the extraordinary fact
that there should be such a large garden (complete
with pink flamingoes wading in a pool) on top of a
building in Central London there is plenty to admire:
well tended borders with substantial shrubs, secluded
sitting places, thoughtfully planted pots, very
attractive paths of old York stone and herring-bone
laid brick, and a knock-out Moorish extravaganza
with more than a whiff of the Alhambra – old
coloured tiles, a scalloped canal with spouting
water-jets and palm trees.

ROYAL BOTANIC GARDENS, KEW
Surrey

Kew Green, Richmond
TW9 3AB
7m SW of Central London.
Tube: Kew Gardens
Tel: 081 940 1171

Owner: Trustees of the
Royal Botanic Gardens

Open: Daily 9.30–4 (6 in
summer). 300 acres

IT IS NOT THE PURPOSE of Kew to be interesting to gardeners but this, despite itself, it effortlessly is. The landscape park with its great Chinoiserie pagoda (designed by Sir William Chambers in 1751) and many specimen trees going back to the 18th century is exquisite; its setting on the Thames wonderful. Most of the plants are wild species rather than garden varieties but it is a perfect place to come on any day of the year and discover new plants, impeccably labelled and well grown. The various glasshouses are immensely rich in non-hardy plants: the palm house designed by Richard Turner and Decimus Burton, the temperate house, and the recently completed Princess Diana Conservatory with tender plants of different climates arranged in naturalistic settings. Among the hardy plants there are several reference collections of great interest to gardeners – they include heathers, bulbs, bamboos and grasses and several others.

SCOTNEY CASTLE
Kent

Lamberhurst, Tunbridge
Wells TN3 8JN
1m S of Lamberhurst by
A21
Tel: 0892 890651

Owner:
The National Trust

Open: Apr to early Nov,
Wed to Fri 11–6 (closed
Good Fri), Sat, Sun and
Bank Hol 2–6 or sunset if
earlier

*Illustration opposite: The
ravine garden at Scotney*

THE GARDENS AT Scotney Castle are a piece of irresistibly romantic picturesque landscape gardening made in the middle of the 19th century by Edward Hussey, with advice from William Sawrey Gilpin. At the same time Hussey built a new house high on a hill, benefitting from wonderful views down towards the moated medieval castle which became an exotic eye-catcher for his landscaping schemes. Walks descend the precipitous and rocky hill with superb trees and shrubs; the flowers of azaleas and rhododendrons, and the new foliage of maples, are dazzling in spring. In the castle forecourt there is a pretty herb garden designed by Lanning Roper and, nearby on an island, a bronze by Henry Moore seems strangely at home in the wild planting.

SHEFFIELD PARK
East Sussex

Uckfield TN22 3QX
Midway between East
Grinstead and Lewes off
A275
Tel: 0825 790655

Owner: The National
Trust

Open: Apr to early Nov,
Tue to Sat 11–6, Sun and
Bank Hol 2–6 or sunset if
earlier; closed Good Fri
and Tue after Bank Hol;
Oct, Sun 1–sunset. 100
acres.

THERE IS SOMETHING dream-like about Sheffield Park and it is certainly one of the most memorable of all gardens. Both 'Capability' Brown and Humphry Repton had a hand in the design but the present appearance of the gardens is due chiefly to Arthur Soames who bought the estate in 1905. The house, a gothic palace designed by James Wyatt in 1775–8, sits on an eminence at the head of a broad valley with a series of four descending lakes extending far into the distance. On the banks of these lakes trees and shrubs are arranged in bold groups with subtle contrast of shape and foliage colour; here conifers and deciduous trees are artfully mingled. Many visitors see only the first two lakes and their immediate banks; this is a pity because, in addition, acres of woods in the hinterland surrounding the lakes are laced with paths and full of marvellous trees and shrubs, with the occasional dazzling piece of herbaceous planting such as a path fringed with gentians. The garden is exquisitely laid out and a slow walk at any time during the long opening season offers some of the most beautiful garden scenes the visitor may ever see.

SISSINGHURST CASTLE GARDEN
Kent

Sissinghurst, nr Cranbrook
TN17 2AB
2m NE of Cranbrook off
A262
Tel: 0580 712850

Owner:
The National Trust

Open: Apr to mid-Oct,
Tue to Fri 1–6.30, Sat, Sun
and Good Fri 10–6.30. 10
acres. House open

THE HISTORY OF this garden is quickly told – it was made by Vita Sackville-West and Harold Nicolson from 1930 onwards and became the most admired English garden of its time. Few great gardens live up to their reputation so effortlessly as this. Whatever superlatives have been heaped on it, Sissinghurst never disappoints and each visit will reveal new pleasures. The National Trust was fortunate to inherit two gardeners, Pamela Schwerdt and Sibylle Kreutzberger, who had worked with Vita Sackville-West before her death in 1963. They not only maintained the garden to perfectionist standards but continued until their recent retirement the

tradition of discerning plantsmanship. Within the disciplined enclosures of old brick walls, cool hedges of yew and linking paths and vistas, here is a profusion of fastidiously chosen plants in which an immense collection of old roses provides a recurring theme. One of the many refreshing things about Sissinghurst is the way in which virtuoso changes in mood are effortlessly achieved – from the hot oranges and reds of the Cottage Garden, for example, to the austere yew alley that separates the formal gardens from the orchard. Despite Vita Sackville-West's aristocratic spirit, it would be wrong to think of Sissinghurst as far from the interests of everyday gardeners. In terms of practical gardening – the pruning, training and feeding of plants, for example – the highest standards were maintained and they are still a delight to observe. Certainly it has the power of enchantment but it is also an unending source of inspiration for all gardeners.

STANDEN
East Sussex

East Grinstead RH19 4NE
2m S of East Grinstead off
B2110
Tel: 0342 323029

Owner:
The National Trust

Open: Apr to Oct, Wed to
Sun and Bank Hol (closed
Tue following) 12.30–5.30.
10 acres. House open

STANDEN HAS a most marvellous position, high on an eminence with views across the Medway Valley to Crowborough Beacon. Below the house, which was designed by Philip Webb, the land falls away on south-facing slopes. An enclosed formal garden is hedged in beech and yew and has square beds edged in catmint with an Irish juniper at each corner and a crab apple at each centre, surrounded by rugosa roses. The rest of the garden consists of terraced lawns and paths that amble through groups of shrubs and trees – azaleas and rhododendrons with maples rising above. A wonderful tulip tree and a very large Scots pine at the foot of a sloping lawn frame distant views of cornfields surrounded by woodland.

STARBOROUGH NURSERY
Kent

Starborough Road, Marsh
Green,
Edenbridge TN8 5RB
Tel: 0732 865614

Open: Daily except Tue
and Wed 10–4

Illustration: Styrax japonica

STARBOROUGH SPECIALISES in acid-loving woody plants of which pride of place is taken by a very wide range of species and hybrid rhododendrons, many of them rarely seen in nurseries. There are also good selections of acers, camellias, daphnes, magnolias, pieris, stewartias, styrax, viburnums and a choice selection of climbing plants. Many unusual plants reflect the discerning taste of the owners who exhibit widely at R.H.S. shows and elsewhere. A catalogue is published and mail orders are fulfilled.

SYON PARK AND GARDENS
London

Brentford TW8 8JF
On the N bank of the
Thames between Brentford
and Isleworth
Tel: 081 560 0881

Owner: The Duke of
Northumberland

Open: Mar to Oct, daily
10–6; Nov to Feb, daily
10–sunset. 55 acres. House
open

IT IS SURPRISING to find a complete great country estate so near to the centre of London. The approach to the house, which was rebuilt by Robert Adam, runs through classic parkland. The chief pleasure gardens lie on one side of the house and are dominated by one of the finest conservatories you will see anywhere, built by Charles Fowler in 1827 in beautiful golden stone. There is an excellent collection of trees – catalpas, holm oaks, sweet chestnuts, acacias and rarer things such as sweet buckeye (*Aesculus flava*). A long narrow lake is edged with trees including some good swamp cypresses. A very large and attractively laid out garden centre has a good stock in all departments and an especially fine selection of garden pots.

TILE BARN NURSERY
Kent

Standen Street, Iden Green,
Benenden TN17 4LB
In the hamlet of Standen
Street 1/2m S of Benenden
Tel: 0580 240221

Open: Wed to Sat 9–5

THIS IS THE kind of nursery that makes converts of even the most unyielding. It specialises in cyclamen and stocks all the most garden-worthy species and varieties of these charmingly seductive plants, several of which are very hard to come by. An excellent list is produced, giving valuable information on their cultivation. Plants are sold by mail order but visitors are welcomed and a few other bulbous plants, such as crocuses, fritillaries and narcissi, are available to callers only.

WAKEHURST PLACE GARDEN
West Sussex

nr Ardingly, Haywards
Heath RH17 6TN
1 1/2m NW of Ardingly on
B2028
Tel: 0444 892701

Owner:
The National Trust

Open: Daily except 25 Dec
and 1 Jan; Nov to Jan
10–4; Feb, Oct 10–5; Mar
10–6; Apr to Sept 10–7. 170
acres

ALTHOUGH THERE IS an attractively planted walled garden and some good borders (albeit with a botanical slant – one is devoted to monocotyledons) Wakehurst Place is really about trees and shrubs. It is the country department of the Royal Botanic Gardens at Kew and it is full of wonderful things. The 16th-century mansion was built for Sir Edward Culpeper and much rebuilt in the late 19th century, and in 1903 the estate was bought by Gerald Loder, 1st Baron Wakehurst. By the house the site is relatively flat and the house looks out onto pools and a water garden fringed with maples and moisture-loving plants. Farther from the house the ground sweeps down into the Himalayan Glade and the precipitous ravine of Westwood Valley and its lake, and beyond that, more woodland. There are wonderful collections of azaleas, magnolias and rhododendrons in the Himalayan Glade and the Westwood Valley, and particularly fine groups of conifers in the Pinetum. The lie of the land adds immensely to the beauty of the trees and this is a wonderful place in which to spend a few hours walking, looking and learning.

WEST DEAN GARDENS
West Sussex

Singleton,
Chichester PO18 0Q2
6m N of Chichester by
A286
Tel: 0243 63301

Owner: The Edward James
Foundation

Open: Mar to Oct, daily
11–6. 50 acres

THE EARLY 19TH-CENTURY gothic house by James Wyatt belonged to Edward James, patron of surrealism, though there is nothing surrealistic about his garden. At its heart is an immense pergola designed by Harold Peto; draped in clematis, roses and wisteria and underplanted with agapanthus, daylilies, ferns, geraniums and lamium, it runs from a gothic flint summer house, incorporates a long rectangular lily pond and ends at a sunken garden with a pool, ornamental grasses, a sea of *Alchemilla mollis*, ferns and roses. The old walled kitchen garden is in the process of being restored and in an outhouse a collection of old lawn-mowers is exhibited. Beyond the garden, handsome parkland spreads across folds in the downs.

WINKWORTH ARBORETUM
Surrey

Hascombe Road,
Godalming GU8 4AD
2m SE of Godalming off
B2130
Tel: 048 632 477

Owner:
The National Trust

Open: Daily, dawn–dusk.
99 acres

WHEN DR WILFRID FOX started this arboretum in 1937 it was a hillside covered in scrub with a certain amount of old oak forest. As arboreta go, then, this is in its early adolescence but there is a great deal to admire. The site, with the land falling to two lakes (one of which has the curious name Rowe's Flashe), and with light, acid loam, is a good one as Dr Fox well realised when he acquired it. His early planting included an immense number of sorbus and maples and this was followed by a continuous stream of acquisitions. There are dogwoods, excellent magnolias, a large number of oaks (of which the scarlet oak, *Quercus coccinea*, is a wonderful sight in autumn), rhododendrons and witch-hazels. A particularly beautiful part of the arboretum is the foliage glade where trees with especially striking leaves have been gathered together, among them hickories, the Japanese walnut and the lovely variegated form of sweet chestnut.

WISLEY GARDEN
Surrey

nr Ripley, Woking
GU23 6QB
6m NE of Guildford by
A3; S of Jnct 10 of the M25
Tel: 0483 224234

Owner: Royal
Horticultural Society

Open: Daily 10–7 (Sun for
R.H.S. Members only).
60 acres

WISLEY IS WHERE the Royal Horticultural Society shows the gardening public how it should be done. Here are the highest standards of practical horticulture deployed over an immense range of different kinds of gardening in the setting of a splendid old site rich in fine trees and a very large number of other plants impeccably labelled. There is a pinetum, an alpine house, a vast and beautifully kept rock-garden, trial grounds of various kinds and practical display areas giving examples of different styles of gardening. It should also be noted that the huge shop contains the largest selection of new gardening books in Britain (and quite probably the world) and there is a large nursery garden with plants of very high quality, many very unusual. As there is no catalogue and no mail order a visit and a deep browse is the only way of buying.

South-Central England

—————— ❧ ——————

Berkshire, Buckinghamshire, Hampshire, Oxfordshire, Wiltshire

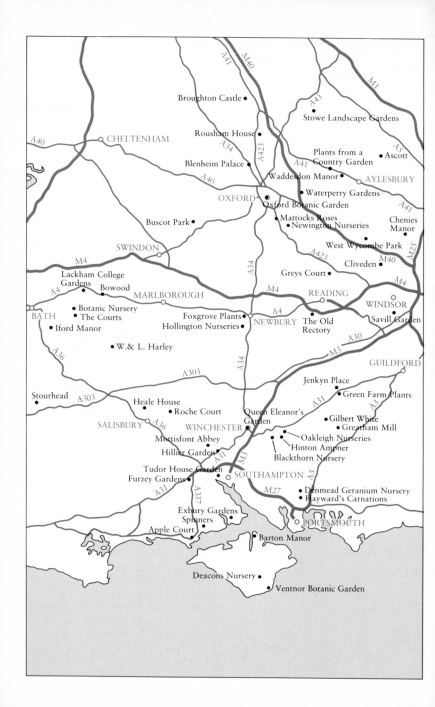

APPLE COURT
Hampshire

Hordle Lane, Lymington
SO41 0HU
3 1/2m W of Lymington by
A337
Tel: 0590 42130

Open: Feb to Nov, daily
except Tue and Wed 10–5;
closed last two weeks in
Aug

THIS IS A VERY attractive nursery with some
outstandingly good plants – hostas (over 70
varieties), daylilies, ferns and ornamental grasses. In
the charming garden (which is under development)
there is a splendid hosta walk where many different
kinds may be seen performing. A catalogue is
produced and a mail order service is provided but a
visit to the garden where many of the plants sold are
displayed so handsomely is particularly worthwhile.

ASCOTT
Buckinghamshire

Wing, nr Leighton Buzzard
LU7 0PS
2m SW of Leighton
Buzzard by A418
Tel: 0296 688242

Owner:
The National Trust

Open: 14 Apr to 17 May
and Sept, Tue, Sun and
Bank Hol (but closed
subsequent Tue) 2–6 ; 20
May to Aug, Wed and last
Sun in month and Bank
Hol 2–6. 39 acres. House
open

THIS IS a rare garden, in which the distinctive late
Victorian character is cherished and made into
something special. The house was a hunting box on
the Rothschilds' Mentmore estate and the gardens
were made at the end of the 19th century. Behind the
house, lawns are terraced down towards a long
double herbaceous border hedged with variegated
holly and golden yew. From the middle of these
borders a path leads to rose beds and a splashing
fountain of Venus designed by Thomas Waldo Story.
To the east there are great topiary pieces in golden
and common yew and a unique topiary sundial.
From the terraces marvellous views of the Vale of
Aylesbury are seen in the distance.

BARTON MANOR
Isle of Wight

Whippingham, Cowes,
Isle of Wight, Hampshire
PO32 6LB
1m SE of Cowes by A3021
next to Osborne House
Tel: 0983 292835

Owner: Mr and Mrs
Goddard

Open: May to mid-Oct,
daily 10.30–5.30. 20 acres

FORMERLY PART of the Osborne House estate, the Barton estate, with its gabled stone manor house, was a particular interest of Prince Albert who laid out the gardens and planted the splendid grove of cork oaks (*Quercus suber*) at the entrance. Today a large part of it is run as a commercial vineyard but the gardens, since 1976, have been very well restored to preserve their Victorian character. By the house there are herbaceous borders and a secret garden of roses and winding paths. An avenue of bushes of St John's Wort leads down to a lake with a romantic 19th-century thatched boat house. Here are many good trees (especially willows relishing the moist ground) and the banks are dazzling with daffodils in spring. A particular interest in summer is the immense collection (over 100 species and cultivars) of red hot pokers (*Kniphofia*) of which Barton Manor holds the National Collection.

BLACKTHORN NURSERY
Hampshire

Kilmeston, nr Alresford
SO24 0NL
6 1/2m SE of Winchester
by A31 and A272
Tel: 0962 79796

Open: Mar to Oct, Fri and
Sat 9–5

Illustration: Geranium
psilostemon

THERE ARE SOME very rare and desirable plants at the Blackthorn Nursery which you will not often see offered for sale. It specialises in herbaceous perennials but among a short list of woody plants is an excellent selection of daphnes. Among the herbaceous plants are many epimediums, an exceptional range of hellebores, ferns and a wide range of alpines. Plants may be supplied by mail order and a good catalogue is produced.

BLENHEIM PALACE
Oxfordshire

Woodstock OX20 1PX
In Woodstock, 8m N of
Oxford by A44
Tel: 0993 811325

Owner: The Duke of
Marlborough

Open: Park daily 9–5.30;
closed Christmas Day;
formal gardens at palace
open at 10.30. 2,000 acres
(including parkland). Palace
open

THE GARDEN at Blenheim has an immensely long
history: in the 12th century it was the site of
Henry II's Rosamond's Bower – and her well still
exists; the garden was remade by Henry Wise in the
early 18th century, and Sir John Vanbrugh who
designed the immense palace also had a hand in it; in
the 1760s the park was landscaped by 'Capability'
Brown; and in the early 20th century new parterres
by the palace were laid out by the French designer
Achille Duchêne. Ingredients from these different
periods are harmoniously interwoven with, at their
heart, the palace and its vista leading north across
Vanbrugh's bridge to the immense Column of Victory
surmounted by a statue of the Duke of Marlborough
clasping a winged victory 'as an ordinary man might
hold a bird'. Brown's park, disposed on gently
undulating land about the vast serpentine lake that he
made by damming the River Glyme, is one of his
masterpieces – a subtle and satisfyingly rural contrast
to the extravagant architecture of the palace.
Duchêne's dapper parterres – the Italian Garden and
the Water Terraces – are fortissimo exercises in the
grand formal manner. A large garden centre sells a
good range of plants.

THE BOTANIC NURSERY
Wiltshire

Rookery Nurseries,
Atworth, nr Melksham
SN12 8NU
9m E of Bath by A4 and
A365
Tel: 0225 706597

Open: Daily except Thur
and Sun 10–5 (10–3 in
winter)

Illustration: Rosa banksiae
alba

TERENCE AND MARY Baker's nursery specialises in lime tolerant plants of which they have an excellently chosen range. Those who garden on alkaline soil will find all sorts of plants that will flourish in their gardens. The nursery concentrates on no particular groups of plants but what they do have is carefully selected – for example a list of species foxgloves. Although their catalogue is full of good, and unusual, plants the Bakers are always on the look out for something new and many items are available in numbers too small to make it worthwhile listing them. This makes a visit all the more valuable and, although there is a limited mail order service, many plants are considered too large or too fragile to be consigned to the post.

BOWOOD
Wiltshire

Calne SN11 0LZ
2 1/2m W of Calne by A4
Tel: 0249 812102

Owner: Earl and Countess
of Shelburne

Open: Apr to Oct, daily
11–6. Garden centre: daily
9–5. 100 acres. House open

THE HOUSE – partly designed by Robert Adam – is a splendid 18th-century confection and very much in keeping with the park which is chiefly of the same period. The park, with its great serpentine lake, spreads out below the house and is enlivened by a picturesque cascade, a hermit's cave and an elegant pillared temple. This is the work partly of 'Capability' Brown and, later, of Humphry Repton

and it is one of the very best of its kind. There are marvellous trees at Bowood and the mid 19th-century pinetum is exceptionally good, with some of the finest specimens of conifers in the country – magnificent cedars of Lebanon, pines, firs and giant redwoods. Immediately alongside the house there are 19th-century formal gardens with beds of roses, balustrades, vases and clipped Irish yews. The particularly good garden centre concentrates on woody plants and also has Haddonstone ornaments and terracotta pots. A catalogue is produced but there is no mail order.

BROUGHTON CASTLE
Oxfordshire

Broughton, nr Banbury
OX15 5EB
2m SW of Banbury by
B4035
Tel: 0295 262624/812027

Owner: Lord Saye and Sele

Open: 18 May to 14 Sept,
Wed and Sun 2–5; Jul and
Aug, also Thur 2–5; also
Bank Hol and preceding
Sun 2–5. 3 acres. Castle
open

THIS SPECTACULAR castle is really a 14th-century moated and fortified manor house and it occupies a beautiful site next to the church. Within the castle walls there are handsome borders on which Gertrude Jekyll advised and which still preserve a fastidious colour harmony – one of white, cream and blue and another in warmer tones of pink and red. In the old walled kitchen garden there is a pretty knot of box and germander planted with pink roses. This is a good garden for roses: there is a border of old shrub roses and climbers scale the old walls to great effect.

BUSCOT PARK
Oxfordshire

Faringdon SN7 8BU
3m NW of Faringdon on
A417
Tel: 0367 20786 (not
weekends)

Owner:
The National Trust

Open: Apr to Sept, Wed,
Thur, Fri and every 2nd
and 4th Sat and Sun
(including Easter) 2–6. 20
acres. House open

*Illustration opposite: The
water garden at Buscot*

EAST OF THE HOUSE, running through woodland towards a lake, is a water garden you will never forget. Designed by Harold Peto before World War I it is in the form of a canal that drops down the incline in gentle steps, dips under occasional little bridges, widens and contracts and from time to time bursts forth in exuberant fountains. The water garden is edged with stately clipped hedges of box and the flanking path is punctuated by Irish yews, statues and urns. Approaching the lake the visitor sees on its far bank a gleaming temple and an ornamental bridge. On the other side of the house, by the kitchen garden, there is a recent development of strongly-designed borders in yellow and blue by the late Peter Coats and, within the walls, Tim Rees has made tunnels of pleached hop hornbeam and Judas trees underplanted with spring bulbs followed by waves of many different daylilies.

CHENIES MANOR
Buckinghamshire

Chenies WD3 6ER
4m E of Amersham on
A404
Tel: 049476 2888

Owner: Lt. Col. and Mrs
MacLeod Matthews

Open: Apr to Oct, Wed,
Thur 2–5 also Bank Hol
2–6. 3 acres. House open

THE MANOR is an early Tudor brick house of tremendous character and the recently made garden is an excellent setting for it. The formal gardens are chiefly behind the house, with a white garden in which a figure of Cupid takes pot shots at plump topiary birds of yew, a cool tunnel of pleached lime and a virtuoso little sunken garden, intricately planted, in which spring tulips are followed by an elaborate summer bedding scheme. Beyond this, a physic garden has beds of medicinal and culinary herbs laid out round a decorative old octagonal wellhouse. To one side of the house an ornamental kitchen garden has gravel paths edged with catmint or box, currants and gooseberries grown in cordons, beautifully tended vegetables and a turf maze in an orchard. The whole garden is impeccably well kept and gives the impression of bursting with horticultural endeavour.

CLIVEDEN
Buckinghamshire

Taplow, Maidenhead
SL6 0JA
2m N of Taplow on B476,
near Jnct 7 of M4 and Jnct
4 of M40
Tel: 0628 605069

Owner:
The National Trust

Open: Daily Mar to Oct
11–6; Nov to Dec 11–4.
375 acres. House open

THE MANSION at Cliveden, built in the 17th century
and rebuilt twice in the 19th century, commands
a spectacular site on a bluff overlooking the snaking
Thames. A giant balustraded terrace looks south to a
vast parterre of box and santolina, first laid out for
the Duke of Sutherland in the 1850s. At its far end
the land falls away in wooded slopes that run down
to the river below. The pleasure gardens lie chiefly to
the north of the house. In the forecourt are excellent
herbaceous borders and, beyond the walls, a hidden
rose garden designed by Geoffrey Jellicoe. A lime
avenue leads to the eyestopping Fountain of Love
commissioned by Lord Astor from the American
Ralph Waldo Story at the turn of the century. To one
side is the magical Long Garden with serpentine box
hedges, whimsical topiary and mysterious stone
figures from the Commedia dell'Arte. Farther up the
drive, the water garden has a pagoda overlooking a
lake fringed with maples and Japanese cherries. In
the woods that surround the house, and by the house
itself, there are many exceptional garden ornaments –
exquisite statues, urns and garden buildings.

THE COURTS
Wiltshire

Holt, nr Trowbridge
BA14 6RR
In Holt village, 3m SW of
Melksham by B3107
Tel: 0225 782340

Owner:
The National Trust

Open: Apr to Oct, daily
except Sat 2–5. 7 acres

CONCEALED BEHIND village walls a pleached lime alley leads up to an ornate Bath stone 18th-century house at the heart of a highly decorative garden in which yew topiary and Irish yews give firm structure. Good shrubs and ornamental trees half conceal an ornamental pool smothered in season with water-lilies, and a billowing hedge of two varieties of holly forms the eastern boundary to a meadow garden. This is a vision of a cottage garden seen through aristocratic eyes and executed with humour and inventiveness.

DEACONS NURSERY
Isle of Wight

Godshill, Isle of Wight,
Hampshire PO38 3HW
In village of Godshill 9m S
of Cowes by A3020
Tel: 0983 840750

Open: Daily except Sun 8–4

DEACONS NURSERY specialises in fruit trees and bushes of which it has an immense collection – around 200 varieties of apples alone, for example, which may be ordered on a choice of five rootstocks. There is virtually no fruit that is hardy in Britain which is not stocked and many of the varieties, especially the old kinds, are very difficult to find elsewhere. Virtually all the business of this nursery is conducted by mail order and an exceptionally informative catalogue is produced. But visitors are welcome and a visit for the spring blossom or the autumn fruit will be especially rewarding.

DENMEAD GERANIUM NURSERIES
Hampshire

Hambledon Road,
Denmead, Portsmouth
PO7 6PS
2m W of Waterlooville
Tel: 0705 240081

Open: Mon to Fri, 8–1,
2–5, Sat 8–12.30 ; May to
Jun, also Sat 8–12.30, 2–5;
Apr, also Sun 9.30–12.30

THERE ARE WELL over 1,500 varieties of pelargoniums commercially available in Britain and this old-established nursery is one of the best places in the country to buy them. Representatives of all the chief groups – with their evocative names like Double Zonals or Stellars – are stocked in variety and many cultivars are available only from Denmead. New cultivars are constantly being added and some varieties have not been propagated in sufficently large quantities to list and may be sniffed out at the nursery where visitors are welcomed. An informative catalogue is produced, with useful hints on cultivation, and a mail order service is provided.

EXBURY GARDENS
Hampshire

nr Southampton SO4 1AZ
From Totton (W of
Southhampton) 14m to
Exbury village by A326 and
B3054
Tel: 0703 891203

Owner: E.L. de Rothschild

Open: Mar to beginning
Jul, Sept to Oct 10–5.30 or
sunset if earlier. 200 acres

THE CLIMATE is particularly mild at Exbury. Lionel de Rothschild came here in 1919 and started to build up the collection of rhododendrons which was to make the garden famous. His son has continued the tradition and has added many new varieties which may be seen growing in this huge garden. But even for those not interested in rhododendrons there is much to see here, especially a very large collection of ornamental trees. Some of these are superb old specimens; a group of cedars of Lebanon are among the most beautiful in England. There is a large garden shop at the garden. A catalogue is produced and there is a mail order service.

FOXGROVE PLANTS
Berkshire

Foxgrove Farm, Enborne, nr Newbury RG14 6RE
1m W of Newbury
Tel: 0635 40554

Open: Wed to Sun and Bank Hol 10–6

THIS LITTLE NURSERY, founded in 1986, has already won several medals at Royal Horticultural Society shows and elsewhere. Its speciality is smaller herbaceous plants, with an emphasis on alpines. Although the stock is small the plants, all of which are propagated and grown on the premises, are particularly well chosen. There are large selections of campanulas, geraniums, primulas, saxifrages, snowdrops (of which a special list is published) and violas. Louise Vockins has an eye for a good plant and the visitor is likely to find something unfamiliar and worth buying. The nursery spills over into her aunt's garden on the other side of the yard where there are some pretty borders.

71

FURZEY GARDENS
Hampshire

Minstead,
nr Lyndhurst SO4 37GL
9m W of Southampton by
A336
Tel: 0703 812464

Owner: Furzey Gardens
Trust

Open: Daily except 25 and
26 Dec 10.30–5 or sunset in
winter. 8 acres

THIS GARDEN was started in 1922 on rough grazing land which benefitted from some good old trees and a rich natural vegetation which in many parts of the garden has been preserved. The site is sloping, the soil is acid and the garden is full of excellent plants, many of them unusual. The layout is informal, with grassy walks descending the hill and winding between groups of shrubs. Herbaceous plantings fringe the paths. In spring an immense number of bulbs – narcissi, dog's tooth violets and fritillaries – is followed by azaleas and rhododendrons, many of them rare and tender and doing exceptionally well in this part of the country. There is a famous heather bed and some good new varieties have originated here, for example the widely grown *Erica* x *darleyensis* 'Furzey'. The garden is outstanding in autumn with brilliant foliage colours from shrubs such as enkianthus and witch-hazels and substantial specimens of *Liquidambar styraciflua* and the scarlet oak, *Quercus coccinea*.

GREATHAM MILL

Hampshire

Greatham, nr Liss
GU33 6HH
7m SE of Alton by B3006
Tel: 0420 7219

Owner: Mrs E.N.
Pumphrey

Open: Mid-Apr to Sept,
Sun and Bank Hol 2–7

MRS PUMPHREY came to this mill house in 1961 and has made a large and seductive garden on a particularly attractive site. To the front the atmosphere is of cottage-garden profusion – an old plum tree sprawls over richly planted beds of shrubs underplanted with herbaceous plants. But here the plants have been fastidiously chosen and there are substantial groups of particular kinds – for example, irises, geraniums and hostas. Mrs Pumphrey also has an excellent eye for what goes with what: a group of intense blue irises associating with glaucous-leafed hostas, a wig-wam of golden hop cooled down by a creamy flowered Scotch rose. This gives the garden harmony rather than jumble. Behind the house impeccable grassy walks lead between beds, old trees, a beautifully planted bog garden, garlands of old roses and the occasional well-placed aristocratic tree such as *Cornus controversa* 'Variegata'. Across a field there is a nursery area with some good plants for sale.

GREEN FARM PLANTS
Hampshire

Bentley, nr Farnham
GU10 5JX
In the village of Bentley 3m
SW of Farnham by A31
Tel: 0420 23202

Open: Wed to Sat 10–6

JOHN COKE'S little nursery is well worth seeking out because he has a connoisseur's eye for a good plant and there are many things here that you will not easily find elsewhere. His specialities are smaller decorative shrubs and herbaceous plants, with an emphasis on more tender kinds. Everything he chooses has something distinguished about it, which gives his range the feeling of a house style. He does not have immense numbers of any particular genus but there are discerningly chosen groups of plants such as toad lilies (*Tricyrtis* spp), sages, curious species mahonias and cistuses. There is no mail order but a catalogue is produced.

GREYS COURT
Oxfordshire

Rotherfield Greys,
Henley-on-Thames
RG9 4PG
3m W of
Henley-on-Thames by A423
Tel: 049 17 529

Owner:
The National Trust

Open: Apr to Sept, daily
except Thur and Sun
(closed Good Fri) 2–6. 9
acres. House open

THE HOUSE, partly Tudor and partly Georgian, built of red brick banded with silvery flint, commands unforgettable views over the valley of beech woods and downland. The garden lies chiefly to the east of the house. Passing through a white garden and a garden of old roses underplanted with pinks, a path leads under a great canopy of *Wisteria sinensis* whose long hanging racemes make a brilliant effect in late spring. In the former kitchen garden, paths are edged with *Rosa mundi* or espaliered fruit trees. Here a pergola veiled with vine and honeysuckle leads to the Archbishop's Maze, an ornamental turf maze designed in 1981 by Adrian Fisher and Randall Coate. Turning back towards the house, by the Cromwellian Stables, is a brilliant little enclosed garden with knots of box hedges and topiary, London pride edging the paths of brick and cobble, beds burgeoning with herbaceous plants, screened by walls of pleached laburnum.

W. & L. HARLEY
Wiltshire

Parham Nursery, The
Sands, Market Lavington,
Devizes SN10 4QA
5m S of Devizes by A360
Tel: 0380 813712

Open: Mar to Nov, Mon,
Tue and Fri 2–5, Sat 10–5

Illustration: Veronica
gentianoides

WILL AND LYNN Harley specialise in hardy perennials and alpine plants. Their list is not large but it is exceptionally well chosen with many things (such as *Acanthus hirsutus*) that are very hard to find elsewhere. Among perennials they sell good ferns, geraniums, violas and many perennial wallflowers and in the alpine department they are especially strong on phlox, saxifrages and sedums. A list is published, with seasonal supplements, and a mail order service is provided.

HAYWARD'S CARNATIONS
Hampshire

The Chace Gardens, Stakes
Road, Purbrook,
Portsmouth PO7 5PL
4m NE of Portsmouth by
A3
Tel: 0705 263047

Open: Mon to Fri 10–12,
2–4; closed first fortnight
Aug, last fortnight Dec and
first week Jan

CARNATIONS AND PINKS are very attractive and versatile garden plants and Hayward's, who sell nothing else, is one of the best places in Britain to buy them. They are constantly adding new things to their list and they sell many cultivars which are nowhere else commercially available. A visit to the nursery in, say, June is a heady experience with the clove-scented ('true old-fashioned') pinks going full blast in the mild south Hampshire climate. A good list is produced, with valuable information on cultivation, and a mail order service is provided.

HEALE HOUSE
Wiltshire

Middle Woodford,
nr Salisbury SP4 6NT
4m N of Salisbury in the
Woodford Valley by minor
roads
Tel: 0722 73207

Owner: Major David and
Lady Anne Rasch

Open: Daily 10–5. 8 acres

ON LOW-LYING LAND on the banks of the Avon Heale House is an irresistibly decorative confection of rosy brick and stone dressings. The garden has a character all of its own and there are few places in England where a gardener is likely to have more fun. The 'landing stage' by the house and the scalloped fish ponds and rose terraces west of the house were designed by Harold Peto in 1910 for the Hon. Louis Greville who installed a Japanese garden with scarlet bridge and fragile tea-house after a tour of diplomatic duty in Japan before World War I. Nearby is a walled vegetable garden which the present owners have transformed with broad tunnels of espaliered apples, clipped mounds of box surrounding a pool and a beguiling mixture of fruit, vegetables and masterly ornamental planting. Everywhere in the garden there are roses – particularly old shrub roses – and the place is an unforgettable sight in late June; but there is always something to admire at other times. There is an excellent nursery and a catalogue is produced but there is no mail order.

THE HILLIER GARDEN AND ARBORETUM
Hampshire

Jermyns Lane, Ampfield, nr Romsey SO51 9PA
3m NE of Romsey by A31
Tel: 0794 68787

Owner: Hampshire County Council

Open: Mon to Fri 10–5; Mar to Oct also Sat, Sun and Bank Hol 1–6. 160 acres

Illustration: Pieris forrestii 'Jermyns'

THIS IS ONE of the greatest collections of woody plants in the country and had its origin as the private arboretum of Sir Harold Hillier. The arboretum holds the National Collection of oaks but its riches are so extensive and various that there is little point in beginning to list them; one can say, however, that the soil is acid, and therefore the arboretum is especially good on acid-loving plants. A visit at any time of the year will be splendidly rewarded and this is a marvellous place for even expert gardeners to learn more; for beginners it is an essential part of gardening education.

HILLIER'S NURSERIES LTD
Hampshire

Ampfield House, Ampfield,
nr Romsey SO51 9PA
Tel: 0794 68733

Open: All branches: Mon
to Sat 9–5.30, Sun 10–5.30;
closed Christmas and New
Year

THIS IS THE headquarters of the Hillier empire from which mail orders are serviced. This nursery has the largest single collection of woody plants commercially available in the country (and quite possibly in the world) and its catalogue is a standard reference book. Herbaceous plants are also sold but there is nothing like the same range and depth. There are several garden centres in Hampshire which include those at Jermyn's Lane, nr Romsey (0794 68407); in Romsey Road, west of Winchester (0962 842288); and at Botley Road, Romsey (0794 513459). These carry a good general stock – but it is only a pale reflection of the treasures available to order by mail or for collection from the headquarters.

HINTON AMPNER
Hampshire

Bramdean, nr Alresford
SO24 0LA
1m W of Bramdean village
by A272
Tel: 0962 771305

Owner:
The National Trust

Open: Apr to Sept, Sat,
Sun, Tue, Wed, Bank Hol
and Good Fri 1.30–5.30. 8
acres. House open

THIS IS AN exciting place to visit – an excellent old garden, redesigned in the 20th century and now being restored. The estate formerly belonged to Ralph Dutton, Lord Sherborne, who rebuilt the house, an 18th-century brick mansion, and laid out a new garden incorporating older features such as a superb lime avenue planted in 1720. He made the best of a marvellous site and opened views into the exquisite parkland that surrounds the house. Within the garden he laid out all sorts of decorative schemes

– a cherry garden with formal hedges of box and yew, a yew walk backed with ramparts of shrub roses, a leafy and mysterious dell, a sunken garden with yew topiary and much else. Throughout the garden there is a brilliant use of ornaments – statues and urns – which direct the gaze and emphasise a vista.

HOLLINGTON NURSERIES
Berkshire

Woolton Hill,
Newbury RG15 9XT
5m SW of Newbury by
A343
Tel: 0635 253908

Open: Mid-Mar to Sept,
Mon to Sat 10–5.30, Sun
and Bank Hol 11–5; Oct to
Mar, Mon to Fri 10–dusk

ALTHOUGH THIS marvellous place certainly sells herbs it is misleading to call it a herb garden because it is of much wider interest that that. Simon and Judith Hopkinson have laid out a series of borders, knots, parterres and raised beds to show their plants in action. All this – beautifully designed and executed – is bursting with ideas for gardeners. In the nursery itself, apart from the very wide range of herbs there are also shrubs and trees with scented foliage, a small selection of conservatory plants and an interesting collection of ready-made topiary in cypress, box, yew and holly. A very good catalogue is produced but seeds only are sold by post and a separate list is available.

IFORD MANOR
Wiltshire

Iford, nr Bradford-on-Avon
BA15 2BA
7m SE of Bath by A36
Tel: 022 16 3146 or 2840

Owner: Mrs
Cartwright-Hignett

Open: Apr and Oct, Sun
2–5; May to Sept, daily
except Mon and Fri 2–5.
2 1/2 acres

*Illustration opposite: The
entrance to the garden at
Iford Manor*

THE ARCHITECT and garden-designer Harold Peto
came here in 1899 and remained until his death
in 1933. On the steep wooded slopes of the Avon
valley, above an 18th-century manor house, he laid
out a terraced garden embellished everywhere by the
collection of classical statuary and architectural
fragments that he amassed over the years. Steep
flights of steps ascend the slope, linking terraces with
pools, fountains, loggias, colonnades, urns and
figures. Cypresses add to the Italian atmosphere and
many trees and shrubs flower among the statues.
Peto was fully aware of the contrasts of his formal
garden with its rural surrounds, and idyllic views
open out everywhere over old woodland and cattle
grazing in meadows. In the woods above the garden
a Japanese garden is being recreated by the present
owners who have done a huge amount of restoration.

JENKYN PLACE
Hampshire

Bentley, nr Farnham
GU10 5JX
In Bentley village, 3m
SW of Farnham on A31
Tel: 0420 23118

Owner: Mrs G.E. Coke

Open: Apr 9 to mid-Sept,
Thur to Sun and Bank Hol
2–6. 6 acres

JENKYN PLACE is in the distinguished 20th-century
tradition of gardens of compartments embellished
with beautifully chosen plants, many rare, lavishly
planted in well designed settings. The garden is laid
out on a gentle slope and divided with hedges of
yew, beech or hawthorn. There are some very grand
ingredients – a pair of exuberant true herbaceous
borders, for example, but many of the most
memorable features are of a simpler kind – waves of
crinums planted under old apple trees, an avenue of
pairs of different species of rowans, a single statue of
a crouching lion at the end of a long, plain enclosure
of beech hedging (copper and common) and a long,
refreshing grassy vista through old trees.
Plantsmanship is a term often used for the urge to
accumulate rare plants. Here, in the foliage garden,
for example, with its groups of plants of striking
foliage, they are used as Gertrude Jekyll
recommended – 'the best plants in the best places'.

LACKHAM COLLEGE GARDENS
Wiltshire

Lacock, Chippenham
SN15 2NY
1m S of Chippenham by
A350
Tel: 0249 443111

Open: Easter to Oct, daily
11–4

LACKHAM IS a college of agriculture and horticulture that occupies an enviable 18th-century house at the heart of an ancient estate. The house overlooks an Italianate rose garden with balustrades, urns and fountains, and parkland beyond. To one side is an old walled kitchen garden, kept to high standards, where there is a herb garden, a bed of ornamental vegetables, displays of annuals, a lily bed and several other display gardens. Superb glasshouses contain tender plants; one is a citron plant which, as recorded by *The Guinness Book of Records*, produced the largest fruit (over 10lbs) ever grown.

MATTOCKS ROSES
Oxfordshire

The Rose Nurseries,
Nuneham Courtenay
OX9 9PY
6m SE of Oxford by A423
Tel: 086 738 265

Open: Mon to Sat 9–5.30
(5 in winter), Sun
10.30–5.30

MATTOCKS, which means roses to many gardeners, was established in 1875 and still has one of the best stocks of roses in the country. The emphasis is on modern cultivars, with regular new varieties introduced by Mattocks itself, but there are worthwhile collections of older types of shrub roses and of species. All these are of high quality and most may be seen growing at the nursery. A good catalogue is produced with much background information including the names of breeders and dates of introduction. A mail order service is provided but nothing beats sniffing them in blooming fragrance in June or July.

MOTTISFONT ABBEY GARDEN
Hampshire

Mottisfont,
nr Romsey SO51 0LJ
4 1/2m NW of Romsey by
A3057
Tel: 0794 41220/40757

Owner:
The National Trust

Open: Apr to Sept, Sun to
Thur 2–6; occasional
evening openings of Rose
Garden late Jun to Jul.
21 acres. House open

MOTTISFONT IS known for its Rose Garden in which an immense collection of shrub roses, with an emphasis on the older varieties, is arranged in the old walled kitchen garden. Here is housed the National Collection of pre-1900 shrub roses. Unlike many rose gardens, however, this is beautifully designed in box-edged beds divided by lawns and gravel paths, and the beds are enriched by all kinds of herbaceous plants which maintain interest when the roses are not performing. Visiting gardeners will not only meet many unfamiliar roses but they will discover an immense amount about their ornamental use in the garden. All this is a tribute to Graham Stuart Thomas who rediscovered so many old roses and supervised the making of this garden. Nearer the house, partly medieval stone and partly Georgian brick, there are other things worth seeing: a pleached lime alley designed by Sir Geoffrey Jellicoe with carpets of chionodoxa in the spring; a dashing box parterre with summer bedding; and, down by the River Test which flows through the grounds, a stupendous London plane tree, one of the most memorable trees you will ever see.

NEWINGTON NURSERIES
Oxfordshire

Old School, Newington,
Oxford OX9 8AW
9m SE of Oxford by B480
Tel: 0865 891401

Open: Sat and Sun 10–4

Newington nurseries sell only conservatory plants and the atmosphere is heady with delicious tropical scents. Chris and Carol Colbourne have a wide range of the sort of outrageously showy plants that make conservatory life exciting – several bougainvilleas, tender buddlejas, hedychiums, mandevillas, oleanders and the mysterious marmalade bush *Streptosolen jamesonii*. A catalogue is issued and orders are supplied by post.

OAKLEIGH NURSERIES
Hampshire

Monkwood,
Alresford SO24 0HB
In the village of
Monkwood 4m SE of
Alresford by A31 and
minor roads
Tel: 0962 773344

Open: Apr to Jul, Mon to
Fri 10–1, 2–4.30; Apr to
Jun, also Sat and Sun
10.30–1, 2–4

The Clarks at Oakleigh sell fuchsias, pelargoniums, epiphyllums and Christmas cacti of which the first two are of most interest to most gardeners. There are now over 1,500 different cultivars of pelargonium on the market and rather more of fuchsia and they need careful selecting. Both are excellent plants for containers and Oakleigh has a wide range. All except hopelessly rabid collectors will probably find what they want here and all the plants are propagated by the nursery. A particularly efficient mail order service sends plants in special containers at the nursery's risk. A well illustrated and informative catalogue is produced.

THE OLD RECTORY
Berkshire

Burghfield, Reading
RG3 3TH
In Burghfield village 5m
SW of Reading

Owner: Mr and Mrs R.R.
Merton

Open: Feb to Oct, last
Wed in month 10–4 (and
by appointment in writing).
4 1/2 acres

THIS WONDERFUL GARDEN gets in only by the skin of its teeth because it is open so rarely, but it is so good that it would be worth planning a visit to these parts to coincide with its opening. The rectory is a 16th-century brick house with a gentlemanly 18th-century pedimented façade and the garden behind it is a dashing mixture of ingredients. Immediately behind the house a marvellous cedar of Lebanon, the supreme garden ornament, is given full breathing space on a lawn. Beyond it a pair of brilliant borders, separated by a crisp turf path and backed by yew hedges, is an object lesson of design in which repeated plantings give structure to the herbaceous profusion. At the end of the borders a pool with a statue of Apollo is fringed with maples, bold foliage planting and flowering shrubs. All about the house are beautifully judged plantings (including some excellent troughs) and there is a splendid kitchen garden. On open days a plant *souk* appears in the yard and many good plants are sold.

OXFORD BOTANIC GARDEN
Oxfordshire

High Street,
Oxford OX1 4AX
In the centre of Oxford,
near Magdalen Bridge
Tel: 0865 276920

Owner: University of
Oxford

Open: Daily except Good
Fri and Christmas Day 9–5
(4.30 in winter)

THIS WALLED GARDEN, with its lovely early 17th-century entrance gate, was founded in 1631, the first botanic garden in England. It still preserves its character of a 'repository of curious plants' but it is extremely attractively laid out and very well maintained. There are rectangular 'order' beds – with plants grouped according to botanical families – and there are also many ornamental trees and shrubs, some of them unusual (like the golden-leafed hop tree, *Ptelea trifoliata* 'Aurea'). Everything is impeccably labelled so it is an admirable place to learn about plants.

PLANTS FROM A COUNTRY GARDEN
Buckinghamshire

The Thatched Cottage,
Duck Lane, Ludgershall, nr
Aylesbury HP18 9NZ
11m W of Aylesbury by
A41
Tel: 0844 237415 (evenings
only)

Open: Mar to Oct, Wed to
Sun and Bank Hol 10–6

Illustration: Campanula
lactiflora alba

DEREK AND JUDY Tolman sell what they describe as 'rare, old-fashioned and desirable plants' which pretty exactly covers the scope of their fascinating nursery. The emphasis is on herbaceous plants and their selections of many groups of plants are among the best you will find. There are many achilleas, species aquilegias, campanulas, hardy geraniums, a marvellous range of Michaelmas daisies (including some rare old cultivars), mints, an irresistible selection of pinks (including some of the oldest cultivars), a wide range of primulas (with an emphasis on species), very many violas and several perennial wall-flowers. It would be hard to imagine any gardener visiting this nursery and coming away empty handed. The Tolmans issue a catalogue that is full of all sorts of interesting information about the plants they collect and sell. Orders are fulfilled by post.

QUEEN ELEANOR'S GARDEN
Hampshire

Winchester Castle,
Winchester
In the centre of Winchester
Tel: 0962 840222

Owner: Winchester City
Council

Open: Daily 10–5

THIS LITTLE recreated 13th-century garden in the authentic medieval setting of Henry III's Great Hall was designed by Dr Sylvia Landsberg at the instigation of the Hampshire Gardens Trust. The planting consists only of plants known in gardens before 1300 and an ornamental fountain and stone seats are based on period survivals found at Winchester. A turf seat, a tunnel arbour of twining honeysuckle and vines, and the old walls of the Great Hall vividly evoke enclosed gardens of the period. No true medieval gardens survive in England and this gives a charming and historically accurate idea of what they looked like.

ROCHE COURT SCULPTURE GARDEN
Wiltshire

Winterslow, nr Salisbury
SP5 1BG
5m E of Salisbury by A30
Tel: 0980 862204

Owner: Mrs M. Ponsonby

Open: Apr to Sept, Sat and
Sun 11–5

THERE IS a renaissance of the use of ornaments in the garden and this is a splendid place to see them in action. The late Georgian house is in a wonderful position with wide views down a wooded valley and the garden itself is rich in excellent old trees, yew hedges and old walls which make a very good setting in which to display ornaments. Roche Court is partly a private garden and partly the country department of a London art gallery (the New Art Centre) in which sculptures and pots are displayed for sale. Some of these are by well known artists such as Eric Gill or Barbara Hepworth, others by the new and little known. Some of the ornaments are part of the owner's permanent collection but most change constantly, giving a new aspect to the place. All benefit from their open air display, and the ensemble of house, garden, views and works of art make it a memorable place to visit.

ROUSHAM HOUSE
Oxfordshire

Steeple Aston OX5 3QX
12m N of Oxford by A423
and B4030
Tel: 0869 47110

Owner: C. Cottrell-Dormer

Open: Apr to Sept, daily
10–4.30. 30 acres. House
open

THERE ARE FEW 18th-century landscape gardens
surviving in England where it is still possible to
see exactly what the designer intended. Rousham was
designed between 1737 and 1741 by William Kent
who devised a virtuoso arrangement of statues,
buildings, water, a serpentine woodland rill and,
above all, made a framework from which to admire
the views over the River Cherwell towards the rural
landscape beyond. Some of the individual garden
buildings are exceptionally beautiful: Praeneste, a
wonderful arcaded curve of golden stone, giving
viewpoints of subtly changing aspect; Kent's little
covered seat of trellis and boards; a solemn gothic
temple half-shaded by the woods. The statues are of
fine quality and almost all of them turn their backs
on the garden and gaze out to the countryside. All
this is done with the effortless ease of a conjuror
pulling rabbits out of a hat. Nearer the house, in the
old kitchen garden with its decorative dovecote, there
is a charming modern arrangement of mixed borders
and a box-edged rose parterre.

SAVILL GARDEN
Berkshire

Windsor Great Park
3m W of Egham by A30
and Wick Road
Tel: None

Owner: Crown Property

Open: Daily 10–6 (closed
for Christmas period). 35
acres

SOME GARDENS set a style and affect the way people make gardens and the Savill Garden has had a strong influence on the tradition of woodland gardening. It was started in 1932 by E.H. (later Sir Eric) Savill who was Deputy Ranger of Windsor Great Park. He invented a natural style of woodland gardening which gave the plants appropriate habitats and made something that was beautiful. The well-watered site with many old trees – especially oaks – was an excellent place for a woodland garden. He planted large numbers of ornamental trees and shrubs – azaleas, camellias, dogwoods, magnolias, rhododendrons – and about the streams moisture-loving plants such as ferns, lysichiton, primulas and rheums. A grove of stately beeches is carpeted with dense, rich moss.

SPINNERS
Hampshire

Boldre, Lymington
SO41 5QE
1m NE of Lymington by
A337
Tel: 0590 73347

Open: Apr to Sept, daily
9–6; Oct to Mar, daily 9–5
or dusk if earlier

ON ACID SOIL and surrounded by woodland, Spinners is both a garden and an outstanding nursery garden. The drive that winds downhill is well planted with ornamental trees and shrubs and nearer the house there are excellent borders. All this, attractive as it is, pales into insignificance compared with the riches of the nursery. Peter Chappell is a plant fanatic and sells an immense range of good things. There are, for example, 90 different species and varieties of magnolia, a huge selection of maples and rhododendrons, many cistuses, rare oaks and witch hazels – and that is only in the woody department. There are also choice riches in herbaceous plants – decorative grasses, dozens of geraniums and a host of hostas. A catalogue is produced but there is no mail order, so you will have to visit – and discover all sorts of things that are not even in the compendious list.

STOURHEAD
Wiltshire

Stourton, Warminster
BA12 6QH
In Stourton village, 3m
NW of Mere by A303 and
B3092
Tel: 0747 840348

Owner:
The National Trust

Open: Daily 8–7 or sunset
if earlier. 40 acres. House
open

ALTHOUGH THIS IS probably the most photographed and certainly the best-known landscape garden in England the experience of visiting it, in different seasons of the year, always provides some new pleasure. It was started in 1741 by the banker Henry Hoare who dammed the River Stour to make a sinuous lake about whose shores he disposed paths, temples, urns, a shivery grotto and, clothing the hillsides, a vast wealth of trees. Although there has been much subsequent planting, continuing in present times, the character of the original layout is unimpaired. Even at rhododendron time it is possible to escape the crush of visitors, ascend the precipitous paths that wind up away from the lake, and experience the authentic feeling of thrilling solitude such gardens inspired in the 18th century.

STOWE LANDSCAPE GARDENS
Buckinghamshire

Buckingham MK18 5EH
3m NW of Buckingham off
A422
Tel: 0280 822850

Owner:
The National Trust

Open: School holidays:
daily 10–6 or dusk if
earlier; Term time: Mon,
Wed, Fri 10–5 or dusk if
earlier (Ansaphone for
dates and additional
openings); closed Good Fri
and 24, 25 Dec. 250 acres.
House open

STOWE MAKES all other gardens seem like light snacks – this is the full banquet. It is a giant 18th-century landscape garden in which the greatest garden designers of the day worked – Charles Bridgeman, William Kent and 'Capability' Brown, who was head gardener in 1741. They made a vast landscape in which grass, trees, water, ornaments, buildings and huge vistas are woven together into a series of exquisite pictures. The monuments and buildings have all sorts of meanings – many of them political – and are often decorated with literary inscriptions. A full understanding of the place means unravelling their significance, but even without that knowledge any visitor can revel in the marvellous shifting scenes that compose the garden. One of its great charms is the contrast of immense views and corners of pastoral intimacy, of grazing cattle and classical temples. To walk about Stowe – and it is a long and exhilarating walk – is one of the greatest of all garden experiences. The National Trust, which recently took over the park, has embarked on a restoration that is already showing brilliant results.

TUDOR HOUSE GARDEN
Hampshire

Tudor House, Bugle Street,
Southampton SO1 OA8
Centre of Southampton;
follow signs to old town
and docks
Tel: 0703 332513

Owner: Southampton
County Council

Open: Tue to Fri 10–5, Sat
10–4

THIS IS a very attractive idea – a dashing recreation of a Tudor period garden, designed by Dr Sylvia Landsberg in 1982 as the annexe to an excellent museum in the old city of Southampton. In the garden there is a knot of box, plants of the period, characteristic columns painted in chevrons and surmounted by heraldic beasts, hives with honey bees, a rose arbour and a tunnel of vines. On a hot summer's day, when the place is heady with herbal scents, the visitor may experience something of the true character of a garden of the period.

VENTNOR BOTANIC GARDEN
Isle of Wight

The Undercliffe Drive,
Ventnor, Hampshire
PO38 1UL
Tel: 0983 855397

Owner: South Wight
Borough Council

Open: Daily 9–5

ON THE SOUTH coast of the Isle of Wight Ventnor has an exceptional microclimate and one of the chief interests of this botanic garden is the large collection of plants from the southern hemisphere and from the Mediterranean countries. These are displayed in sweeping beds and fine old Holm oaks (*Quercus ilex*) and strawberry trees (*Arbutus unedo*) provide a handsome evergreen background. A large temperate house protects more tender subjects, where there are well arranged collections from South Africa and Australia and also from less familiar regions like the island of St Helena which has a fascinating flora.

WADDESDON MANOR
Buckinghamshire

Waddesdon,
nr Aylesbury HP18 0JH
6m NW of Aylesbury by
A41
Tel: 0296 651211

Owner:
The National Trust

Open: 18 Mar to 23 Dec,
Wed to Fri 12–5; Easter
weekend and Bank Hol
12–6. 160 acres. House
open (but closed for
restoration until 1993)

*Illustration opposite: Statue
at Waddesdon Manor*

THIS IS a Rothschild garden and a splendid one. The house is a fantasy pastiche of a Loire château, finished in 1889 for Baron Ferdinand de Rothschild and built on a wonderful site – the top of a hill commanding views over the Vale of Aylesbury. The slopes of the hill are encircled with walks and clothed in splendid trees. A marvellous collection of statues animates the scene. To the south of the house are terraced gardens which are now being restored with elaborate bedding schemes to their original high Victorian splendour. To one side of the house a superb aviary of delicate tracery and rococo curlicues houses a collection of exotic birds.

WATERPERRY GARDENS
Oxfordshire

nr Wheatley OX9 1JZ
9m E of Oxford by A40
Tel: 0844 339254

Owner: School of
Economic Science

Open: Apr to Sept, daily
10–5.30 (6 at weekends);
Oct to Mar 10–4.30.
83 acres

WATERPERRY WAS started in 1932 as a pioneer horticultural college for women by the extraordinary Miss Beatrix Havergal. Although still providing courses for amateurs, it is today chiefly a nursery garden and a very attractive pleasure garden. The nursery has an excellent range of all the essential garden plants – including a comprehensive collection of fruit trees, bushes and canes. Alpine plants are a particular speciality and the garden holds the National Collection of porphyrion (kabschia) saxifrages. The ornamental gardens have giant herbaceous borders, an alpine garden, fine trees and the beautifully tended stock beds for the nursery.

WEST WYCOMBE PARK
Buckinghamshire

West Wycombe HP14 3AJ
2m W of High Wycombe
by A40
Tel: 0494 524411

Owner:
The National Trust

Open: Apr to May, Sun
and Wed 2–6; Easter, May
and Spring Bank Hol 2–6;
Jun to Aug, Sun to Thur
2–6. 46 acres. House open

THE PARK at West Wycombe, made for the
Dashwoods in the 18th century, is among the
smaller English landscape gardens and is an excellent
place to understand the particular charms of that
style. The 18th-century pillared and portico'd house
stands on a wooded eminence overlooking a lake
with an island on which is an airy Music Temple
and, nearby on the shore, a gothic boathouse. The
lake feeds a cascade guarded by two recumbent
nymphs and a stream winds across meadow land. In
the woods about the lake an exotic Temple of the
Winds marks the meeting point of two vistas. All the
ingredients are harmoniously interrelated and form a
series of shifting and seductive views.

GILBERT WHITE MUSEUM
Hampshire

Selborne,
nr Alton GU34 3JH
In the village of Selborne,
5m SE of Alton by B3006
Tel: 042 050 275

Owner: Oates Memorial
Trust

Open: Mar to Oct, daily
except Mon (open Bank
Hol) 10–5.30

GILBERT WHITE was as passionately observant
about gardening as he was about natural history
and this place – his former house and garden – is
sacred ground. Behind the house, which is in the
village high street, the garden has wonderful views
across to the wooded ridge known as the Hanger.
A rose garden, yew hedges and topiary, a laburnum
tunnel and herbaceous borders are well cared for.
These are relatively modern features but there still
remains much from White's time – the ha-ha he
made in 1761, his fruit wall and a decorative sun-dial.

SOUTH-WEST ENGLAND

—————— ཛ ——————

Avon, Cornwall, Devon, Dorset, Somerset

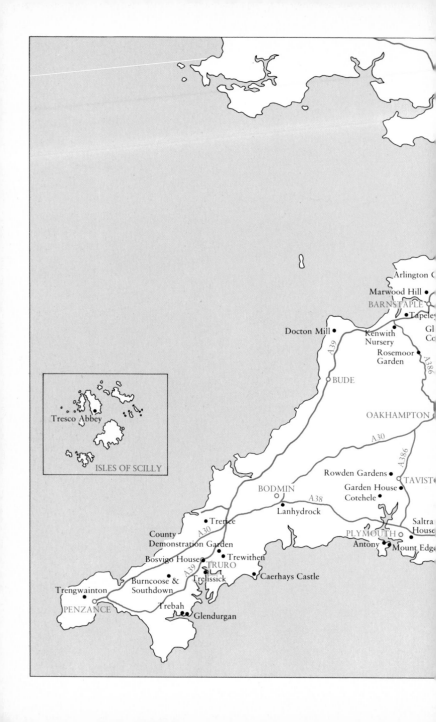

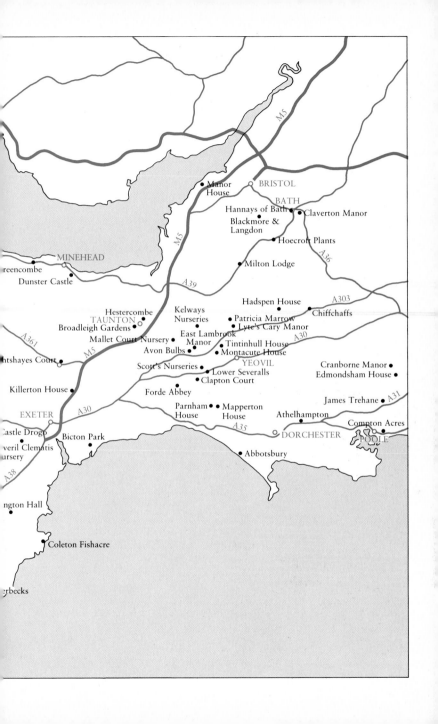

BRISTOL

BATH

Manor House

Hannays of Bath

Claverton Manor

Blackmore & Langdon

Hoecroft Plants

MINEHEAD

Milton Lodge

reencombe

Dunster Castle

Hadspen House

Kelways Nurseries

Chiffchaffs

Hestercombe

TAUNTON

Patricia Marrow

Broadleigh Gardens

Lyte's Cary Manor

Mallet Court Nursery

East Lambrook Manor

Tintinhull House

Avon Bulbs

Montacute House

htshayes Court

YEOVIL

Scott's Nurseries

Cranborne Manor

Lower Severalls

Edmondsham House

Killerton House

Clapton Court

Forde Abbey

James Trehane

EXETER

Parnham House

Mapperton House

Athelhampton

Compton Acres

astle Drogo

Bicton Park

DORCHESTER

POOLE

veril Clematis
ursery

Abbotsbury

ngton Hall

Coleton Fishacre

rbecks

ABBOTSBURY SUB-TROPICAL GARDENS

Dorset

Abbotsbury, nr Weymouth
DT3 4LA
1/2m W of Abbotsbury
village, 9m NW of
Weymouth by B3157
Tel: 0305 87387

Owner: Ilchester Estates

Open: Daily except Mon in
winter 10–6. 20 acres

BENEFITING FROM a remarkably mild microclimate, Abbotsbury Gardens have an immense range of plants. The garden was started in the 1760s but the 4th Earl of Ilchester introduced many new plants in the 19th century. From the original walled garden with its beautiful wingnut (*Pterocarya fraxinifolia*), paths lead to the valley garden, a gentle combe with camellias, magnolias and rhododendrons in old woodland. Asiatic primulas enliven the banks of the stream in spring followed later by the vast leaves of gunnera, petasites, rodgersias and rheums. Everywhere there is something to catch the eye in the surrounding jungle-like luxuriance. National Collections of eucalyptus and salvia are held at Abbotsbury and there are some good plants for sale.

ANTONY HOUSE

Cornwall

Torpoint PL11 2QA
5m W of Plymouth by
Torpoint car ferry and A374
Tel: 0752 812191

Owner:
The National Trust

Open: Apr to Oct, Tue,
Wed, Thur and Bank Hol
1.30–5.30; Jun to Aug, also
Sun 1.30–5.30. 25 acres.
House open

WHEN A HOUSE is as beautiful as Antony there is always a danger that any garden will be outfaced. As it is, helped by the genius of Humphry Repton, the two go together in perfect harmony. The house – an early 18th-century dream of silver Pentewan stone – presents its north façade to land which slopes gently towards the distant Tamar estuary. The view from the house, over shallow rose-planted terraces, is towards an immense lawn broken in the middle ground only by a superb old black walnut (*Juglans nigra*). Far beyond this, Repton pierced an opening through a deep belt of woodland to give glimpses of the shimmering water in the distance. In the woods there are marvellous trees, including some ancient holm oaks which Repton admired and was careful to preserve. To the west of the house a grassy walk runs between high yew hedges. A flower garden, and a recently made knot of box and germander, are enclosed in yew, and in the

old vegetable garden there is an immense collection of daylilies of which Antony holds a National Collection. South of all this is a giant cork oak (*Quercus suber*), the largest in Britain, and a marvellous thing to see.

ANTONY WOODLAND GARDEN AND WOODS
Cornwall

Torpoint PL11 2QA
5m W of Plymouth by
Torpoint car ferry and
A374

Owner: Carew Pole
Garden Trust

Open: Woodland garden:
mid–Mar to mid–Jun, Aug
to Oct, Mon to Sat
11–5.30, Sun 2.30– 5.30;
Woodland walk: mid–Mar
to Oct, same times. 100
acres

ADJOINING THE HOUSE and garden at Antony, and still owned by the family that built it, is an atmospheric woodland garden. Sir John Carew Pole started to plant it before World War II but was interrupted by active service. Since then he has added an immense number of magnolias and rhododendrons which flourish in the naturalistic setting of a wooded combe protected to the west by windbreaks. The woods fringe the estuary of the River Lynher and an idyllic walk gives glimpses of the mainland and the castellated silhouette of Ince Castle.

ARLINGTON COURT
Devon

Arlington, nr Barnstaple
EX31 4LP
7m NE of Barnstaple by
A39
Tel: 0271 850296

Owner:
The National Trust

Open: Apr to Oct, daily
except Sat (open Sat Bank
Hol weekends) 11–5.30.
25 acres. House open

THE PLEASURES of Arlington are not dramatic but they are distinctive. The best thing here is a little Victorian garden with, as its central ornament, a handsome gabled glasshouse crowned with a decorative metal heron, the crest of the Chichester family who owned the estate for many centuries. The garden is backed by a high wall and the ground descends in bold turfed terraces to the entrance steps which are flanked by a pair of cast-iron herons holding wriggling worms in their beaks. On either side of a central pool and fountain, arbours are festooned with roses in summer. The Victorian garden is some distance from the house which is set in lawns with fine specimen trees including the recent addition of a collection of species of ash. The lake was made at about the same time as the Victorian garden and a classical urn on a plinth to its north-east is in memory of Miss Rosalie Chichester who gave the estate to the National Trust.

ATHELHAMPTON
Dorset

Athelhampton DT2 7LG
5 1/2m NE of Dorchester
by A35
Tel: 0305 848363

Owner: Lady Du Cann

Open: Easter to Oct, Wed,
Thur and Sun 2–6; May to
Sept, also Tue; Aug, also
Mon. 10 acres. House open

Illustration opposite:
*Looking through the gates
of the enclosed gardens at
Athelhampton*

THE GREAT THING about the garden at Athelhampton is the beauty of its design. This is a late medieval manor house of rare character and the garden, which was designed in the 1890s by F. Inigo Thomas, fits it to perfection. A balustraded terrace ornamented with two elegant summer houses overlooks a narrow canal and beyond, disposed on a sunken lawn with a pool, are twelve giant pyramids of clipped yew. On the far side a gate leads through to a series of enclosed gardens – cunningly connected to the house by penetrating vistas – which are richly ornamented with statues, fountains, obelisks, beautifully detailed walls and gate piers in golden Ham stone. A new cloister garden – a circle of pleached lime round an octagonal pool with a fountain – has recently been added in keeping with the rest. The whole place is a virtuoso performance: a garden harmoniously related to house and site.

AVON BULBS

Somerset

Burnt House Farm, Mid
Lambrook, South Petherton
TA13 5HE
10m W of Yeovil by A3088
and A303 to South
Petherton
Tel: 0460 42177

Open: Mid–Feb to
mid–Apr; end Sept to
mid–Nov, Thur to Sat
9–4.30 (check by telephone;
also by appointment)

BECAUSE OF the restricted opening times this wonderful place only just qualifies for inclusion. Avon Bulbs wins Gold Medals at Chelsea regularly and its list is stuffed with good things. There is an emphasis on species or natural forms and many genera are represented in quantity (e.g. 16 species and forms of fritillary and over 20 snowdrops). The nursery's business is overwhelmingly bulbs but it occasionally strays into other desirable areas such as hellebores, of which a choice selection is offered. The list is one of the best, full of meticulous detail about the plants, including advice on cultivation. A mail order service is provided.

BICTON PARK

Devon

East Budleigh, Budleigh
Salterton EX9 7DP
6m NE of Exmouth by
A376
Tel: 0395 68465

Owner: Bicton Park Trust
Company

Open: Apr to Oct, daily
10–6. 50 acres

IT WOULD be a pity if garden visitors were deterred from coming to Bicton because of the family fun park with its ghost train and adventure playground, for there is a fascinating garden here as well. At the heart of it is a formal arrangement, the Italian Garden, which in essence dates from the early 18th century but now has a jolly Victorian character with bedded-out parterres, fountains, urns and palm trees. To the north is a range of glasshouses with collections of pelargoniums and orchids and, to the west, a stunning curvaceous palm house, like a ship's prow seen from below. Recently restored, this very early building dates from 1820, and has been planted with a splendid range of conservatory plants. To one side of the Italian Garden there is an ornamental shell-house set in a ferny rock garden and, another relic of the early 19th century, an American garden in which plants from North America were grown. A woodland railway rambling through the grounds gives views of a fine arboretum and the old house.

BLACKMORE & LANGDON LTD
Avon

Pensford, Bristol BS18 4JL
6 1/2m S of Bristol by A37
Tel: 0272 332300

Open: Mon to Fri 9–4.30;
Easter to Jun, also Sun
1–4.30

Illustration: Delphinium
'*Cassius*'

OLD-ESTABLISHED FAMILY firms such as this are becoming very rare. Blackmore & Langdon was founded in 1901 and has won over 60 Gold Medals at the Chelsea Flower Show and countless others elsewhere. It is best known for delphiniums, border phlox and begonias, and many varieties of these are available only from Blackmore & Langdon whose catalogue every year advertises interesting new cultivars. It also sells tender cyclamen, freesias, gloxinias, nerines and polyanthus. The catalogue is particularly informative and excellent specialist pamphlets on growing some of these plants are issued. A mail order service is provided and special wire supports for delphiniums are available.

BOSVIGO HOUSE
Cornwall

Bosvigo Lane, Truro
TR1 3NH
In the western suburbs of
Truro by A390
Tel: 0872 75774 (after dark)

Owner: Michael and
Wendy Perry

Open: Jun to Sept, daily
11–6; nursery throughout
year, daily 11–dusk. 3 acres

BOSVIGO HOUSE is a surprising and very attractive place to find on the edge of Truro with bungaloid growth gnawing all about. In the garden, however, all that seems far away. The Perrys are perfectionists, and although the garden is still being developed, they seem to be doing all the right things. To one side of the handsome 18th-century house is a new woodland garden of exceptional charm. There are good trees and shrubs here but the main interest lies in the fastidiously chosen herbaceous plants which thrive under their canopy. The Perrys also sell an excellent range of plants, some very rare. There is a very good catalogue but no mail order.

BROADLEIGH GARDENS
Somerset

Bishops Hull, Taunton
TA4 1AE
3m SW of Taunton by A38
Tel: 0823 286231

Open: Mon to Fri 9–4.
Mail order sales only

*Illustration: Crown
imperials* (Fritillaria
imperialis lutea)

THIS IS AN outstandingly good nursery specialising in bulbs. Although the business is mail order only, you may visit the garden and view the plants on the spot. Spring is, of course, a good time but Lady Skelmersdale has all sorts of bulbous treats in store throughout the year – a rare selection of colchicums and autumn-flowering crocuses, for example. This is not a place for instant gardeners but you can go round, notebook and pencil in hand, making a shopping list to order from the excellent catalogue which is issued twice a year.

BURNCOOSE & SOUTHDOWN NURSERIES
Cornwall

Gwennap, Redruth
TR16 6BJ
3m SE of Redruth by A393
Tel: 0209 861112

Open: Mon to Sat 8.30–5,
Sun 2–5. Garden: 30 acres

THE NURSERY is in the ownership of the Williams family, famous plant collectors who also own Caerhays Castle. It carries a varied stock but there are specialities for which it is outstanding, some of which would be considered hopelessly tender anywhere outside the privileged south-west (for example, *Metrosideros*). There are groups of plants (such as camellias, magnolias and rhododendrons) of which it has especially good selections. Several rarities are stocked (for example *Pittosporum tenuifolium* 'Silver Magic') which are scarcely to be found anywhere else. A very good catalogue is published from which mail orders may be placed. Alongside the nursery is a fine old woodland garden in which camellias, magnolias and, above all, magnificent rhododendrons are attractively displayed.

CAERHAYS CASTLE
Cornwall

nr Gorran FA1 7DE
In the village of Caerhays
10m S of St Austell by
minor roads
Tel: 0872 501310

Owner: F.J. Williams

Open: 30 Mar to 8 May,
Mon to Fri 11–4.30; also
Suns 29 Mar and 19 Apr
and 4 May Bank Hol
2–5.30. 100 acres

THIS IS a special place for the three greatest groups of ornamental Asiatic shrubs: camellias, magnolias and rhododendrons. The Williams family who own it sponsored some of the great plant hunters – such as George Forrest and Frank Kingdon-Ward – and their discoveries found a marvellous home, climatically and aesthetically, in this wild coastal setting. North of the early 19th-century castle designed by John Nash, woodland sweeps up the hill. It is above all a place for the observant visitor because the garden's chief glories may lie hidden in the jungle and it is the excitement of discovery that is one of the exceptional pleasures of the place. Apart from the great trio of shrubs there are many others, some of them exceptionally rare and first planted here – such as the exotically scented *Michelia doltsopa* with its flowers of creamy yellow. The lavish feast of spring blossom, in this wildly romantic place, is one of the great garden sights.

CASTLE DROGO
Devon

Drewsteignton EX6 6PB
21m W of Exeter by A30
Tel: 0647 433306

Owner:
The National Trust

Open: Daily 10.30–5.30.
12 acres. Castle open

CASTLE DROGO, the last castle to be built in Britain, was designed by Edwin Lutyens and started before World War I. It occupies a dramatic position near Dartmoor on a rocky bluff commanding wide views over the wild country with the River Teign in the distance. The garden, to the north of the drive, is concealed behind ramparts of yew strongly echoing the bold forms of the castle. A huge circular croquet lawn enclosed by yew hedges, devoid of ornament and with powerful atmosphere, is linked by granite steps and a path to a rectangular sunken garden. Here, in each corner, is a shady arbour of *Parrotia persica* trained over a framework, and around two central lawns are mixed borders. In late spring an immense old wisteria snakes along the terrace walls, its flowers dripping to the beds below.

CHIFFCHAFFS
Dorset

Chaffeymoor, Bourton, Gillingham SP8 5BY
3m E of Wincanton by A303
Tel: 0747 840841

Owner: Mr and Mrs K.R. Potts

Open: Garden: 22 Mar to 27 Sept, Sun, Wed and Thur (except 2nd Sun, Wed and Thur in month) and Bank Hol weekend 2–5.30; Nursery: Tue–Sat 10–1, 2–5, and whenever garden is open. 11 acres

THIS GARDEN, in a surprisingly secluded valley just off the A303, was started from nothing 12 years ago and the owners recently incorporated within it their nursery garden, Abbey Plants. The

sloping site has been skilfully terraced and linked with stone paths and steps. The soil is acid and a very wide range of plants is grown in beds separated by curving lawns. The different levels, and secluded nooks and crannies, provide a variety of sites in an attractively informal setting. Across a field is a woodland garden threaded with streams where moisture-loving plants such as primulas, gunnera and rheums thrive in the shade of rhododendrons and many ornamental trees. All this is an exceptional example of what can be achieved by skilled gardeners in a remarkably short time. The nursery has an excellent general range of plants at modest prices and a visit is essential as no mail order service is provided.

CLAPTON COURT

Somerset

Clapton, nr Crewkerne
TA18 8PT
In the village of Clapton
3m S of Crewkerne by
B3165
Tel: 0460 73220

Owner: Captain S.J. Loder

Open: Feb to Nov, Mon to
Fri 10.30–5, Sun 2–5.
10 acres

THERE IS PLENTY to see at Clapton Court – two gardens of different character and a good nursery. The formal part has lively terraced garden rooms walled with yew, hornbeam and cotoneaster. Beyond the house, following a stream with some good planting, there is a woodland garden with outstanding trees underplanted with rhododendrons and other ornamental shrubs. The nursery has very large collections of fuchsias and pelargoniums and a wide general stock. A catalogue is produced but there is no mail order, so a visit is recommended.

CLAVERTON MANOR
Avon

Claverton, nr Bath
BA2 7BD
4m SE of Bath by A36
Tel: 0225 460503

Owner: The American
Museum in Britain

Open: Apr to Oct, daily
except Mon 2–5, Bank Hol
Sun and Mon 11–5. 10
acres. House open

CLAVERTON MANOR, with its wonderful views across the Avon valley, is an elegant Bath stone mansion designed by Sir Jeffry Wyatville. The position of the garden, on south-facing slopes, is beautiful, with excellent old trees – evergreen oaks, limes and beeches – providing a backdrop for the gardens made here since the American Museum came in 1961. Under the walls of the house the American garden designer Lanning Roper laid out an effective mixed border punctuated by Irish yews. A further transatlantic flavour is given by a collection of herbs used in colonial times, disposed in box-edged beds with a bee-skep at the centre. To the west of the house, overlooked by terraces, is a George Washington garden, influenced by Washington's Virginian estate of Mount Vernon. Here are sweeping beds edged in brick or box, gravel paths and an elegant octagonal pepper-pot gazebo. Farther down the slopes an arboretum planted with American trees and shrubs vividly reminds the visitor of the debt owed by British gardens to American flora. All this is impeccably maintained. A small selection of well-grown herbs is offered for sale.

COLETON FISHACRE GARDEN
Devon

Coleton, Kingswear,
Dartmouth TQ6 0EQ
4m S of Brixham off B3205
Tel: 080 425 466

Owner:
The National Trust

Open: Apr to Oct, Wed to
Sun (except Sat) 10.30–5.30
or dusk if earlier; also 1, 8,
15, 22, 29 Mar, 2–5. 18
acres

THIS IS a remote corner of south Devon and to find a garden here at all seems pretty unlikely; to find one of such special charm as this is amazing good fortune. The house, built by Oswald Milne, a follower of Edwin Lutyens, for the D'Oyly Carte family, looks down a narrow valley that descends to the sea. The garden has a very warm microclimate and the sea adds to the humidity. Plants flourish here and many tender things, tricky if not impossible to grow elsewhere in Britain, seem luxuriantly at home. A stream runs the whole length of the garden, occasionally breaking out into little pools whose banks are finely planted with moisture-loving herbaceous perennials. The sides of the valley, threaded with winding paths, are densely planted with trees and shrubs. There are many camellias and rhododendrons but also far more exciting things – tender exotics such as the crape myrtle (*Lagerstroemia indica*), *Mandevilla suaveolens* and great thickets of mimosa (*Acacia dealbata*).

COMPTON ACRES
Dorset

Canford Cliffs, Poole
BO1 9LS
1 1/2m W of Bournemouth
by A35 and B3065
Tel: 0202 700778

Owner: Mr and Mrs L.
Green

Open: Apr to Oct, daily
10.30–6.30. 10 acres

IN SPITE of Compton Acres' popularity, garden snobs should not turn their backs on it for it has an immense amount to offer. The precipitous site, with old pine woods close to the sea, reveals occasional splendid views to the Isle of Purbeck. The garden is arranged in a series of thematic episodes, each of which is beautifully arranged to give surprise: an Italian garden with a long pool, splashing fountains, clipped hedges and statues; a palm court with a Moorish flavour; an elaborate water garden with conifers and paths winding over rocks; and an immense Japanese garden of great character, shady, richly ornamented and dramatic. There are many excellent plants – in particular rhododendrons in a valley garden and many conifers and heathers in the heather dell. All this is done with panache and maintained to exemplary standards.

COTEHELE
Cornwall

St Dominick, nr Saltash
PL12 6TA
8m SW of Tavistock off
A390
Tel: 0579 50434

Owner:
The National Trust

Open: Daily 11–5.30 or
dusk if earlier. 10 acres.
House open

THE GABLED and towered courtyard house, built in late Tudor times of moody grey granite by the Edgcumbe family, is at the centre of a garden that has many different faces. The house itself and its splendid outhouses and courtyards provide sheltered corners for all sorts of tender things such as the yellow-flowered *Jasminum meznyi*. North-west of the house is a meadow which in spring is bright with daffodils. From here a gate leads through to a garden of more formal atmosphere, with a pool at the centre and a good border running along the northern wall. East of the house a series of terraces are planted with wallflowers in spring, followed in summer by roses, and there are some superb magnolias on the lower lawn. From the bottom terrace a secret passage leads through to a complete change of atmosphere. Here is a woodland garden in a steep valley with a pool and ancient dovecote shaped like a giant beehive. In the woods paths amble among many camellias, magnolias and rhododendrons richly underplanted with ferns and moisture-loving plants; hostas, primulas and the bold foliage of *Gunnera manicata* relish the banks of a rushing stream.

COUNTY DEMONSTRATION GARDEN
Cornwall

Probus, Nr Truro
TR1 3BA
8m SW of St Austell by
A390
Tel: 0872 74282

Owner: Cornwall County
Council

Open: May to Sept, daily
10–5; Oct to Apr, Mon to
Fri 10–4.30

IT IS HARD to imagine any gardener failing to learn something interesting, diverting or useful at this ambitious and well-organised place. It has many displays of particular groups of plants – roses, herbs, lilies, dahlias, ivies, conifers and so on – but also of plants for specific sites (e.g. windy places) and purposes (e.g. shrubs giving shade or acting as a mulch). There are many exhibitions showing horticultural techniques – for example comparing the results of different types of digging; different kinds of nourishment; the correct way to plant and prune trees; how to support and train climbers, and an immense number of other things. There is no particular emphasis on organic techniques but if this is what interests you, you can learn about them here. All this is vividly displayed and more quickly grasped and easily digested than by reading even the very best of gardening manuals.

CRANBORNE MANOR GARDENS
Dorset

Cranborne, nr Wimborne
BH21 5PP
In the village of Cranborne
16 1/2m SW of Salisbury
by A354 and B3081
Tel: 072 54 248

Owner: Viscount and
Viscountess Cranborne

Open: Garden: Apr to Sept,
Wed 9–5; Garden centre:
Mar to Dec, daily 9–5 (Sun
2–5). 10 acres

THE MANOR house, once a medieval hunting lodge, has been in the Cecil family since the 16th century. The garden has ancient origins but was given a new breath of life by the Marchioness of Salisbury. There are excellent borders, a pretty knot garden, waves of pinks under espaliered apple trees, a 17th-century mount and the exceptional charm of an ancient place embosomed in even more ancient woods. The garden centre next door to the manor is in fact a nursery garden and a particularly good one. It carries a wide general stock but with especially good collections of old and shrub roses and clematises. It also sells modern Italian stone ornaments, made in the traditional way, furniture, trellis-work and some very good pots. A mail order service service is provided for roses only and a catalogue of them is issued.

DARTINGTON HALL
Devon

Dartington, nr Totnes
TQ9 6EL
2m NW of Totnes by A384
Tel: 0803 862271

Owner: Dartington Hall
Trust

Open: Daily, dawn–dusk.
30 acres

THE HOUSE is one of the most spectacular medieval mansions in Devon and the garden which lies chiefly to the south-west of it is designed on a heroic scale. The natural combe has been sculpted into great grassy terraces looking down onto an expanse of turf – supposedly a medieval jousting lawn. These terraces, and a formal arrangement to the north, were designed by the American garden designer Beatrix Farrand, her only work in England. On the highest terrace, in the shade of immense old sweet chestnuts, a splendid stone carving by Henry Moore of a reclining woman turns her back on the terraces below. Nearby, a vertiginous flight of steps sweeps down the hill and giant magnolias ornament each side. At the far end of the terraces more steps lead up to an ornamental pond with a fountain of carved swans in the shade of a very large *Elaeagnus umbellata* 'Parvifolia', and farther to the west glades open out in old woodland. This powerful shaping of the land and sensitive planting is entirely worthy of the great house.

DOCTON MILL
Devon

Spekes Valley, nr Hartland
EX39 6EA
3m S of Hartland follow
signs to Elmscott and
Lymebridge Cross
Tel: 0237 441369

Owner: Mr and Mrs N.S.
Pugh

Open: Mar to Sept, daily
10–5. 8 acres

THIS GARDEN has been made since 1980 and is a model of sensitive planting and design in an exceptionally beautiful site. Less than a mile from the coast, it is set in a secluded valley and possesses a favourable microclimate well protected from the coastal winds. Water is a central theme – running from the mill-stream and pond, and also from drainage pipes put in by the Pughs to feed an attractive pool. In spring the garden explodes into life with an immense collection of daffodils and the upper slopes of the valley sparkle with the young foliage of many shrubs and ornamental trees. There is an excellent bog garden and the banks of streams are planted with moisture-loving plants – lysichitons, ligularias, candelabra primulas and hostas, with bold

contrasts of foliage shape and colour. Farther from the house, natural woodland and an old orchard have an authentically rural character which contrasts well with the fastidious plantsmanship so evident nearer the house.

DUNSTER CASTLE

Somerset

Dunster, nr Minehead
TA24 6SL
3m SE of Minehead by
A396
Tel: 0643 821314

Owner:
The National Trust

Open: Feb, Mar, Oct to
Dec, daily 11–4; Apr to
Sept, daily 11–5.
17 acres. Castle open

THE MICROCLIMATE here is very privileged and the spectacular rocky crag on which the castle is built provides shelter to tender plants. The garden, which is informally arranged to spiral up the wooded slopes to a secluded plateau at the summit, has many plants from Australasia – such as pittosporums, mimosas and olearias. On a sunny terrace there is a large lemon tree, over 150 years old, which with winter protection fruits handsomely. The National Trust has been restoring and adding to this garden in recent years – planting an unusual grove of strawberry trees, for example.

EAST LAMBROOK MANOR
Somerset

East Lambrook, South
Petherton TA13 5HL
3m N of the A 303 to
South Petherton
Tel: 0460 40328

Owner: Mr and Mrs
Andrew Norton

Open: Garden: Mar to Oct,
daily except Sun (open
May Bank Hol weekend)
10–5; Nursery, daily except
Sun 10–5. 1 1/2 acres

*Illustration: Winter
aconites* (Eranthis hyemalis)
at East Lambrook Manor

THE GARDEN was made by Margery Fish from
1938 and, publicised by her excellent books,
became one of the best known gardens in England.
Mrs Fish invented a style of inspired cottage
gardening, often using carefully chosen forms of wild
plants. The design is informal and, although it is
given structure by clipped evergreens and pollarded
willows, there is scarcely a straight line in the place.
All this is a well-judged setting for the Ham stone
Elizabethan manor house. Her garden, superbly
restored since 1985 by new owners, is full of excellent
plants very well grown and some exceedingly rare. It
is also full of lessons for all gardeners about the
importance of siting plants and choosing those that
perform in every season; which makes the garden
well worth visiting at any time. It is especially strong
on herbaceous plants and contains the best collection
of cultivars of hardy geraniums (a National

Collection) in the country. An excellent nursery sells a very good range of the kind of plants grown in the garden, chiefly herbaceous and many of them unusual, at excellent prices. The nursery produces a catalogue and does mail order.

EDMONDSHAM HOUSE
Dorset

Edmondsham, nr Wimborne BH21 5RE 17m SW of Salisbury by A354 and B3081
Tel: 07254 207

Owner: Mrs J. Smith

Open: Apr to Jun, Oct, Wed to Sat 10–12. 5 acres

THE HOUSE at Edmondsham is marvellous, and splendidly two-faced – ornately Tudor and Jacobean on one side, suavely Georgian on the other. It is framed by excellent old trees, and there is no planting on the lawns to detract the eye. The chief garden interest here is an old 1-acre walled kitchen garden which is cultivated entirely organically. Fruit and vegetables are bursting with vigour, and broad double herbaceous borders – with delphiniums, peonies, poppies and campanulas – flank a path. With its impeccable potting shed, its old well and pump and its beautifully restored pit-house, this is a fascinating example of the kitchen gardens of the past. A hexagonal dairy (with extra shade on the south side), a root-store and an apple loft are also part of this intricately productive world.

FORDE ABBEY
Somerset

Chard TA20 4LU 7m W of Crewkerne by B3165
Tel: 0460 21366

Owner: M. Roper

Open: Daily 10.30–4.30. 20 acres. House open

THE LATE medieval monastic buildings at Forde are spectacular, and near the house old yew hedges with wambly tops and a procession of sentinel clipped yews provide suitably unfussy and venerable ornament. At some distance, across undulating turf with many fine specimen trees, a lake is overlooked by a curious summer house of pleached beech; beyond, is a fine bog garden. Extending from the south front of the house the beginning of a young lime avenue is marked by statues. In the old kitchen garden a nursery garden, The Abbey Nursery, sells a wide range of excellent plants with an emphasis on the tender and the unusual.

GARDEN HOUSE
Devon

Buckland Monachorum,
Yelverton PL20 7LQ
5m S of Tavistock by A386

Tel: 0822 854769

Owner: The Fortescue
Garden Trust

Open: Apr to Sept, daily
12–5. 2 acres

O N THE VERY edge of Dartmoor the Garden House is hidden in a wooded valley. Here, around some romantically decaying monastic ruins, Lionel Fortescue made a suitably romantic garden, surrounded by old walls and built on precipitous terraces. Clematis and roses scale the stone walls and there are wonderful riches of plants, especially herbaceous, artfully disposed. Here are no cold and calculating vistas – everything depends on the quality of the planting and meticulous upkeep. There is an exceptional small nursery selling ornamental trees and shrubs and herbaceous plants, none commonplace and all good value. There is a catalogue from which plants may be ordered by mail.

GLEBE COTTAGE PLANTS
Devon

Pixie Lane, Warkleigh,
Umberleigh EX37 9DH
6m W of South Molton by
B3226
Tel: 07694 554

Open: Wed to Thur 10–5
(check by phone)

Illustration: Geranium
pratense '*Mrs Kendall
Clark*'

C AROL KLEIN specialises in herbaceous plants with a few woody herbs. She sells exactly the kind of plants that many people want to grow in their gardens and she has excellent collections – campanulas, pinks, a long and distinguished list of hardy geraniums, many penstemons and a marvellous range of primulas. Most of these may be seen growing in her garden next to the nursery. An elegantly hand-lettered list is produced, from which plants may be supplied by mail.

GLENDURGAN GARDEN

Cornwall

Helford River, Mawnan
Smith, nr Falmouth
TR11 5JZ
4m SW of Falmouth on
road to Helford Passage
Tel: 0208 74281

Owner:
The National Trust

Open: Mar to Oct, Tue to
Sat and Bank Hol (closed
Good Fri) 10.30–5.30.
25 acres

THE FOXES are a great Cornish family and their garden exploits contributed immensely to the horticultural life of the county. Glendurgan was bought by Alfred Fox in 1821 and his family have been here ever since. The glen is a deep ravine which tumbles down to the sparkling water of the Helford estuary. On either side of the steep banks paths follow the contours but the bottom of the valley is not so densely planted as to obscure the marvellous views across to trees and shrubs on the other side of the ravine. Deftly infiltrated into the informal planting is a wandering maze of cherry laurel, planted in 1833 by Alfred Fox, and making a lively evergreen garden ornament. Like other Cornish gardens Glendurgan is abundantly rich in camellias, magnolias and rhododendrons but it also has exceptional trees such as an unforgettable tulip tree with wide spreading branches, one of the largest in the country. The view from the terrace of the house, at the head of the glen, perfectly composed, is one the visitor will not quickly forget.

GREENCOMBE

Somerset

Porlock TA24 8NU
1/2m W of Porlock by road
to Porlock Weir
Tel: 0643 862363

Owner: Greencombe
Garden Trust

Open: Mid-Apr to mid-Jul,
Sat, Sun and Mon 2–6. 10
acres

MUCH OF THE character of this remarkable garden is determined by its site – on slopes overlooking Porlock Weir and the Bristol Channel with a very benign microclimate. The garden was started after World War II by Horace Stroud but it is under Miss Joan Loraine, who made the present garden and passed it over to the Trust that now owns it, that it has come to full and unforgettable life. Near the house there are beds and flowing lawns with strong contrasts of shapely plants – mounds of Japanese maple and soaring spires of cypress. Above them, roses pour down slopes and walls; to the west, paths lead into ancient woodland in which immense hollies, oaks and old coppiced sweet chestnuts provide the background to wonderful magnolias, rhododendrons and maples underplanted with all kinds of shade-loving plants. There is nothing fiddly or fussy; the whole place has an air of marvellous inevitability.

HADSPEN HOUSE

Somerset

nr Castle Cary BA7 7NG
2m SE of Castle Cary by
A371
Tel: 0963 50939

Owner: N. A. Hobhouse

Open: Mar to Oct, Thur to
Sun and Bank Hol 9–6.
8 acres

THE VERY PRETTY late 18th-century house in its park-like setting is sheltered by wooded slopes rising to the north behind it. The romantic garden has 18th-century origins but most of its present distinction is owed to Penelope Hobhouse who restored and replanned it after 1968, laying down a bold design and introducing vast numbers of new and distinguished plants. The formal parts are well away from the house, on the far side of the lawn and approached by grassy walks and paths among fine trees and shrubs. In the old walled kitchen garden a dazzling but subtle double border of hostas and mixed planting backed with beech hedges descends the hill, and borders round the walls are full of good things. Nearby, above a huge rectangular pool a high brick wall affords protection to many tender plants. There is also an excellent nursery with a particularly well chosen range of plants, some of which are rare and handsome cultivars bearing the 'Hadspen' name. The present gardeners, Nori and Sandra Pope, know a good plant when they see one and excellent new introductions are constantly being made. A catalogue is produced but there is no mail order.

THE HANNAYS OF BATH

Avon

Sydney Wharf Nursery,
Bathwick, Bath BA2 4ES
In Bath at bottom of
Bathwick Hill via Sydney
Mews
Tel: 0225 462230

Open: Wed, Fri to Sun 10–5

THE HANNAYS are mad about plants and a visit to their nursery is always rewarding because you will certainly find excellent and unfamiliar ones. Some may come from the Hannays' own plant collecting expeditions; from South Africa, for example, where they recently collected the newly introduced and very pretty climbing cranesbill *Geranium robustum*. They are especially good on herbaceous plants and on their wild forms; aquilegias, diascias, euphorbias and geraniums are well represented. Among woody plants buddlejas, cistuses, honeysuckles and sages are outstanding. A very good catalogue is produced, with much valuable information, but there is no mail order.

HESTERCOMBE
Somerset

Cheddon Fitzpaine, nr
Taunton TA2 8LQ
2m NE of Taunton off
A358
Tel: 0823 337222

Owner: Somerset County
Council

Open: Mon to Fri 9–5.
1 1/2 acres

THE GARDEN at Hestercombe was designed by Gertrude Jekyll and Edwin Lutyens just before World War I and is one of their great masterpieces. Since 1973 it has been rescued from the brink of irretrievable collapse by Somerset County Council who have restored it with authenticity. Here is a marvellous distillation of the essence of the Lutyens/Jekyll garden wizardry – an enclosed area of shifting levels with lively stonework, a symmetrical parterre-like 'Great Plat', iris-fringed rills fed by water-spouting masks, and Miss Jekyll's boldly unfussy planting of massed grey-leafed plants, glossy bergenias, ramparts of rosemary and a pergola of roses and clematis. In addition to all this, there is a round pool in a round walled garden filled with wintersweet and roses, a Dutch garden of lamb's ears, lavender and roses, and the most beautiful orangery of the 20th century. Everywhere there are details of design and planting from which any gardener can learn.

HOECROFT PLANTS
Avon

Fosse Lane, Welton,
Midsomer Norton
BA3 2UZ
In the centre of Midsomer
Norton, 10m SW of Bath
by A367
Tel: None

Open: Mar to Nov, Fri
9.30–1, 2–5.30, Sat 2–5.30

THIS IS A NEW and very attractive nursery – a medal winner at Chelsea – with a highly original stock. Nigel Taylor's speciality is plants, and especially grasses, with coloured or variegated foliage. This interest gives a special focus to the range of plants carried and there are many marvellous and unusual things here. The list includes virtually every single category of plant, with over 200 plants with variegated foliage and even more than that of those with coloured leaves. Grasses, sedges and rushes have become very fashionable garden plants and Hoecroft's collection is outstanding. The catalogue is full of interest and is particularly informative about the garden uses and cultivation of the plants it describes. Although primarily a mail order nursery, visitors are welcome.

KELWAYS NURSERIES
Somerset

Langport TA10 9SL
In Langport, 10m E of
Taunton by A358 and
A378
Tel: 0458 250521

Open: Mon to Fri 9–1, 2–5

THIS IS ONE of the best of all nurseries for peonies and irises, and the many cultivars bearing the 'Langport' or 'Kelway' name are evidence of the work of this famous place in the raising of garden-worthy plants. They also sell a very wide range of bulbs and herbaceous perennials, and excellently illustrated catalogues are issued twice a year from which orders are fulfilled by post.

KENWITH NURSERY
Devon

The Old Rectory,
Littleham, Bideford
EX39 5HW
In the village of Littleham
1m S of Bideford
Tel: 02372 473752

Open: Wed to Sat 10–12,
2–4.30

Illustration: Cedrus
deodarus '*Golden Horizon*'

GORDON HADDOW, who moved here quite recently from another site, sells only conifers, about which he is immensely knowledgeable. There are trees here, many of them dwarf, which you will not often come across – for example his is the only nursery in Britain to supply several different American forms of the dwarf *Pinus banksiana*. He produces an outstandingly informative catalogue, rich in background information about his plants, from which he fulfils orders by mail. In front of the house, to one side of the nursery, there are several display beds containing many rarely seen specimens.

KILLERTON

Devon

Broadclyst, Exeter
EX5 3LE
5m NE of Exeter by B3181
and B3185; or by Jnct 28
on M5
Tel: 0392 881345

Owner:
The National Trust

Open: Daily dawn–dusk.
22 acres. House open

THE CHARMS of Killerton reveal themselves gradually and because of that tend to stick in the mind. Behind the stucco house, land slopes up towards the north and the garden lies chiefly to the west. Near the house a gravel path leads between a pair of fortissimo mixed borders – originally planted with the advice of William Robinson – ornamented with elegant Coade stone urns. Beyond, the lawn unrolls, interrupted by countless trees and shrubs of an acid-loving type – magnolias, rhododendrons, stewartias, styrax and maples. A half-hidden rustic summer house, with a touch of Grimm's fairy tales, has a wonderful interior of rattan and wickerwork, and a ceiling with patterns of pine cones. Behind it is a masterly rock garden, recently restored, of a naturalistic kind built in an old quarry; hellebores, hostas, geraniums and many other herbaceous plants flourish among mossy rocks under a canopy of old camellias, maples and daphnes. In late spring the air is scented with sheets of *Cyclamen repandum*. Do not miss the especially good plant shop which also has a selection of good pots.

KNIGHTSHAYES COURT
Devon

Bolham, Tiverton
EX16 7RQ
2m N of Tiverton by A396
Tel: 0884 254665

Owner:
The National Trust

Open: Apr to Sept, daily
10.30–5.30; Oct 11–5. 40
acres. House open

THE GARDENS at Knightshayes have two faces, both of them very handsome. Near the house are generously planted borders and a formal garden with yew hedges, standard wisterias, lead figures and a cool pool overhung by a weeping pear. East of this is one of the best small woodland gardens in the country, in which exceptional shrubs and ornamental trees are disposed to brilliant effect. At first sight it seems just a very attractive piece of woodland but the more you look the more you will see rare plants used with rare skill. A small selection of very good plants is for sale.

LANHYDROCK
Cornwall

Bodmin PL30 5AD
2 1/2m SE of Bodmin by
A38 or B3268
Tel: 0208 73320

Owner:
The National Trust

Open: Daily dawn–dusk.
25 acres. House open

THE HOUSE, a romantic mixture of the 17th and 19th centuries, is set in exquisite parkland, and an avenue of sycamores and beeches marches to the castellated entrance lodge. Beyond it a formal courtyard garden has rows of vast clipped Irish yews, beds of modern roses and ornate bronze urns. Behind the house and church is a yew-hedged circular garden with herbaceous beds containing many cultivars of crocosmia, of which the garden holds the National Collection. Beyond this is a woodland garden with flowering shrubs and trees, especially rhododendrons and exceptionally fine magnolias of which there are 120 different kinds many of which have grown to a great height.

LOWER SEVERALLS HERB NURSERY

Somerset

Lower Severalls, nr
Crewkerne TA18 7NX
1 1/2 NE of Crewkerne by
A30
Tel: 0460 732 34

Open: Daily except Thur
10–5 (Sun 2–5)

Illustration: Geranium
renardii

MARY PRING'S nursery is arranged in the garden of a very attractive Ham stone farmhouse. As well as medicinal and culinary herbs she is particularly interested in those with especially good scents – of lemon, pineapple and so on. She also has a selection of tender and half-hardy plants for containers and bedding. There is a well-chosen range of herbaceous perennials – including over 50 cranesbills and some very good sages (around 25 varieties). Orders are fulfilled by mail order and a catalogue is produced

LYTE'S CARY MANOR

Somerset

Charlton Mackrell,
Somerton TA11 7HU
4m SE of Somerton by
B3151
Tel: 045822 3297

Owner:
The National Trust

Open: Apr to Oct, Mon,
Wed and Sat 2–6 or dusk if
earlier. 3 acres. House open

THE ENTRANCE to the late medieval manor house is through a forecourt with a central path flanked by yew topiary clipped into cottage-loaf shapes. This mixture of formality and simplicity characterises the garden. A door leads through to a lavish mixed border of herbaceous plants under old roses, while, on the other side of the path, a yew hedge is clipped into buttresses with decorative finials. Beyond a formal orchard, open lawns and statues lead to a shady tunnel of hornbeam and a secret garden.

MALLET COURT NURSERY
Somerset

Curry Mallet, nr Taunton
TA3 6SY
In village of Curry Mallet
5m SE of Taunton by A358
and A378
Tel: 0823 480748

Open: Mon to Fri 9–1, 2–5

JAMES HARRIS is known among tree-lovers as 'Acer' Harris and sells one of the finest selections of maples commercially available – almost certainly the largest in the country. His nursery is primarily devoted to trees and shrubs, with a particular emphasis on those grown from seed collected in the wild. He sells, for example, a vast range of oaks, many birches, rowans and magnolias and shrubs, from China, Korea and Japan. Although a catalogue is produced and orders are supplied by post a visit is always worthwhile to discover treasures that have not yet found their way onto the list.

THE MANOR HOUSE
Avon

Walton-in-Gordano, nr
Clevedon BS21 7AN
2m NE of Clevedon by
B3124
Tel: 0272 872067

Owner: Mr and Mrs Simon
Wills

Open: Mid-Apr to
mid-Sept, Wed and Thur
10–4; May and Aug Bank
Hol 2–6. 4 acres

PROTECTED BY wooded hills to the north, this garden has a balmy microclimate which allows the owners to grow a very wide range of plants. This is a plant spotter's garden in which both herbaceous and woody plants are well represented and where something new is always happening, often as a result of plant-hunting expeditions particularly in the Mediterranean. A few plants propagated in the nursery, some unusual, are for sale at modest prices.

MAPPERTON HOUSE GARDEN

Dorset

Beaminster DT8 3NA
2m SE of Beaminster by
B3163
Tel: 0308 862645

Owner: The Montagu
family

Open: Mar to Oct, daily
2–6. 14 acres. House open
by appointment to groups
only

To THE EAST of the fine 16th-century house, the garden, hidden in a long combe, comes as a surprise – a splendid formal arrangement of descending terraces and cross vistas. At the head of the valley a Ham stone orangery looks down flagged paths past a rose-festooned pergola and along the central vista which ends with two long rectangular pools guarded by stone eagles. All this is copiously ornamented with topiary of yew and box, handsome urns and statues, and plenty of places to sit and admire the garden and the gabled house rising above it. This lively pastiche of a 17th-century garden, with all the trimmings, was laid out as recently as the 1920s. It makes an entirely unexpected and wonderful contrast to idyllic views of cattle grazing in the park-like countryside beyond.

PATRICIA MARROW

Somerset

Kingsdon, nr Somerton
TA11 7LE
In the middle of Kingsdon,
2m SE of Somerton off
B3151
Tel: 0935 840232

Open: Daily, dawn–dusk
but check by phone

As SO MANY of the old-established nursery gardens cut back on their stock, much smaller, specialist nurseries have become one of the best sources of more unusual plants. Mrs Marrow is a gardening institution in the West Country – a demon propagator who chooses her plants with great care. There is nothing commonplace here and much that you will not find easily elsewhere. She stocks a very large number of hardy plants, woody and herbaceous, some of which may not be quite so hardy in the frozen north. She issues no catalogue and provides no mail order service but part of the essential charm of the place lies in meeting her. She does not bully customers but she talks about her plants so seductively that you will certainly bear away more than you bargained for.

MARWOOD HILL GARDENS
Devon

Barnstaple EX31 4EB
4m NW of Barnstaple by
A39 and B3230
Tel: 0271 42528

Owner: Dr J.A. Smart

Open: Garden: daily,
dawn–dusk; Nursery: daily
11–1, 2–5. 20 acres

THERE ARE many reasons for visiting Marwood Hill but the chief interest of the garden lies in the very large number of plants grown in appropriate habitats in the attractive valley setting. The garden was started in 1949 by Dr Jimmy Smart who took over the neglected garden of a Georgian house. Flowering shrubs and ornamental trees clothe the slopes of the upper garden and at the bottom of the valley small lakes are linked together by streams. A bog garden between two of the lakes burgeons with ligularias, candelabra primulas and irises. In high summer the banks are covered by the plumes of an immense number of astilbes – 135 different species and cultivars, a National Collection. There is also a large and excellent nursery whose chief speciality is camellias, of which it has one of the best selections commercially available. A catalogue is produced but there is no mail order, so a visit is essential.

MILTON LODGE

Somerset

nr Wells BA5 3AQ
1/2m N of Wells off A39
Tel: 0749 672168

Owner: D.C. Tudway
Quilter

Open: Easter to Oct, Mon
to Sat 2–6. 15 acres

HERE IS a garden that takes full advantage of its exquisite position – with the city of Wells and its great cathedral below it to the south, and Glastonbury Tor in the distance beyond the vale of Avalon. On the south side of the Georgian house a wide terrace overlooks the steeply sloping site with its mixed borders, yew hedges and vertiginous descents giving way to parkland with excellent ornamental trees. At some distance from the house, on the other side of the Old Bristol Road, is a real rarity – the Combe, a late 18th-century gentleman's arboretum now in splendid maturity. This walled and bosky valley, full of fine old trees to which the present owner adds, has immense charm.

MONTACUTE HOUSE

Somerset

Montacute TA15 6XP
In the village of
Montacute, 4m W of
Yeovil by A3088
Tel: 0935 823289

Owner:
The National Trust

Open: Daily except Tue
11.30–5.30 or dusk if
earlier. 12 acres. House
open

THE LATE Tudor house, a marvel of golden Ham stone, is well situated in a garden to match. To the east of the house a walled forecourt has good herbaceous borders. The Tudor walls are ornamented with stone finials and, in each corner, an airy Elizabethan gazebo gives views to the deer park beyond. North of the house a raised walk overlooks a deep border planted with shrub roses and a stately lawn surrounded by clipped Irish yews with a circular poool at its centre. All about are venerable yew hedges, some handsomely blowsy with age, and the view is constantly drawn to the great house.

MOUNT EDGCUMBE
Cornwall

nr Plymouth
2 1/2m SE of Torpoint
Tel: 0752 822236

Owner: City of Plymouth and Cornwall County Council

Open: Park and formal garden: daily dawn–dusk; Earl's Garden: Apr to Oct, Wed to Sun and Bank Hol 11–5.30. 100 acres. House open

IT IS HARD to pin down the rare character of this place – but there is certainly nowhere like it. The site, on a sloping headland overlooking Plymouth Sound, is beautiful, and the castellated mansion turns its face to this, down an immense triple avenue of limes. The Edgcumbe family, also of Cotehele, came here in the mid 16th century and their estate became so famous that Admiral Medina Sidonia vowed that he would live there after his Armada had beaten the English. At the foot of the hill there is a conservatory and Italianate garden with double staircase ornamented with flamboyant statuary, a pool, bedding schemes and orange trees in Versailles boxes. The parkland that runs to the very edge of the cliffs – interrupted with picturesque ruins and a columned temple from which there are marvellous views of the sea – has countless fine trees including some of the largest cork-oaks (*Quercus suber*) in the country.

OVERBECKS GARDEN

Devon

Sharpitor,
Salcombe TQ8 8LW
1 1/2m SW of Salcombe by
minor roads
Tel: 054 884 2893

Owner: The National Trust

Open: Daily 10–8 or sunset
if earlier. 6 acres

OVERBECKS IS a very unusual place, lost on the precipitous heights above Salcombe estuary. It was the creation of Otto Overbecks who left it to the National Trust in 1937. It enjoys a remarkably mild microclimate and, with views through trees of shimmering water, it is fairly easy to imagine yourself on the *corniche* on the Côte d'Azur. Even the steps leading down into the garden, with their sinuous handrail, have a Mediterranean feel to them. The garden is terraced and its very sharp drainage and abundant sunshine permits many tender plants to flourish as they do in few other places on mainland Britain – callistemons, Chusan palms, mimosa, olearias, olives and tender pittosporums. On the lower slopes, an old *Magnolia campbellii*, planted in 1901, is a famous sight in spring, covered with its hot pink flowers. The earlier part of the year is a wonderful time to visit, when the garden is extraordinarily floriferous and the air laden with sweet scents. In high summer it takes on the character of an exotic jungle.

PARNHAM HOUSE
Dorset

Beaminster
1m S of Beaminster by
A3066
Tel: 0308 862204

Owner: John Makepeace

Open: Apr to Oct, Wed,
Sun and Bank Hol
weekends 10–5. House open

SWARMING WITH decoration – gables, castellations
and bristling chimneys – Parnham House is a
Tudor mansion comprehensively done over by John
Nash in the early 19th century. The estate was
acquired by the famous furniture maker, John
Makepeace, who has restored it with energy and
imagination. To the south, a deep terrace with stone
gazebos at each end overlooks an immense lawn with
rows of giant yew cones and water runnels. Beyond,
superb woodland is framed by great cedars of
Lebanon. On the east side of the house the entrance
forecourt has decorative walls crowned with finials
and borders planted with roses. Beyond the house,
behind old yew hedges and brick walls, Mrs
Makepeace has been breathing new life into
herbaceous borders. To one side of this, a little glade
of cherry trees contains an oddity – a much bigger
than life-size fibreglass statue of Morecambe and
Wise caught forever in mid-quip.

PEVERIL CLEMATIS NURSERY
Devon

Christow, Exeter EX6 7NG
9m SW of Exeter by B3212
and B3193
Tel: 0647 52937

Open: Daily except Thur
10–1, 2–5.30

Illustration: Clematis
'Countess of Lovelace'

THIS IS ONE of the best collections of clematis in the country and as there is no mail order service a visit is the only way to sample its riches. It is well worth getting a copy of the excellent catalogue which, apart from the delights of the list, has much valuable information about care and cultivation. There are constant new introductions and several cultivars which are unique to Peveril – either of their own hybridising or rediscoveries of ancient varieties such as *Clematis viticella* 'Mary Rose' which was found at a Devon manor house and mentioned by Parkinson in 1629.

ROSEMOOR GARDEN
Devon

Great Torrington
EX38 8PH
1m SE of Great Torrington
by B3220
Tel: 0805 24067

Owner: The Royal
Horticultural Society

Open: Daily dawn–dusk.
40 acres

THERE ARE two gardens at Rosemoor: one was made in the early 1960s by Lady Anne Palmer, an intimate woodland garden with less informal planting nearer the house; the other is a more razzamatazz affair complete with Visitors' Centre, ambitious formal rose gardens and giant borders, all of which have been made by the Royal Horticultural Society since it became the owner in 1988. The two gardens, which have a fundamentally different character, are separated by the B3220 under which visitors may pass by an underground passage. A

newly made stream garden, when its planting has matured, will make an attractive prelude to the tunnel. Lady Anne's garden has an excellent collection of trees and shrubs of the kind which relish the acid soil – rhododendrons, dogwoods, eucryphias, maples, pieris and vacciniums. By the house there are lawns, borders and a tennis court that has been transformed into an alluring coniferous jungle. At the Visitors' Centre there is a plant shop with many good plants for sale.

ROWDEN GARDENS

Devon

Brentor, nr Tavistock
PL19 0NG
SW of village of Brentor
Tel: 0822 810275

Open: Apr to Sept, Sat,
Sun and Bank Hol 10–5

SOMETHING NEW always seems to be happening at Rowden Gardens which has in the past specialised in aquatic plants but now has a wider range – in all, over 2,000 species and varieties with a strong emphasis on herbaceous perennials. There are particularly good collections of rheums, primulas and crocosmias. Some of the plants are very rare, including those bred at the nursery and bearing the 'Rowden' name. This is the home of probably the largest collection of polygonums in the country, of which Rowden holds the National Collection. Behind the nursery there are rows of slender canal-like pools, displaying the nursery's wares in very decorative fashion. An informative list is produced and there is a mail order service. Many plants that are not listed are to be seen at the nursery and John Carter will probably seduce you into buying them

SALTRAM
Devon

Plympton, Plymouth
PL7 3UH
3m E of Plymouth by A38
Tel: 0752 336546

Owner:
The National Trust

Open: Apr to Oct, daily
except Fri and Sat
10.30–5.30. 21 acres. House
open

Illustration opposite:
Rhododendrons at Saltram
House

ALTHOUGH WITHIN sight of the urban sprawl of Plymouth, Saltram still preserves its character of a gentlemanly house set in parkland. The early 18th-century house was enriched by spectacular new rooms by Robert Adam for the Parker family. The parkland – in the 18th-century grazed by deer to the very walls of the house – is now embellished with ornamental trees, superb sweet chestnuts and the Spanish plane (*Platanus* x *hispanica*) among them. The lawn west of the house, smooth as finest Wilton carpet, is interrupted by thickets of shrubs, especially camellias, many fine magnolias and rhododendrons. From the stately pedimented orangery built in 1775 paths lead to a dapper gothic pavilion. Beyond the house, a long avenue of limes, carpeted with pale narcissi in spring, forms a boundary. All this is understated and, of its kind, perfect.

SCOTT'S NURSERIES LTD
Somerset

Merriott TA16 5PL
2m N of Crewkerne on the
A356
Tel: 0460 72306

Open: Mon to Sat 9–5, Sun
11–5

Illustration: Rosa 'New
Dawn'

THIS OLD-ESTABLISHED nursery is one of the best in the West Country. It sells a very wide range of plants with especially good collections of old-fashioned and species roses and of fruit – there are many old cultivars of apples, pears, plums and soft fruit that are not often found. Good trees and flowering shrubs are stocked and a wide range of herbaceous plants and alpines. An outstanding catalogue is issued and there is a mail order service.

TAPELEY PARK

Devon

Instow EX39 4NT
2m N of Bideford by A39
Tel: 0271 860528

Owner: H.T.C. Christie

Open: Easter to Oct, daily
except Sat 10–6. 10 acres.
House open

TAPELEY PARK deserves to be much better known.
The house, a mid 18th-century tycoon's mansion
of pink brick, occupies an unforgettable position in
parkland, with wonderful views down to the River
Torrington. South of the house is a dazzling Italian
garden designed by the neo-classical architect John
Belcher in the early 20th century. Terraces gently
descend the hill, with a fountain at the centre, and a
row of sentinel Irish yews guards the lowest terrace
to the west. Handsome statues decorate the walls and
others, on the far side of the lawn, gaze out towards
the countryside. The lowest terrace wall is lined with
lively borders in which tender plants such as *Sophora
japonica* and *Feijoa sellowiana* flourish. To the east a
pedimented brick and flint tool-house, with busts in
niches, was designed by a former head gardener. To
one side vertiginous steps flanked by statues climb up
under the shade of old Monterey pines towards a
sundial and a domed ice-house. Beyond, is an old
walled kitchen garden.

TINTINHULL HOUSE

Somerset

Tintinhull,
nr Yeovil BA22 8PZ
In village of Tintinhull, off
A303 5m SW of Yeovil
Tel: 0985 847777

Owner:
The National Trust

Open: Apr to Sept, Wed,
Thur, Sat and Bank Hol
2–6. 3/4 acre. House open

THE DESIGN of this small garden is so clever that it provides an inexhaustible model for gardeners. Divided into separate 'rooms' by walls or hedges, each area has a distinctive atmosphere. The Eagle Court west of the Queen Anne façade of the house has a central flagged path edged with clipped mounds of box and, under the walls, richly planted borders. The path leads to a little white garden, hedged in yew, in which white anemones, roses and lilies glow under miniature silvery willows. An opening leads through to a decorative kitchen garden with an orchard beyond. The pool garden above it, with its slender canal planted with irises, and pillared summer house at one end, has a pair of masterly borders – one with hot colours of red and yellow and the other with cool silvers and mauves. On either side of the summer house high walls give protection to tender plants and pots decorate the terrace. The garden, chiefly the work of Phyllis Reiss between the wars, is now expertly cared for by Penelope Hobhouse and her husband, Professor John Malins.

TREBAH
Cornwall

Mawnan Smith,
nr Falmouth TR11 5JZ
4m SW of Falmouth by minor
roads
Tel: 0326 250448

Owner: Major and Mrs J.A.
Hibbert

Open: Apr to Aug, daily
11–5. 25 acres

TREBAH IS the creation of Charles Fox who came here in 1831 and also made the neighbouring Glendurgan which enjoys a very similar site. By 1981 when the present owners started to restore it, the place had all but collapsed. Set in a long, slender ravine, the garden sweeps down south to the Helford river. Paths run along each side of the valley, with vertiginous views over great rhododendrons, magnolias and palms. At the bottom of the valley pools and moist ground provide a perfect site for an immense collection of hydrangeas and a huge grove of the giant Brazilian rhubarb, *Gunnera manicata*. Things grow well here and one of the great attractions is the contrast of different exotic foliage, viewed from above or below. A nursery based at the garden but in separate ownership, Hardy Exotic Plants, sells rare, often tender, plants. It issues an interesting catalogue and supplies by mail order.

JAMES TREHANE & SONS LTD
Dorset

Stapehill Road,
Hampreston,
Wimborne BH21 7NE
3m E of Wimborne Minster
by B3073
Tel: 0202 873490

Open: Mon to Fri 9–4.30;
Mar to mid-May, Sat and
Sun 10–4.30; closed week
after Christmas

THIS FAMILY firm is famous for its camellias although it does sell a few other woody plants including a good selection of azaleas, magnolias and one of the most comprehensive selections of pieris cultivars available in Britain. The camellias, however, are the nursery's greatest glory and the Trehanes are constantly looking for new varieties. Here is an immense range of cultivars of *Camellia japonica* and of other species, some available only here, but other gardeners will be bowled over by the less showy but exquisite species An excellent catalogue is produced and a mail order service is provided.

TRELISSICK GARDEN
Cornwall

Feock, nr Truro TR3 6QL
4m S of Truro by B3289
Tel: 0872 862090/865808

Owner:
The National Trust

Open: Mar to Oct, Mon to
Sat 10.30–5.30, Sun 1–5.30
(5 in Mar and Oct); Nov to
Mar, woodland walk open.
25 acres

THE GARDEN here is in the tradition of Cornish woodland gardens but it is a fairly recent creation and is a more manicured, gentler kind of place. The terrain is gently rolling, and smooth lawns, edged with sweeping mixed borders, give way to densely shaded woodland walks. There are many fine trees, outstanding rhododendrons, and a hydrangea walk leading from the main lawn with many different species and cultivars. Near the house there is a collection of fig cultivars and a sheltered garden of choice plants, many of them scented.

TRENGWAINTON GARDEN
Cornwall

Madron,
nr Penzance TR20 8RZ
2m NW of Penzance by
B3312
Tel: 0736 63021

Owner: The National
Trust

Open: Mar to Oct, Wed to
Sat, Bank Hol and Good
Fri 10.30–5.30 (5 in Mar
and Oct). 15 acres

S IR EDWARD BOLITHO was the chief creator of
this garden in the 1920s when he added to it some
of the spectacular new discoveries of the plant
hunters, especially those of Frank Kingdon-Ward.
From the entrance lodge a very long drive running
from east to west provides the main axis of the
garden. Immediately on the right is an extraordinary
walled kitchen garden now turned over to growing
especially tender exotics. These flourish among rare
magnolias and other ornamental trees and shrubs
such as *Styrax japonica*, eucryphias, stewartias,
michelias and other choice and rare things. On the
left-hand side of the drive there is an excellent stream
garden beautifully planted with candelabra primulas,
meconopsis, ligularias and skunk cabbage. Beyond it
in the woodland are immense rhododendrons – with
spectacular examples of some of the large-leafed
species such as *R. sino-grande*, *R. macabeanum* and
R. falconeri and rare trees such as *Podocarpus
salignus*. At the end of the drive the house looks out
across a lawn to far views of St Michael's Mount, a
splendid eye-catcher.

TRERICE
Cornwall

nr Newquay TR8 4PG
3m SE of Newquay by
A392 and A3058
Tel: 0637 875404

Owner:
The National Trust

Open: Apr to Oct, daily
except Tue 11–5.30 (5 in
Oct). 6 acres. House open

T HIS IS THE perfect small manor house, built of
silver-grey limestone with fanciful curlicues on
the gables and a handsome walled forecourt. The
essential charm of the garden is that it is so perfectly
in tune with the rural intimacy of the house. In the
forecourt a pair of ancient granite lions guard the
gate and borders on either side have plants with
purple or gold foliage, making a lively contrast with
the silver of the house. Lawns are punctuated by four
great Irish yews and a gate leads to a pair of borders
separated by a grass walk with a chinoiserie bench at
the end. In an outhouse a collection of old
lawnmowers will fascinate those taking an interest in
antique garden implements.

TRESCO ABBEY
Cornwall

Tresco,
Isles of Scilly TR14 0QQ
Access by helicopter or
ferry from Penzance
Tel: 0720 22849

Owner: R. Dorrien Smith

Open: Daily 10–4. 16 acres

THERE IS certainly no other garden like this in the world. Tresco, one of the Scilly Isles, has an extraordinarily benign microclimate with moderate rainfall but high humidity from the sea. The garden was started by Augustus Smith in 1834, whose first priority was to plant trees to shelter his garden from its greatest enemy, the wind. He gradually built up a terraced garden in which he was able to cultivate a staggering range of plants, with a strong emphasis on those of the Southern Hemisphere. This, greatly added to by his descendants, is the garden that visitors may see today. It is primarily a collection of plants, but the garden is craftily designed with gravel paths leading along terraces and cross vistas giving thrilling views through the sub-tropical luxuriance. There is no point in beginning to list plants – there are so many things here which you will see in no other British garden. There are, however, emphatic repeated plantings – of different kinds of palms, of the splendidly architectural *Echium wildpretii* with its soaring spires of flowers, and of the giant purple-flowered *Geranium maderense* – which give structure to the tropical abundance. It is unlikely that you, or anyone else, will ever make a garden like this and it gives unique and exhilarating pleasure.

TREWITHEN
Cornwall

Grampound Road,
nr Truro TR2 4DD
7m W of St Austell by
A390
Tel: 0726 882418/882763

Owner: A.M.J. Galsworthy

Open: Mar to Sept, Mon
to Sat 10–4.30. 25 acres.
House open

TREWITHEN IS another Cornish garden with an
outstanding collection of camellias, magnolias
and rhododendrons, but it is strikingly unlike any of
the others. Behind the elegant 1723 house there is an
immense lawn, 200 yards long, with trees and shrubs
crowding in on either side. From the far end of the
lawn, this is seen to provide a marvellous setting for
the house, like an immensely deep stage framed in
wonderful plants. The garden was made by George
Johnstone who came here in 1903 and cleared
existing woodland, enriching the planting with many
of the Asiatic plants newly introduced in the 1920s.
Paths wind through this woodland and at every turn
there is something wonderful to see. It is at its most
spectacular in early to late spring but it has many
pleasures to offer later in the year. The entrance to
the garden is through a formal walled garden which
should not be overlooked; with its wisteria-draped
pergola, Irish yews and beautifully planted borders it
is an admirable piece of work. There is an excellent
plant shop selling many of the plants particularly
associated with the garden (e.g. the beautiful
Ceanothus arboreus 'Trewithen Blue').

WALES AND WEST-CENTRAL ENGLAND

——— ❧ ———

Cheshire, Gloucestershire, Hereford & Worcester, Shropshire

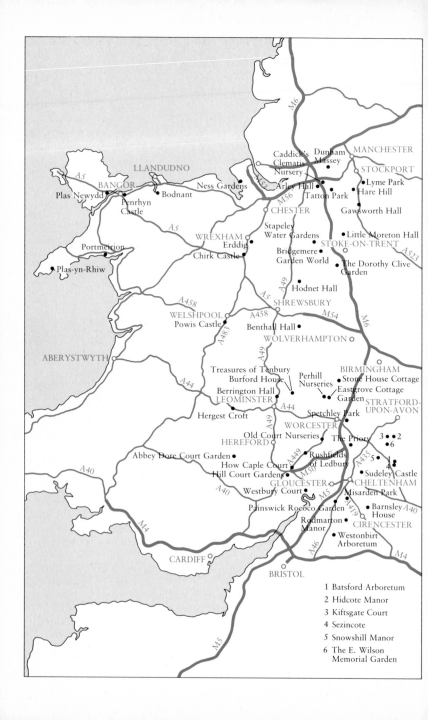

MANCHESTER

STOCKPORT

Caddick's
Clematis
Nursery

Dunham
Massey

Lyme Park
Hare Hill

LLANDUDNO

BANGOR

Ness Gardens

Arley Hall

Plas Newydd

Bodnant

Tatton Park

Gawsworth Hall

Penrhyn
Castle

CHESTER

A5

Little Moreton Hall

Stapeley
Water Gardens

WREXHAM

STOKE-ON-TRENT

Portmeirion

Erddig

A523

Bridgemere
Garden World

Plas-yn-Rhiw

Chirk Castle

The Dorothy Clive
Garden

A49

A5

Hodnet Hall

A458

SHREWSBURY

WELSHPOOL

A458

Powis Castle

M54

M6

Benthall Hall

ABERYSTWYTH

WOLVERHAMPTON

A483

A49

BIRMINGHAM

Treasures of Tenbury

A44

Perhill
Nurseries

Stone House Cottage

Burford House

Berrington Hall

Eastgrove Cottage
Garden

STRATFORD-
UPON-AVON

LEOMINSTER

A44

Hergest Croft

A49

Spetchley Park

WORCESTER

Old Court Nurseries

The Priory

3 2

HEREFORD

6

Abbey Dore Court Garden

A449

Rushfields
of Ledbury

A435

5   1

How Caple Court

A40

Hill Court Gardens

M50

4

Sudeley Castle

Westbury Court

GLOUCESTER

CHELTENHAM

Painswick Rococo Garden

M5

Misarden Park

A419

Rodmarton
Manor

Barnsley
House

A40

CIRENCESTER

Westonbirt
Arboretum

M4

CARDIFF

M4

BRISTOL

1 Batsford Arboretum

2 Hidcote Manor

3 Kiftsgate Court

4 Sezincote

5 Snowshill Manor

6 The E. Wilson
Memorial Garden

ABBEY DORE COURT GARDEN
Hereford & Worcester

Abbey Dore,
nr Hereford HR2 0AD
11m SW of Hereford by
A465
Tel: 0981 240419

Owner: Mrs C.L. Ward

Open: 3rd Sat in Mar to
3rd Sun in Oct, daily
except Wed 11–6. 4 acres

O N THE BANKS of the River Dore Abbey Dore Court is both an attractive garden and a nursery garden with a good range of woody and herbaceous plants that may be seen growing in the garden. There is no catalogue and no mail order service, so a visit is essential. Abbey Dore keeps National Collections of euphorbias, those fashionable and valuable greenery-yallery plants (45 species and cultivars) and of sedums (273 species and cultivars).

ARLEY HALL
Cheshire

Arley, nr Northwich
CW9 6NA
5m W of Knutsford by
minor roads, between Jncts
19 and 20 of M6
Tel: 0565 777353

Owner: The Hon. M.L.W.
Flower

Open: Apr to Oct, Tue to
Sun and Bank Hol 2–6; Jun
to Aug, 12–6. 12 acres

A PAIR OF herbaceous borders was laid out at Arley in 1846, a great novelty, and they survive to this day, beautifully maintained: pairs of topiary yew 'dumb waiters' form entrances at each end and a broad grass path separates the borders which have yew buttresses on each side, breaking up an otherwise uncomfortably long stretch of planting. From June to the end of the gardening season they are one of the great garden sights of England. A path leads from the borders to a procession of giant columns of clipped holm oak and views over fields. There are also borders of shrub roses, old walled gardens with good mixed borders, a simple terraced walk above a ha-ha and much else to see. Still in private ownership, Arley Hall preserves the atmosphere of a garden kept for its own delight.

BARNSLEY HOUSE
Gloucestershire

Barnsley, nr Cirencester
GL7 5EE
In Barnsley village 4m N of
Cirencester by A433
Tel: 0285 74281

Owner: Mrs D.C.W. Verey

Open: Mon, Wed, Thur
and Sat 10–6 or dusk if
earlier. 2 acres

THIS IS a famous garden, made by Rosemary Verey since she came to live here in 1951. Influenced by her knowledge of garden history she has contrived a heady mixture of such ingredients as a pleached lime walk, knot gardens, an ornamental *potager*, temples and statuary. The real distinction, however, lies in the planting, especially in the use of herbaceous plants and subtle associations of form and colour. Barnsley House is well known through Mrs Verey's own excellent books – but there is no substitute for a visit to the garden itself, which is in a constant state of gentle but stimulating change as new discoveries are made. A nursery sells an excellent stock of choice and often rare plants of the sort grown in the garden.

BATSFORD ARBORETUM
Gloucestershire

Moreton-in-Marsh GL56 9QF
1m NW of Moreton-in-Marsh
by A44
Tel: 0386 700409/0608 50722

Owner: The Batsford
Foundation

Open: Mar to Oct, daily 10–5.
50 acres

Illustration opposite: Simon
Verity's figure of Diana at
Batsford

THIS ARBORETUM, started in the 1880s, has recently been revitalised with an enormous amount of new planting. It is now well worth visiting at any time of the year and even demon dendrologists will find marvellous things – like the largest specimen in Britain of the Macedonian oak, *Quercus trojana*. But for less rarified tastes the place is full of interest with all trees well labelled and the landscape enlivened by statues (including a good carving by Simon Verity of Diana) and ornamental buildings. There is also a large nursery which carries a good general stock.

BENTHALL HALL
Shropshire

Broseley TF12 5RX
6m SW of Telford by
minor roads
Tel: 0952 882159

Owner:
The National Trust

Open: Apr to Sept, Wed,
Sun and Bank Hol
1.30–5.30. 3 acres. House
open

BENTHALL HALL is a 16th-century gabled stone house which was inhabited in the 19th century by George Maw, a devoted amateur botanist with a particular passion for crocuses on which he wrote a famous, very rare book. His naturalised plantings of spring and autumn crocuses survive to this day. He went on plant-collecting expeditions and made new introductions; the charming pale blue *Chionodoxa luciliae*, from western Turkey, first flowered in England at Benthall in 1877. A subsequent tenant was Robert Bateman, son of James Bateman of Biddulph not far away. Robert Bateman made the terraced Pixie Garden with a pool and topiary of yew and box. This is not a dramatic garden but it has many good plants and an agreeably intimate atmosphere.

BERRINGTON HALL
Hereford & Worcester

nr Leominster HR6 0DW
3m N of Leominster by
A49
Tel: 0568 615721

Owner:
The National Trust

Open: Apr, Sat, Sun and
Bank Hol 1.30–5.30; May
to Sept, daily except Mon
and Tue (open Bank Hol)
1.30–5.30; Oct, Sat, Sun
1.30–4.30. 10 acres. House
open

THE BROWN STONE mansion was designed by Henry Holland and completed in 1781 and the unspoilt landscape park was laid out by his partner and father-in-law 'Capability' Brown. There was no house or garden here before so this is an unusual period piece. From the vast Arch of Triumph at the entrance an avenue of clipped mounds of golden yew leads towards the front door of the house. On one side a magnificent brick-walled 18th-century kitchen garden has a newly planted collection of historic varieties of apple and, leading up to the wrought-iron entrance gate, a pair of good mixed borders. The walls provide protection for some unusual tender plants including the grandest of all buddlejas, *B. colvillei*, with huge panicles of red flowers.

BODNANT
Gwynedd

Tal-y-Cafn, Colwyn Bay,
Clwyd LL28 5RE
8m S of Llandudno by
A470
Tel: 0492 650460

Owner:
The National Trust

Open: Mid-Mar to Oct,
daily 10–5. 80 acres

BODNANT WAS started in the late 19th century at the height of the rhododendron craze. The steep slopes of the Conwy valley provided a wonderfully romantic site for their cultivation, and with the rushing waters of the River Hraethlyn at his feet, the visitor today may convincingly imagine himself in a dream-like valley of the Himalayas. Rhododendrons and camellias flourish under a high canopy of conifers. Nearer the house there is a completely different garden – formal terraces descend in stately progression to a vast lily pool and the crispest yew hedges you will ever see. At the upper level is one of the most photographed garden sights in Britain – a curved tunnel of laburnum which in May and June drips gold and still has the power to take your breath away. There is a large nursery with an especially strong selection of acid-loving shrubs; plants may be supplied by mail order.

BRIDGEMERE GARDEN WORLD
Cheshire

Bridgemere, nr Nantwich
CW5 7QB
6m SE of Nantwich by A51
Tel: 093 65 381

Open: Mon to Sat 9–8, Sun
10–8; closes 5 or dusk in
winter

NO GARDEN CENTRE has the sense of horticultural excitement that you will find here. It is a huge place – 25 acres in all – and there are enormous numbers of plants of every kind; it probably carries the greatest commercially available range in the country. They are grouped in a way that is useful to the gardener – both under type of plants (herbaceous, roses, etc) or by use in the garden (ground-cover, shade-loving, etc). A separate 3-acre display garden, 'The Green Kingdom', shows the plants in use. There is no mail order, but all gardeners will enjoy visiting Bridgemere to see excellent and unfamiliar plants.

BURFORD HOUSE
Hereford & Worcester

Tenbury Wells WR15 8HQ
1m W of Tenbury Wells by
A456
Tel: 0584 810777

Owner: Treasures of
Tenbury Ltd

Open: Mid-Mar to
mid-Oct, Mon to Sat 11–5,
Sun 2–5. 4 acres

THIS IS THE GARDEN that John Treasure made since 1954, alongside his famous nursery. The gentlemanly Georgian brick house has formal arrangements near the house – a rectangular pool, a paved terrace, a long straight vista through an opening in a yew hedge and double borders. Farther from the house sweeping lawns are interrupted by an ambling stream with excellent planting along its banks, island beds of trees and shrubs fringed by herbaceous plantings and some fine specimen trees.

CADDICK'S CLEMATIS NURSERIES

Cheshire

Dyer's Lane, Rushgreen Road, Lymm WA13 9QL
On the northern edge of the village of Lymm
Tel: 0925 757196

Open: Daily 10–5

Illustration: Clematis 'William Kennett'

IF YOU VISIT Caddick's do not allow yourself to be deterred by an unpromising approach that seems to lead to a builder's yard. Press on and you will find a wonderful collection of clematises, beautifully displayed. Caddick's sells nothing but these essential garden plants and their list is one of the best in the country. A mail order service is provided.

CHIRK CASTLE

Clwyd

Chirk LL14 5AF
1/2m W of Chirk village by A5
Tel: 0691 777701

Owner:
The National Trust

Open: Apr to 27 Sept, daily except Mon and Sat (open Bank Hol) 12–6; Oct, Sat and Sun 12–6. 5 acres. Castle open

CHIRK IS A 13th-century border castle and its massive defensive towers are echoed in the billowing old topiary cones of yew that march down its east side. An opening cut into a yew hedge guarded by a pair of bronze nymphs leads through to the upper lawn and a deep mixed border punctuated by groups of flowering cherries. On this windy site woodland provides protection for magnolias, rhododendrons and more unusual plants such as the Chilean firebush (*Embothrium coccineum*) with its scarlet flowers, and *Eucryphia glutinosa*.

153

THE DOROTHY CLIVE GARDEN
Shropshire

Willoughbridge, nr Market
Drayton TF9 4EU
9m NE of Market Drayton
by A53 and A51
Tel: 0630 81237

Owner: Willoughbridge
Garden Trust

Open: 29 Mar to Oct, daily
10–5.30. 20 acres

FEW GARDENS have such diversity of interest as this. The garden was started in 1937 by Col. Harry Clive who realised the attractions of the site; a former gravel pit with acid soil on a fine south-facing, well watered slope which provides habitats for a very wide range of plants. At the very top of the hill, in the old quarry, Col. Clive's original woodland garden is now fully mature; it is rich with azaleas, maples, rhododendrons and other ornamental trees and shrubs. A rushing multi-tiered waterfall is a brilliant sight in high summer, fringed with the coloured plumes of astilbes and ligularias. On the slopes below the old quarry a garden of a completely different character, planned by the garden designer John Codrington, was developed after Col. Clive's death. In the upper reaches, broad grassy paths running along the contours of the hill divide mixed borders lavishly planted with woody and herbaceous plants. Paths then run downwards at a brisker pace, between informal and scree beds with a lily pond at the bottom.

DUNHAM MASSEY

Cheshire

Altrincham WA14 4SJ
3m W of Altrincham by
A56
Tel: 061 941 1025

Owner:
The National Trust

Open: Apr to Oct, daily
12–5.30 (Sun and Bank Hol
11–5.30). 250 acres. House
open

ONE OF THE great successes of many National Trust gardens is their willingness to give full emphasis within a single garden to garden styles of different periods. At Dunham Massey, with its grand early 18th-century house, there are remains of a pattern of formal avenues of the same period, charging towards the horizon. Much replanting of beeches, limes and oaks has given this new life. From the house a double staircase leads to a sprightly Edwardian parterre, bedded in summer with zonal pelargoniums mixed with verbena and edged with rich blue lobelia. Clipped mounds of holm oak and hedges of golden yew give permanent ornament. To one side of the house informal lawns spread out, overlooked by an 18th-century orangery with, half-concealed in the woods behind, a well house disguised as a rustic retreat. Grassy walks lead along a moat whose banks are densely planted with astilbes, ferns, hostas, irises and rodgersias. The walk continues to a simple lawn from which views are suddenly revealed of the house reflected in the tranquil waters of the moat.

EASTGROVE COTTAGE GARDEN
Hereford & Worcester

Sankyns Green, Little
Witley WR6 6LQ
8m NW of Worcester by
A443 and B4196
Tel: 0299 896389

Owner: Malcolm and
Carol Skinner

Open: Apr to Oct, Thur to
Mon 2–5. 1 acre

*Illustration opposite: A
rose arbour at Eastgrove
Cottage*

IF YOU DID NOT know what a cottage garden should look like this would be a good place to learn. The cottage itself, tiled and ancient, is set in lovely countryside and the garden, flawlessly kept, is full of lively planting and cunning design. There are formal ingredients – a splendid zigzagging hedge of the neatest possible *Lonicera nitida*, carefully placed benches in enclosures and a great rose arbour; the garden itself is chiefly composed of curving borders and sweeps of lawn. A very wide range of plants, some extremely unusual, are grown in the borders and also in little scree beds. Malcolm and Carol Skinner, who made the garden, also run an outstanding nursery which concentrates on herbaceous perennials and in which even the keenest gardeners will make discoveries. A very good list is produced but there is no mail order service.

ERDDIG
Clwyd

nr Wrexham LL13 0YT
2m S of Wrexham by A525
Tel: 0978 355314

Owner:
The National Trust

Open: Apr to Sept, daily
except Thur and Fri (open
Good Fri) 11–6. 13 acres.
House open

THE FORMAL GARDEN to the east of the long low early 18th-century house is one of the very few in Britain to survive the craze for landscape gardens in the second part of the 18th century. It has now been sensitively restored by the National Trust and is full of delights. It is enclosed in brick walls on which are espaliered old varieties of fruit trees. These are underplanted with many varieties of daffodil and in the central area there are formal orchards of apple trees. A gravel path leads from the Edwardian parterre under the east windows of the house towards a slender canal flanked with old limes. At its end, exquisite wrought-iron gates give views of the country beyond. Parallel to this, to the south, a path runs along an avenue of Irish yews, with, on the north-facing wall, many varieties of ivy of which Erddig holds the National Collection. The path continues through a recreated flowery Victorian parterre to a memorably gloomy moss walk in the woods beyond.

GAWSWORTH HALL
Cheshire

Gawsworth, nr
Macclesfield SK11 9RN
3m S of Macclesfield by
A536
Tel: 0260 223456

Owner: Mr and Mrs
Timothy Richards

Open: Apr to Oct, daily
2–5. 20 acres. House open

Gawsworth Hall is a lovely late Elizabethan house with the inventive patterns of timbering associated with Cheshire architecture. In front of the house lawns with specimen trees run down to a pool and from the forecourt a paved path leads to a formal garden of rose beds, hedges of holly and yew and an ornamental bronze fountain. All this is quite modern but beyond the house lie the ghostly remains of a princely garden of the same date as the house. Magnificent Tudor brick walls survive, enclosing a great space, and the pattern of terraces, the site of a wilderness garden and of a formal canal are still visible. All this has been the subject of an archaeological dig which is very well described in a booklet on sale at the house. No plants survive from this early garden but it still has great atmosphere.

HARE HILL
Cheshire

Hare Hill has a touch of the Marie Céleste about it – as though the inhabitants might return at any moment and the place would burst into life. It is a woodland garden, approached across meadows and parkland, with sandy paths running under a high canopy of beech, oak and sycamore and glades of azaleas, maples and rhododendrons. Hidden in the middle of the wood is a large walled garden with rose beds, weeping silver pears and a trellis-work

nr Macclesfield SK10 4QB
3m NW of Macclesfield by
B5087
Tel: 0625 828981

Owner:
The National Trust

Open: Apr to late Oct,
Wed, Thur, Sat, Sun and
Bank Hol 10–5.30; 18 May
to 5 Jun also daily 10–5.30;
Nov to Mar, Sat and Sun
10–5.30. 10 acres

arbour draped in clematis. Deeper still into the
woodland a rustic bridge spans the neck of a lake
whose banks are densely planted with the wilder
moisture-loving plants such as *Gunnera manicata*.
From the path running along the southern edge of the
wood glades occasionally open out offering lovely
views of the peaceful countryside.

HERGEST CROFT
Hereford & Worcester

Kington HR5 3EG
1/2m W of Kington by A44
Tel: 0544 230160

Owner: W.L. Banks and
R.A. Banks

Open: Easter to Oct, daily
1.30–6.30. 50 acres

T HIS IS ONE of the best private collections of
woody plants in Britain and has an exceptionally
attractive atmosphere. The house was built in 1896
by William Hartland Banks who also started the
collection of plants, many of which were raised from
seed gathered in the wild. The garden falls into two
chief parts – that near the house and the separate
woodland garden which lies across some fields and
contains a fine collection of rhododendrons. It is
useless to attempt to list the great riches of this place.
There are marvellous plants everywhere and of
particular interest are the National Collections of
maples (excluding *Acer japonicum* cultivars) and of
birches. There is also an exceptionally pretty walled
kitchen garden with good borders, peonies under old
apple trees and proper vegetable beds. Although no
catalogue is issued and there is no mail order, there
are excellent plants for sale at the garden.

HIDCOTE MANOR GARDEN
Gloucestershire

Hidcote Bartrim, nr
Chipping Campden
GL55 6LR
4m NE of Chipping
Campden by B4632
Tel: 0386 438333

Owner:
The National Trust

Open: Apr to Oct, daily
except Tue and Fri 11–7 or
sunset if earlier. 10 acres

ALTHOUGH AMONG the best-known gardens in Britain, Hidcote still has the power to startle. It was begun before World War I by an American, Major Lawrence Johnston, who devised a type of garden that many think of as quintessentially English. First, it is a garden built up of separate 'rooms', each connected to the next but often with dramatic contrasts. For example, a pair of blazing red borders leads through to a cool green alley of pleached hornbeams. Second, the firm layout provides a disciplined setting for an immense range of plants of which Johnston was a pioneer rediscoverer – especially of old roses – and which he used in a swashbuckling manner in contrast with the crisp authority of his layout. Everywhere something enticing is glimpsed through an opening, across a pool, down steps or framed by a distant gate.

HILL COURT GARDENS AND GARDEN CENTRE
Hereford & Worcester

Hom Green,
Ross-on-Wye HR9 5QN
2 1/2m SW of
Ross-on-Wye by B4228
Tel: 0989 763123

Owner: Christopher
Rowley

Open: Daily 9.30–5.30.
3 acres

THE HOUSE at Hill Court is a dashing pedimented brick creation of the mid 18th century. The gardens, now almost entirely contained in the old walled vegetable garden of the house, have been beautifully restored by the present owner. Round the walls, in deep borders, shrubs are arranged according to the month in which they best perform – an unusual and fascinating exercise. Old espaliered fruit trees give great character and there are impeccable beds of roses, a large collection of delphiniums and gravel paths edged with box. At the centre of the garden there is a pair of sinuous herbaceous borders with, as a centrepiece, a fine sundial and four tall pyramids of clipped yew. A lively nursery sells a carefully chosen range of plants, pots and ornaments.

HODNET HALL
Shropshire

Hodnet, nr Market Drayton TF9 3NN
5 1/2m SW of Market Drayton by A53
Tel: 0630 84202

Owner: Mr and the Hon. Mrs Heber-Percy

Open: Apr to Sept, Mon to Sat 2–5, Sun and Bank Hol 12–5.30. 70 acres

THE HEBERS have been at Hodnet for an immense time but the garden can never have been in a better state than it is today. The main house is a neo-Elizabethan extravaganza built in 1870 by Anthony Salvin on an eminence with views south over a lake; a decorative Tudor dovecote forms an eye-catcher in the distance. Immediately below the south terrace of the house there are good mixed borders and steps lead down towards the lake which is part of a chain of pools whose banks have been brilliantly planted with with moisture-loving plants – primulas, hostas, rodgersias, *Gunnera manicata*, astilbes and ferns. By the east end of the lake, partly concealed by woodland, is a circular bed with a figure of Father Time surrounded by concentric beds of hydrangeas, roses and peonies.

HOW CAPLE COURT GARDENS
Hereford & Worcester

nr Ross-on-Wye HR1 4SX
4m N of Ross-on-Wye by
A449 and B4224
Tel: 0989 86626

Owner: Mr and Mrs Peter
Lee

Open: Apr to Oct, Mon to
Sat 9–5.30; May to Sept,
also Sun 10–5. 11 acres

THIS MARVELLOUS PLACE is undergoing restoration but already so much has been done that it is well worth visiting. The house is an ancient one with medieval origins, rebuilt in the early 17th century and once again at the turn of the century. The present owner's grandfather was mad about gardens and laid out an ambitious and exciting scheme thoroughly appropriate to the spectacular site. On one side of the house he made a series of dramatic terraces linked by steps with views across the Wye valley towards the Brecon Beacons to the south. The bottom terrace has a pool, Italianate statues, sentinel Irish yews and cascades of old roses. In the wooded valley alongside the house there is a dell garden, a vast circular pool and the splendid remains of a Florentine garden with a pattern of canals, the remains of a huge pergola and a loggia. A small nursery in the stable yard sells some good plants, particularly shrub roses.

KIFTSGATE COURT
Gloucestershire

Chipping Campden
GL55 6LW
3m NE of Chipping
Campden by B4632
Tel: 0386 438777

Owner: Mr and Mrs A.H.
Chambers

Open: Apr to Sept, Wed,
Thur and Sun 2–6; Jun to
Jul, also Sat and Bank Hol
2–6. 6 acres

THE NAME KIFTSGATE means to many gardeners that beautiful and embarrassingly vigorous rambling rose *R. filipes* 'Kiftsgate', and although the garden, started in the 1920s by Heather Muir, is certainly full of roses there is much else to admire. The house has a splendid setting, teetering on the edge of a precipitous valley across which, through the woods, are views of the Vale of Evesham. About the house is a series of enclosed gardens in which formality is blurred by generous planting. Four Squares has peonies, rodgersias and penstemons among indigofera, berberis and kolkwitzia. The rose borders have a central path hedged in *Rosa versicolor* behind which rise ramparts of shrub roses, and the Kiftsgate rose zips 50 feet into the branches of a copper beech. Below all this, paths wind steeply down the valley side where, under the canopy of trees, cistuses, hebes, phlomis and senecio relish the dry conditions. A choice selection of plants is for sale.

LITTLE MORETON HALL
Cheshire

Congleton CW12 4SD
4m SW of Congleton by
A34
Tel: 0260 272018

Owner:
The National Trust

Open: Apr to Sept, Wed to
Sun (closed Good Fri)
12–5.30; Bank Hol 11–5.30;
Oct, Wed, Sat and Sun
12–5.30. 1 acre. House open

THE HALF-TIMBERED famously wambly 15th-century house is surrounded by a moat. Little is known about what sort of garden the house had in its heyday but there are the remains of an artificial mound of the sort that might have been used for viewing a formal knot or parterre. With this in mind Graham Stuart Thomas laid out a charming little knot garden of box hedges, gravel and topiary yew obelisks based on a 17th-century pattern. At each side a pattern of square beds hedged in box contains a standard gooseberry bush underplanted with blocks of a single herbaceous plant – germander, strawberries, woodruff or London pride. All this is perfectly appropriate to the setting and a model of what may be done in a small space.

LYME PARK
Cheshire

Disley,
Stockport SK12 2NX
6 1/2m SE of Stockport by
A6
Tel: 0663 762023

Owner:
The National Trust

Open: Daily except 25 and
26 Dec; summer 11–5;
winter 11–4. 15 acres.
House open

AT LYME PARK the best parts of the garden have an exciting Victorian flavour that contrasts strikingly with the grand Frenchified house of the early 18th century. To one side of the house a well planted orangery of 1862 overlooks a parterre with Irish yews and urns, whose beds are planted in spring and summer with bright bedding schemes. On a terrace above, a rose garden with flagged paths and a central pool is enclosed in yew hedges and partly shaded by a pair of beautiful old limes. To one side a

path sweeps uphill between deep herbaceous borders whose colour-scheme modulates from oranges and yellows to blues and violets as it recedes from the house. North-west of the house, suddenly revealed below a high terrace, is an eye-stopping sight: the so-called Dutch garden, a dazzling arrangment of a fountain, statues of the four seasons, and a geometric pattern of beds edged in tightly clipped ivy and planted with single blocks of begonias, yellow or orange marigolds, santolina or purple verbena.

MISARDEN PARK
Gloucestershire

Miserden, Stroud GL6 7JA
7m SE of Gloucester
Tel: 028 582 1303

Owner: Major M.T.N.H. Wills

Open: Apr to Sept, Wed and Thur 10–4.30. 12 1/2 acres

T HE HOUSE is of the early 17th century with additions in 1920 by Sir Edwin Lutyens who also influenced the style of the terrace garden and forecourt alongside the house. The site is marvellous, on the edge of a valley with long views over wooded country. South and east of the house are excellent ornamental trees, and pleasure gardens are disposed on the slopes above. At their heart is a long walk of yew hedges whose tops are decorated by a series of undulating topiary humps. On one side a pair of great mixed borders is separated by a broad grass walk and on the other a formal rose garden is backed with elegant trellis fencing. The garden is extremely well kept and is full of interest. There is also a nursery selling the kinds of plants seen in the garden.

NESS GARDENS
Cheshire

Ness, Neston, South Wirral
L64 4AY
11m NW of Chester by
A540
Tel: 051 336 2135

Owner: The University of
Liverpool

Open: Daily except 25 Dec
9.30–sunset. 63 acres

NESS GARDENS were founded by A.K. Bulley, who sponsored the first expeditions of two of the greatest plant hunters of the 20th century – George Forrest to western China in 1904 and Frank Kingdon-Ward to Yunnan in 1911. Other expeditions followed and the plants that they introduced are among the most splendid specimens that may be seen in the gardens to day. The site of the garden was good – with undulating land, acid soil and natural outcrops of stone. Bulley planted windbreaks of holly, evergreen oak, pines and poplars and built up a very wide range of plants. Some parts of the collection – such as azaleas, rhododendrons and sorbus – are particularly good. From the gardener's point of view, however, there are other valuable features: a heather garden, herbaceous borders, a large rock garden, many roses, immense numbers of flowering trees and shrubs, and a woodland garden.

OLD COURT NURSERIES LTD
Hereford & Worcester

Colwall, nr Malvern
WR13 6QE
3m SW of Malvern by
A449 and B4218
Tel: 0684 40416

Open: Apr to Oct, Wed to
Sun 10–1, 2.15–5.30; Nov
to Mar, Wed to Fri and
Sun 2.15–5.30 or dusk if
earlier

Illustration: Astrantia
'*George Chiswell*'

THE GREAT GLORY of Old Court Nurseries is the collection of Michaelmas daisies, one of the National Collections and a wonderful sight in September and October. But the nursery also sells an excellent collection of herbaceous perennials and rock garden plants. These are handsomely displayed in the adjoining Picton Garden which is open at the same times as the nursery. Nursery and garden together make an extremely attractive place to visit. Paul Picton has an excellent eye for a good plant and any gardener will find something desirable. Michaelmas daisies only are sold by mail order and a list of them is issued for that purpose.

PAINSWICK ROCOCO GARDEN
Gloucestershire

Painswick, nr Stroud
GL6 6TH
1/2m N of Painswick by
B4073
Tel: 0452 813204

Owner: Lord Dickinson

Open: Feb to mid-Dec,
Wed to Sun and Bank Hol,
11–5

THIS IS ONE of the most ambitious restorations of a private historic garden ever undertaken. The garden had all but disappeared but has now been almost entirely restored, using a painting of it by Thomas Robins of 1748. In a secret combe behind the house are wonderful garden buildings, woodland walks, pools and a snowdrop grove to take your breath away. A mysteriously two-faced gothic gazebo looks down a yew alley towards a distant pond. Paths snake up and down the wooded slopes of the combe, giving glimpses of alcoves, temples and pools. The Eagle House, an airy gothic gazebo with pinnacles, crockets and pointed windows, has recently been beautifully reconstructed.

167

PENRHYN CASTLE
Gwynedd

Bangor LL57 4HN
1m E of Bangor by A5122
Tel: 0248 353084

Owner:
The National Trust

Open: Apr to Oct, daily
except Tue 11–6. 47 acres.
House open

THE GIANT CASTLE – commissioned from Thomas Hopper in 1827 by a local millionaire quarry owner – is in neo-Norman style, built on a bluff with marvellous views north to Beaumaris Bay and south towards Snowdon. Parkland surrounds the castle but the chief horticultural interest lies in the old kitchen garden to the south. This is built on a steep slope with a formal terrace, parterres of roses and penstemons and a rose arbour at the top; at a lower level are ornamental trees and shrubs – eucryphias, magnolias, sophoras and styrax; at the lowest level are trained fuchsias on a long pergola with clematis intertwining and views to the stream garden below with, in summer, the huge leaves of *Gunnera manicata* splendidly placed against groves of elegant purple-leafed maples.

PERHILL NURSERIES
Hereford & Worcester

Worcester Road, Great
Witley WR6 6JT
On A443 1/4m SE of
village
Tel: 0299 896329

Open: Mon to Sat 9–6, Sun
9–5. No mail order

Illustration: Phygelius
'Winchester Fanfare'

ALPINES AND HERBACEOUS perennials are the speciality of this nursery which carries a stock of around 1,800 different species and varieties. There are particularly good collections of campanulas, penstemons, phlox, pinks, silenes and sisyrinchiums. Perhill also has other interests including herbs – with, for example, a dozen different kinds of basil, sixteen lavenders and some marvellous sages. There are always too many plants to be listed so a visit and a rummage around will always reveal something new and desirable. A mail order service is provided and an exceptionally good catalogue is produced, with much information on the plants and useful lists of plants for particular purposes or places.

PLAS NEWYDD
Gwynedd

Llanfairpwll, Anglesey
LL61 6EQ
1m S of Llanfairpwll by A5
Tel: 0248 714795

Owner:
The National Trust

Open: Apr to 27 Sept, daily except Sat 12–5 (Jul to Aug, 11–5); Oct, Fri and Sun 12–5. 31 acres. House open

THE HOUSE of Plas Newydd is a famously decorative piece of gothic fantasy built in 1793 by James Wyatt overlooking the waters of the Menai Strait. This is a mild but windy place and one of the striking things about the garden is the decorative use of unfamiliar hedging plants – grisellinia, potentilla and fuchsia. There is a pretty little formal terraced garden between the house and the strait but the real garden excitement comes with the parkland to the west, known as 'West Indies', in the design of which Humphry Repton had a hand. Here countless good ornamental trees and shrubs – camellias, magnolias, maples and the Chilean firebush – flourish among older cedars, an exceptional sycamore and Monterey cypresses. A rhododendron garden, three-quarters of a mile to the north of the house, has recently been restored and is open only during flowering time from the beginning of April to the end of May.

PLAS-YN-RHIW
Gwynedd

Rhiw, Pwllheli LL53 8AB
12m from Pwllheli on S
coast road to Aberdaron
Tel: 075 888219

Owner:
The National Trust

Open: Apr to 27 Sept, daily
except Sat 12–5; Oct, Sun
12–4. 1 acre. House open

THE LLEYN PENINSULA is the most westerly part of Wales and this enchanting little garden is one of the most remote on the mainland of Britain. The elegant stone house is built on precipitous wooded slopes giving beautiful views over Hell's Mouth Bay. Cobbled paths and box hedges divide the densely planted garden and old plants of sweet bay, a fig, myrtles and artemisias give a Mediterranean air. The microclimate is very benign here so plants like *Euphorbia mellifera* grow to great size and the tender climber *Lapageria rosea* flourishes.

PORTMEIRION
Gwynedd

Penrhyndeudraeth
LL48 6ET
2m SE of Porthmadog
Tel: 0766 770228

Open: Daily 9.30–6

Illustration opposite:
Portmeirion village

IN A WOODED COMBE overlooking the estuary of Traeth Bach towards the Harlech hills the architect Clough Williams-Ellis let rip with a fantasy Italianate village. He incorporated old architectural fragments into his buildings – cupolas, colonnades, statues and enough balconies to meet the needs of the world's population of Romeos and Juliets. Among these buildings there is interesting planting with a Mediterranean feeling – Chusan palms and Italian cypresses punctuate the scene and cistus and artemisias flourish on the rocky slopes. Portmeirion has a mild microclimate so tender plants such as *Echium pininana* do particularly well. There is a hotel in the village and houses are available for rent.

POWIS CASTLE

Powys

Welshpool SY21 8RF
1m S of Welshpool by
A483
Tel: 0938 554336

Owner:
The National Trust

Open: Apr to Jun, Sept to
Oct, daily except Mon and
Tue 11–6; Jul to Aug, daily
except Mon (open Bank
Hol) 11–6. 24 acres. Castle
open

THERE ARE FEW historic gardens that have so much to offer the gardener as Powis Castle. The place is historic because it preserves the splendid remains of a great formal garden of the 17th century – with grand terraces and immense old yews. But on these terraces the National Trust has laid out a brilliant series of borders with wall plants and climbers forming a background to fortissimo displays of border perennials; these are designed to provide interest throughout the summer into early autumn. Another particular interest in the gardens is the exceptional collection of pots beautifully planted with carefully judged combinations. A small woodland garden below the castle has great atmosphere, and a mysterious sculpture by Vincent Woropay of a disembodied foot lying in the grass.

THE PRIORY

Gloucestershire

Kemerton GL20 7JN
6m S of Pershore by B4080
Tel: 0386 89258

Owner: The Hon. Mrs
Peter Healing

Open: May to Sept, Thur
2–7. 4 acres

THE HOUSE at Kemerton is an elegant Georgian box of brick but the priory ruins are visible among the densely planted borders. On the south-facing slopes of Bredon Hill the garden has a protected site where Mrs Healing and her late husband laid out a series of brilliant borders in which colour harmony – some of it refreshingly bold – was the essential principle. Unusual plants chosen with an artist's eye fill these borders and they flower over an extended period. Providing contrast are broad sweeps of lawn with beautiful ornamental trees (especially maples), yew hedges, a pergola of roses and vines and discreetly used ornaments. A nursery sells some excellent plants but there is no mail order.

RODMARTON MANOR
Gloucestershire

Rodmarton, nr Cirencester
GL7 6PF
In village of Rodmarton 6
miles SW of Cirencester by
A433
Tel: 028 584 219

Owner: Mrs Anthony
Biddulph

Open: Mar to Aug, Thur
2–5. 3 acres

THE ARCHITECT Ernest Barnsley started Rodmarton in 1909 and it became a shrine of the Cotswolds crafts movement. The grey, gabled house has an intricate garden which was partly designed by Ernest Barnsley and his brother Sidney. It is formal in spirit but the lavish planting has a cottage-garden informality. A flagged path separates double borders overflowing with old roses, peonies and campanulas, backed with stone walls and a yew hedge and enlivened with topiary of yew and box. Behind the house a pattern of enclosures separated by yew hedges and a pleached lime walk frames unspoilt views of the rural landscape.

RUSHFIELDS OF LEDBURY
Hereford & Worcester

Ross Road, Ledbury
HR8 2LP
1 1/2m SW of Ledbury by
A449
Tel: 0531 2004

Open: Wed to Sat 11–5

Illustration: Helleborus
orientalis *form*

T HIS IS A small nursery carrying a choice stock
with an emphasis on herbaceous perennials.
There are good collections of hardy geraniums,
hostas, penstemons and interesting grasses. The very
rare double-flowered sweet rocket is stocked and
there is a splendid selection of the exquisite
hellebores cultivated by Helen Ballard. An
informative catalogue is produced from which plants
may be ordered by post.

SEZINCOTE
Gloucestershire

nr Moreton-in-Marsh
GL56 9AW
1 1/2m W of
Moreton-in-Marsh by A44

Owner: Mr and Mrs D.
Peake

Open: Jan to Nov, Thur,
Fri and Bank Hol 2–6 or
sunset if earlier. 10 acres.
House open

T HE HOUSE at Sezincote was built in around 1810
by Sir Charles Cockerell and has a wonderful
Indian character. A formal garden with soaring Irish
yews is overlooked by a grand sweeping conservatory
with minarets, ending in an octagonal domed
pavilion. Farther from the house an Indian temple
overlooks an ornamental lake from which a stream
flows whose banks are richly planted with hostas,
rodgersias and skunk cabbage, relishing the moisture.

The stream flows under an exotic Oriental bridge surmounted by statues of bulls, and old woodland spreads all around studded with ornamental trees. This heady mixture of subtle layout, excellent plants and orientalist decoration deep in the Cotswold countryside is a unique experience.

SNOWSHILL MANOR
Gloucestershire

Snowshill, nr Broadway
WR12 7JU
In village of Snowshill 3m
S of Broadway
Tel: 0386 852410

Owner:
The National Trust

Open: Apr and Oct, Sat,
Sun and Bank Hol 11–1,
2–5; May to Sept, Wed to
Sun and Bank Hol 11–1,
2–6. 2 acres. House open

CHARLES WADE, antiquarian and architect, was responsible for this extraordinary place where the garden was partly designed by the Arts and Crafts architect M.H. Baillie Scott. The house is a pretty stone-tiled Cotswold manor and the garden lies on steep west-facing slopes to one side. Wade terraced the slope and linked the separate spaces with stone steps and a bold descending avenue of Irish yews. Within the various garden enclosures Wade deployed a rich repertoire of garden ornaments – sundials, an armillary sphere, a gilt figure of George and the Dragon, pools, and benches painted in the distinctive 'Wade blue'. Flower beds and climbing roses look wonderful against the honey-coloured stone. The charm of this modestly sized garden lies in its different levels and endlessly shifting viewpoints.

SPETCHLEY PARK
Hereford & Worcester

nr Worcester WR5 1RS
3m E of Worcester by A422
Tel: 0905 65224/65213

Owner: Mr and Mrs R.J.
Berkeley

Open: Apr to Sept, Tue to
Fri and Bank Hol, 11–5,
Sun 2–5. 25 acres

*Illustration opposite: The
fountain garden at Spetchley*

THE HEART of the garden is a maze of walks, borders and hedged enclosures which are so full of excellent plants that one's attention is repeatedly drawn by some lovely specimen, making it easy to lose one's orientation. The Berkeleys have been here a long time but, from the gardening point of view, the most important event was the marriage in 1891 of Robert Berkeley to Rose Willmott of Warley Place, the older sister of the famous gardener Ellen Willmott who designed the fountain garden at Spetchley. Here a fountain lies at the centre of four large squares enclosed in yew hedges and densely planted. Running along one side is an immense border in which roses, philadelphus and other shrubs are densely underplanted with herbaceous perennials – among them peonies, campanulas, geraniums and delphiniums. In a walled garden a nursery sells a good general stock of plants.

STAPELEY WATER GARDENS LTD
Cheshire

London Road, Stapeley,
Nantwich CW5 7LH
2 1/2m SE of Nantwich by
A51
Tel: 0270 623868

Open: Mon to Fri 9–6, Sat,
Sun and Bank Hol 10–7;
closes at 5 in winter. 53
acres

THERE IS nothing at all quite like this anywhere in Britain. It is a tremendous celebration of water gardens and their plants where the visitor may see and buy and, indeed, quite possibly spend the whole day. Although there is plenty of razzamatazz there is also nurserymanship of a high order and the gardens display the largest collection of hardy and tender water-lily varieties in the world – over 160 varieties are grown. Apart from these there are also very many other moisture or water-loving plants displayed in immense glasshouses and out-of-doors. In addition to their watery activities Stapeley are building up National Collections of begonias and bromeliads. A mail order service is provided and the very well illustrated catalogue tells you probably all you need to know about making, stocking and maintaining a water garden.

STONE HOUSE COTTAGE
Hereford & Worcester

Stone, nr Kidderminster
DY10 4BG
2m SE of Kidderminster by
A448
Tel: 0562 69902

Owner: Major and the
Hon. Mrs Arbuthnott

Open: Mar to Nov, Wed to
Sat 10–6 ; May to Jun, also
Sun 10–6. 3/4 acre

JAMES ARBUTHNOTT is a demon bricklayer and his
wife Louisa a brilliant propagator. The garden, an
old walled kitchen garden, now bristles with look-out
towers, gazebos, arcades and other charming
architectural geegaws which make ornaments as well
as supports for the countless climbing, twining and
ramping plants that are a speciality of the garden.
Hedges of yew and purple plum divide the space, and
at the centre there is a pair of burgeoning borders
culminating in a sundial. Ornamental trees and
shrubs are planted in grass and near the house raised
beds contain alpines and smaller plants. There is an
excellent nursery which specialises in wall plants,
some very unusual, and many with reputations for
dubious hardiness that have proved remarkably tough
in this not particularly mild climate. An informative
catalogue is produced but there is no mail order.

SUDELEY CASTLE
Gloucestershire

Winchcombe, nr
Cheltenham GL54 5JD
8m NE of Cheltenham by
B4075 and B4632
Tel: 0242 604357/602308

Owner: Lord and Lady
Ashcombe

Open: Apr to Oct, daily
11–5.30. 10 acres. Castle
open

THIS IS a spectacular place with a grand late medieval castle with later additions and a garden that takes full advantage of the architectural setting. Roses are the great thing at Sudeley and they look wonderful against the old stone walls. At the entrance a long lily pool runs in front of the ruins of the 15th-century great barn whose roof-less walls are draped with climbing roses and clematis. Beyond the castle, a recently replanted formal Victorian garden has a pool surrounded by L-shaped beds with old shrub roses underplanted with herbs. On either side are immense old tunnels of yew and the surrounding lawns are studded with topiary shapes of golden and common yew. Old trees – walnuts, limes and a vast cedar of Lebanon – stand out superbly against the castle walls. Although there is plenty of history at Sudeley the garden is full of new vigour. A good nursery sells a general stock but has an especially distinguished collection of roses.

TATTON PARK
Cheshire

Knutsford WA16 6QN
3 1/2m N of Knutsford
signposted from the centre
of the town
Tel: 0565 654822

Owner:
The National Trust

Open: Apr to Sept, daily
except Mon (but open
Bank Hol) 12–4; Oct to
Mar, daily except Mon
12–3. 60 acres. House open

THE HOUSE was designed in the early 19th century for the Egerton family by Lewis Wyatt who also had a hand in the gardens which have an exuberant 19th-century flavour. South of the house, on a terrace with grand views, a dapper parterre designed by Joseph Paxton has recently been beautifully restored and is brilliantly bedded out in summer. Her Ladyship's Garden, by the house, is a sunken garden with a pergola and rose-beds. Fine mixed borders with buttresses of yew are backed by the old heated walls of the kitchen garden. Nearby, a unique fernery designed by Wyatt houses tender ferns and an orangery protects citrus plants and sub-tropical climbers. On sloping land south of the house a long walk pierces well-wooded lawns with glimpses to the west of a serpentine network of lakes. Humphry Repton landscaped the park in the early 19th century. On the edge of one of the lakes is an exceptional Japanese garden, built in 1910 by Japanese gardeners, in which maples, moss-covered stones, an arched bridge and a Shinto temple make a convincing picture under a canopy of old trees.

TREASURES OF TENBURY LIMITED
Hereford & Worcester

Tenbury Wells WR15 8HQ
1m W of Tenbury Wells by
A456
Tel: 0584 810777

Open: Mon to Sat 10–6,
Sun 2–6

TREASURES CARRIES a large general stock but it is for clematis that the nursery is best known: well over 200 species and varieties are stocked and the nursery holds a National Collection. The list is especially strong in the species and their choice forms although it by no means disdains the glamorous large-flowered cultivars. A list of clematis only is published and a mail order service for them is provided. The list is a mouth-watering browse with much detail on each variety and valuable information about cultivation. John Treasure's own garden at Burford House next door to the nursery is also open.

WESTBURY COURT GARDEN
Gloucestershire

Westbury-on-Severn
GL14 1PD
9m SW of Gloucester by
A48
Tel: 045 276 461

Owner:
The National Trust

Open: Apr to Oct, Wed to
Sun and Bank Hol 11–6
(closed Good Fri); also by
appointment. 4 acres

THIS LATE 17TH-CENTURY formal water garden, for a house that was destroyed, survived by the skin of its teeth and has now been beautifully restored. On low-lying land on the banks of the Severn formality is given by two parallel canals edged with yew hedges whose crests are decorated with yew and holly topiary. An elegant Dutch-style pavilion overlooks the head of one canal and a boundary wall is covered in pre-1700 varieties of espaliered fruit. In one corner is a secret walled garden, overlooked by a charming little summer house, in which box-edged beds burgeon with plants in cultivation before 1700 and the paths are shaded by an arbour of honeysuckle and clematis. Nearby a parterre of box topiary and annuals has been recreated from an 18th-century print. On the way out keep an eye open for an unforgettable sight behind the pavilion – an immense holm oak (*Quercus ilex*), probably the oldest in the country.

WESTONBIRT ARBORETUM
Gloucestershire

Westonbirt, nr Tetbury
GL8 8QS
3m SW of Tetbury by the
A433
Tel: 0666 88220

Owner: The Forestry
Commission

Open: Daily 10–8 or sunset
if earlier. 600 acres

THIS IS ONE of the greatest collections of trees in the country but it is much more than a collection. It was started in 1829 by Robert Holford who had a brilliant eye for arranging the huge quantities of trees which he so energetically collected. Planting has been continued by subsequent members of his family and, since 1956, under the ownership of the Forestry Commission. Today it is not only a marvellous place to learn about and admire trees but it is also a landscape of rare beauty. The arboretum has the National Collections of *Acer japonicum* and of lowland species of willow but in most of the major groups, and many of the minor, it has wonderful trees, some of them fine old specimens.

THE ERNEST WILSON
MEMORIAL GARDEN
Gloucestershire

High Street, Chipping
Campden
In the centre of the town

Open: Daily, dawn–dusk.
1/4 acre

THE GREAT plant hunter E.H. 'Chinese' Wilson was a native of Chipping Campden and this charming little garden, entered by a gothic arch through a stone wall, reminds gardeners of how much we owe him. It is planted entirely with his introductions – from China and Japan – which consist chiefly of shrubs and trees with a few perennials. It may come as a surprise to some that *Lilium regale*, the sweetly scented cottage-garden stalwart, was a Wilson introduction in 1905.

The Heart of England

—— ❧ ——

Derbyshire, Leicestershire, Northamptonshire, Nottinghamshire,
Staffordshire, Warwickshire, West Midlands

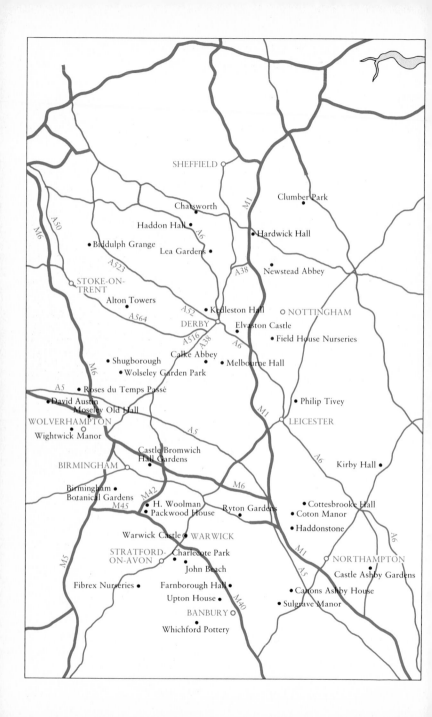

SHEFFIELD

Clumber Park

Chatsworth

Haddon Hall

Hardwick Hall

Biddulph Grange

Lea Gardens

Newstead Abbey

STOKE-ON-TRENT

Alton Towers

Kedleston Hall

NOTTINGHAM

DERBY

Elvaston Castle

Field House Nurseries

Shugborough

Calke Abbey

Melbourne Hall

Wolseley Garden Park

Roses du Temps Passé

David Austin

Philip Tivey

Moseley Old Hall

LEICESTER

WOLVERHAMPTON

Wightwick Manor

Castle Bromwich
Hall Gardens

BIRMINGHAM

Kirby Hall

Birmingham
Botanical Gardens

H. Woolman

Ryton Gardens

Cottesbrooke Hall

Packwood House

Coton Manor

Warwick Castle

WARWICK

Haddonstone

STRATFORD-
ON-AVON

Charlecote Park

John Beach

NORTHAMPTON

Castle Ashby Gardens

Fibrex Nurseries

Farnborough Hall

Canons Ashby House

Upton House

Sulgrave Manor

BANBURY

Whichford Pottery

ALTON TOWERS
Staffordshire

Alton ST10 4DB
18m E of Stoke-on-Trent
Tel: 0538 702200

Owner: Alton Towers Ltd

Open: Daily 10–5.30. 100
acres

A RING-A-DING family leisure park, the busiest in Britain, is not a place where you would expect much by way of a garden. The gigantic house was designed for the 16th Earl of Shrewsbury in the first half of the 19th century by a bevy of architects of which the chief was A.W.N. Pugin whose wild gothic palace was said to sacrifice 'domestic comfort to showmanship'. The gardens were made on a similarly lavish scale. In a precipitous dell north of the house huge numbers of conifers clothe the slopes which are animated by exotic buildings, most of which were designed by Robert Abraham: a palatial mosque-like conservatory with many domes and beautiful stone-work; a gothic prospect tower on the heights; a memorial to the 15th Earl; and, best of all, a fountain in a lake disguised as a Chinese pagoda. A shady terrace runs in front of the conservatory, with urns and a topiary tunnel of yew. J.C. Loudon thought the whole place was 'in excessively bad taste', and that is exactly what many people will love. The gardens are splendidly well cared for.

185

DAVID AUSTIN
West Midlands

Bowling Green Lane,
Albrighton,
Wolverhampton WV7 3HB
7m NW of Wolverhampton
by A41 and A464 nr Jnct 3
of M54
Tel: 0902 372142

Open: Mon to Fri 9–5, Sat,
Sun and Bank Hol 10–6

Illustration: Rosa 'Mary
Rose'

ALTHOUGH DAVID AUSTIN grows other things (irises, peonies and daylilies, for example) he is overwhelmingly a rose specialist and one of the very best in the country. He is known above all for old roses and his own 'English Roses' which combine the beauty of flower and form of the old varieties with the repeat flowering of the modern ones. In fact he does not disdain modern roses and has a carefully chosen selection of Hybrid Teas, some of which are now hard to find. Go, of course, in late June or July and be bowled over by the beauty and scent. He produces an excellent and informative catalogue and sells by mail order.

JOHN BEACH LTD
Warwickshire

9 Grange Gardens,
Wellesbourne CV35 9RL
(office); Thelsford Farm,
Charlecote (nursery)
4m S of Warwick by A429
Tel: 0926 624173

Open: Daily except Sun
10.30–1, 2.30–5 (or dusk in
winter)

THE BEST PART of John Beach's nursery is the marvellous collection of clematises – well over 150 different kinds with a particularly good selection of the species and smaller-flowered varieties. An excellent catalogue has invaluable information on the care and cultivation of these sometimes tricky customers. Although clematises loom largest on Beach's list he also sells shrubs, trees and herbaceous perennials. Among these there are some interesting things, with unusual selections of, for example, fuchsias and hibiscus cultivars and an unexpectedly good range of grape vines – for both wine and dessert. A mail order service is provided.

BIDDULPH GRANGE
Staffordshire

Biddulph, nr
Stoke-on-Trent ST8 7SD
5m SE of Congleton by
A527
Tel: 0782 517999

Owner:
The National Trust

Open: Apr to Oct, Wed to
Fri 12–6 (closed Good Fri),
Sat, Sun and Bank Hol 11–
6 or dusk if earlier. 15 acres

GARDENS THAT ARE snatched from the brink of extinction always have a special charm and Biddulph is an exceptionally fine example. It was made by James Bateman and Edward Cooke over a long period from 1842, when tastes in garden design turned to the exotic and a flood of newly introduced conifers fuelled the gardening imagination.

A frightening rocky tunnel lit by a glimmer of candle-light leads suddenly into a glittering gold, scarlet and white interior of a Chinese pagoda overlooking a pool fringed with maples. Stone sphinxes and monumental clipped yews guard the mysterious entrance to Egypt. A sprightly dahlia walk marches up to a sombre avenue of deodars piercing deeply into the woodland. This has been superbly restored by the National Trust; more work is still being done but the results already make Biddulph a truly exciting place.

BIRMINGHAM BOTANICAL GARDENS
Birmingham

Westbourne Road,
Edgbaston B15 3TR
2m SW from city centre
Tel: 021 454 1860

Owner: Birmingham
Botanical and Horticultural
Society Ltd

Open: Daily except
Christmas Day 9 (10 on
Sun)–8 or dusk if earlier.
15 acres

THERE IS a zip about the Birmingham Botanical gardens. First, they are beautifully gardened – even the bedding schemes manage brilliantly to avoid municipal plodding. Second, although they call themselves botanical gardens, they are treated by locals, and those from farther afield, as a public park and there are plenty of horticultural diversions. Glasshouses of several different climates protect a very wide range of tender plants. Collections of particular groups of plants – introductions by E. H. 'Chinese' Wilson, rhododendrons, rock and water plants, and roses, are displayed in the undulating site which was landscaped by J.C. Loudon in 1832.

CALKE ABBEY
Derbyshire

Ticknall DE7 1LE
9m S of Derby by A514
Tel: 0332 863822/864444

Owner:
The National Trust

Open: Apr to Oct, Sat to
Wed 11–5.30. House open

*Illustration: Bedding in the
Victorian garden at Calke*

THE EARLY 18th-century grey stone mansion seems almost like an after-thought when the visitor has traversed the many acres of wonderfully unspoilt ancient parkland that surrounds it. The garden, at some distance from the house, as was often the case in the 18th century, consists of a walled formal garden which has been restored with a pattern of borders containing bedding schemes of Victorian appearance. In one corner is a rare 'auricula theatre' – shelves on which to display auriculas in pots – which in summer is used for pelargoniums. The walled physic garden to one side has been restored as a working kitchen garden in which are grown many old varieties of vegetables and fruit in box-edged beds.

CANONS ASHBY HOUSE
Northamptonshire

Canons Ashby, Daventry
NN11 6SD
11m NE of Banbury by
A361, A422 and B4525
Tel: 0327 860044

Owner:
The National Trust

Open: Apr to Oct, Wed to
Sun and Bank Hol (closed
Good Fri) 1–5.30 or dusk if
earlier. 70 acres. House
open

THE BEGUILING brick and stone house, the home of the Dryden family, was started in the 1550s and substantially rebuilt in the early 18th century. The essential layout of the garden as it is today is a rare survival from the same period. The Green Court by the west façade, with its decorative stone walls and gates, is ornamented with giant cones of clipped yew and a lead statue of a fluting shepherd boy which was probably made by John Van Nost. A door leads under a vast cedar of Lebanon to the garden proper in which terraces descend towards decorative gates. Here there has been much replanting with formal rows of Portugal laurels and ancient varieties of fruit trees, among which is a 16th-century plum cultivar. The Drydens were an old-fashioned family and rejected the late 18th-century craze for landscaping, so preserving the gentlemanly formality of an earlier period that may be seen today.

CASTLE ASHBY GARDENS
Northamptonshire

Castle Ashby NN7 1LT
5m E of Northampton by
A428
Tel: 060 129 234

Owner: The Marquess of
Northampton

Open: Daily 10–6. 19 acres.
Terrace garden by
appointment only

CASTLE ASHBY was built for the Compton family between 1574 and 1640 and it is still in their hands, surrounded by thousands of acres of land. The Marquess of Northampton has recently undertaken an ambitious programme of restoration – of house and garden – and the results are strikingly successful. A Victorian terraced garden below the house has been brilliantly restored with scalloped fountains, ribbon carpet bedding and elaborate arabesques of gravel cut into the turf. Marvellous parkland lying below the balustrades to the south-west was laid out by 'Capability' Brown in 1761 and a comprehensive replanting of trees has been carried out. The Italian garden has a glamorous conservatory designed by Matthew Digby Wyatt, overlooking formal gardens with a pond, yew topiary and terracotta urns. A path leads downhill to an arboretum with some fine trees, especially the specimens of weeping beech.

CASTLE BROMWICH HALL GARDENS
Birmingham

Old Chester Road, Castle
Bromwich B36 9BT
6m NE of city centre by
A47, near Jnct 5 of M6
(northbound only)
Tel: 021 749 4100

Owner: Castle Bromwich
Hall Gardens Trust

Open: Apr to Sept, Mon to
Thur 1.30–4.30, Sat, Sun
and Bank Hol 2–6. 10 acres

CASTLE BROMWICH HALL is a fine brick mansion built in the 17th century for the Bridgeman family. The gardens are an exciting survival from the heyday of English formal garden design of the late 17th and early 18th century and are in the process of restoration by a privately formed trust. Already much has been done and this is a very rare opportunity to see an authentic restoration of a garden of this period in a mavellous setting of old brick walls and fine garden buildings. The site is a west-facing slope divided down the centre by a holly walk – a broad turf path lined with regularly spaced variegated hollies – the 'Gilded ever Green' mentioned in surviving records. One end of the walk is punctuated by an elegant pedimented brick orangery and the other by the remains of a corresponding music room. Above the walk is an area of 'wilderness', formal shubberies with winding walks, and below, kitchen gardens and a holly maze. Work on other features is going ahead and it will be fascinating to follow this restoration as it progresses.

CHARLECOTE PARK
Warwickshire

Wellesbourne, Warwick
CV35 9ER
5m E of Stratford-on-Avon
by B4086
Tel: 0789 470277

Owner:
The National Trust

Open: Apr to Oct, daily
except Mon and Thur
(open Bank Hol, closed
Good Fri) 11–6. 3 acres.
House open

THE APPROACH to Charlecote – across an ancient deer-park – has wonderful atmosphere. The house, originally an Elizabethan mansion, was comprehensively done over in the 19th century. The garden has been revitalised in recent years by the National Trust, with lively mixed borders in the walled forecourt with its ornate turreted gate-tower. Flanking the steps in the forecourt are a pair of lead statues – an early 18th-century shepherd and shepherdess by John Cheere. Charlecote has associations with Shakespeare – he is supposed to have poached here as a lad – and a border of flowers mentioned in his plays commemorates him. Behind the house the River Avon curves across flat parkland.

CHATSWORTH
Derbyshire

Bakewell DE4 1PP
4m E of Bakewell by A6 or
A619 and minor roads
Tel: 0246 582204

Owner: Chatsworth House
Trust

Open: Easter to Oct, daily
11–5. 100 acres. House open

*Illustration opposite: Pool
and crinkle-crankle beech
hedges at Chatsworth*

THE CAVENDISHES first made a garden at
Chatsworth in the 16th century and it was
subsequently added to by many of the greatest garden
designers and architects of the day. In the late 17th
century London and Wise were called in; in the 18th
century 'Capability' Brown landscaped the garden,
undoing one of the greatest of all formal gardens; in
the 19th century Joseph Paxton was head gardener,
adding great conservatories and rockeries. Today, the
garden is full of reminders of the past – a handsome
formal scheme of lime walks and pools to the south;
Paxton's 'conservative' wall; an exquisite orangery of
1698; the dazzling cascade house of 1703 over whose
domed roof water pours as though off an umbrella.
But this is not a museum and there are lively new
borders in front of the orangery shop; the charming
caprice of a miniature ornamental *potager*, and
Wendy furniture trimmed with yew – a bed with a
coverlet of red begonias and a pillow of white, and
table lamps of clipped ivy. Above all, views across
the valley beyond the great house to exquisite
pastoral scenery, provide an incomparable setting. A
good range of plants is sold, and Chatsworth makes
its own garden furniture which is of very high quality.

CLUMBER PARK
Nottinghamshire

The Estate Office, Clumber
Park, Worksop S80 3AZ
4 1/2m SE of Worksop by
B6034 or A614
Tel: 0909 476592

Owner:
The National Trust

Open: Park: daily
dawn–dusk; Walled kitchen
garden: Apr to Sept, Sat,
Sun and Bank Hol 10–5.
20 acres

ONE OF THE approaches to Clumber Park, carved
out of Sherwood Forest in the 18th century, is
lined with a marvellous double curving avenue of
limes. The grounds were landscaped by both
'Capability' Brown and by Humphry Repton, and
many fine trees date from those times. The great
house was destroyed by fire but the walled kitchen
garden survives, with an immense glasshouse running
along one wall, in which there is an interesting
collection of the paraphernalia of kitchen gardening.
The old potting shed and gardener's bothy, full of
atmosphere, are also shown.

COTON MANOR
Northamptonshire

nr Guilsborough NN6 8RQ
10m NW of Northampton
by A50
Tel: 0604 740219

Owner: Mr and Mrs Ian
Pasley-Tyler

Open: Garden: Easter to
Sept, Wed, Sun and Bank
Hol 2–6; Nursery: Mon to
Fri 10–5; Apr to Oct, also
Sun 2–6. 10 acres

A T COTON MANOR the gardens are adorned by many different kinds of rare birds, some enclosed in aviaries and others, black-necked swans, for example, at home in one of the many pools in the garden. The land slopes away from the old gabled stone house and is divided into enclosures of varying character. Terraces, overhung with the 'Seven Sisters' rose, with cerise flowers changing to the palest of pinks, lead to a long herbaceous border hedged in holly. Behind this is a formal rose garden. At a lower level a peaceful pond is edged with lawns with an old 'Kanzan' cherry, and paths lead through an intricate water garden well planted with moisture-loving plants. A very good small nursery has excellent selections of hebes, viburnums, hepaticas and roses. There is no mail order.

COTTESBROOKE HALL
Northamptonshire

nr Northampton NN6 8PF
9m NW of Northampton
by A50
Tel: 060 124 808

Owner: Captain John
Macdonald-Buchanan

Open: Jun to Sept, Thur
and Aug Bank Hol 2–5.30.
25 acres. House open

S OME GARDENS deserve to be better known and Cottesbrooke is a prime example. The beautiful early 18th-century brick and stone house has a garden which matches it for beauty and interest. It looks out over wonderful 18th-century parkland and a central vista is aligned on the distant spire of

Brixworth church. The garden today is the result of many different influences – the present owner's mother, Lady Macdonald-Buchanan, the Arts and Crafts designer Edward Schultz, Dame Sylvia Crowe and Sir Geoffrey Jellicoe. Around the house there is a cornucopia of formal gardens: a pair of fortissimo herbaceous borders; a statue walk with yew hedges and figures by Scheemakers from Stowe; enclosed gardens with pools and a pergola; and a stately south-facing terrace with statues and plantings of roses and agapanthus. All about is splendid parkland and countless good trees. At a distance from the house, but not to be missed, is a wild woodland garden with a beautifully planted stream; arched bridges and many Japanese maples give an eastern atmosphere. There are few gardens anywhere with so much to admire as Cottesbrooke.

ELVASTON CASTLE
Derbyshire

Elvaston, Derby DE7 3EP
6m SE of Derby by A6 and
B5010
Tel: 0332 571342

Owner: Derbyshire County
Council

Open: Daily 9–sunset. 200
acres

THE GOTHIC CASTLE is the work of James Wyatt in the early 19th century and sets the scene for the thoroughly romantic if slightly dishevelled gardens which were laid out for a reformed Regency buck, 'Beau' Petersham, in the 1830s. They were designed by a Scot, William Barron, who concocted a heady mixture of the latest conifers and Italianate parterres and 'bowers' with much topiary of box and golden yew. A new addition is the 'old English garden' of herbaceous and rose borders, in the walled former kitchen garden.

FARNBOROUGH HALL
Warwickshire

nr Banbury, Oxfordshire
OX17 1DU
6m N of Banbury off A423

Owner:
The National Trust

Open: Apr to Sept, Wed
and Sat 2–6; also 3 and 4
May 2–6. 16 acres

FARNBOROUGH is a very unusual intimate landscape garden laid out in the 18th century – delicate chamber music rather than resounding symphony. William Holbech inherited the property with its handsome late 17th-century house in 1717 and, with the help of the elusive Sanderson Miller, laid out the grounds in the new landscape taste. A long serpentine terrace of grass running along a ridge is embellished with two pavilions, one of which is an unusual oval in section, with an open loggia, and the other in the form of a columned temple. Punctuated also by a slender obelisk, the terrace leads to a new rose garden and a yew alley.

FIBREX NURSERIES LTD
Warwickshire

Honeybourne Road,
Pebworth, nr
Stratford-upon-Avon
CV37 8XT
5m NW of Chipping
Camden by B4081 and
minor roads
Tel: 0789 720788

Open: Jan to Mar, Aug to
Nov, Mon to Fri 12–5; Apr
to Jul, Tue to Sat 12–5;
closed Dec

Illustration: Helleborus
orientalis *form*

THE NURSERY has four specialities, in each of which it offers marvellous collections. First, its pelargonium list is enormous, essential browsing for anyone with an interest in those plants. Second, there is a rich selection of ivies with, for example, over 130 different varieties of *Hedera helix*. Third, it has a particularly attractive collection of hardy and tender ferns for which a good catalogue is issued with much valuable information. Lastly, there is a unique selection of very rare cultivars of *Helleborus orientalis*, known as the Raithby hybrids, with lovely and unusual colouring. Mail order is provided and lists of each speciality are published.

FIELD HOUSE NURSERIES
Nottinghamshire

Leake Road, Gotham
NG11 0JN
10m SW of Nottingham by
A453 (Jnct 24 of M1)
Tel: 0602 830278

Open: Wed to Mon 9–5

Illustration: Phlox nana
'*Chameleon*'

FIELD HOUSE NURSERIES specialise in alpines, rock garden plants and auriculas, of which an especially attractive range is grown; gardeners taking an interest in these formerly fashionable and charming plants will find much to attract them. Lists are provided and both plants and seeds are supplied by post. At the nursery a huge alpine house – one of the biggest in the country – is beautifully laid out with naturalistic arrangements of a wide variety of plants displayed in raised beds.

HADDON HALL
Derbyshire

Bakewell DE4 1LA
2m SE of Bakewell by A6
Tel: 0629 812855

Owner: The Duke of
Rutland

Open: Apr to Jun, Sept,
Tue to Sun 11–6 (open
Bank Hol); Jul and Aug,
Tue to Sat (open Bank
Hol) 11–6. 6 acres. House
open

HADDON HALL is an intensely romantic place: a vast castle, built between the 12th and 17th centuries, with turrets, crenellations and tracery windows. It is set in wooded countryside and the garden still has some of the character of the formal gardens of the 17th century. The south garden, a series of terraces with balustrades, dates from the very early 17th century. Buttresses at the lowest level make an attractive and protected setting for roses and other flowering shrubs and climbers. There is a fountain and a rose garden but the eye is constantly drawn to the old stone of the castle and the rural landscape on the slopes below.

HADDONSTONE LTD
Northamptonshire

The Forge House, East
Haddon, Northampton
NN6 8DB
8m NW of Northampton
off A428
Tel: 0604 770711

Open: Mon to Fri 9–5.30

Garden ornaments and buildings made of reconstituted stone have a long and honourable history. Haddonstone is one of the leading manufacturers and produces a very wide range of statues, urns, columns, garden buildings and architectural detailing. It also undertakes to make individual pieces to customers' specifications. Many of the designs are faithful copies of surviving examples in historic gardens. A show garden displays many of the products in a setting planned to display their ornamental use. A beautiful catalogue is produced and ornaments may be supplied by Haddonstone's own delivery service.

HARDWICK HALL
Derbyshire

Doe Lea, Chesterfield
S44 5QJ
6 1/2m W of Mansfield by
A6175 and minor roads, nr
Jnct 29 of M1
Tel: 0246 850430

Owner:
The National Trust

Open: Apr to Oct, daily
12–5.30. 7 acres. House
open

Bess of Hardwick married successfully (four times) and this is her final architectural flourish, built in the late 16th century when she was in her seventies and Countess of Shrewsbury. She ornamented the parapet of her great house with her initials, E.S., carved in fretted stone against the sky. The gardens are disposed in the Elizabethan stone courts to the west and south of the house. The entrance court, with a fine old cedar of Lebanon on the lawn, has splendid new mixed borders in which colour and foliage have been cunningly chosen. Repeated plantings of the sprawling, elegant *Aralia elata* 'Aureovariegata' and in late summer of the arching fronds of miscanthus give structure to a colour scheme which modulates from hot reds, oranges and yellow near the house to blues, whites and yellow farther away. The south court is divided into four by yew and hornbeam hedges. One of the divisions is a virtuoso herb garden in which pillars of golden and ordinary hop rise magnificently from a sea of angelica, lavender, sage, sweet cicely and thyme.

KEDLESTON HALL
Derbyshire

Derby DE6 4JN
5m NW of Derby by A52
and minor roads
Tel: 0332 842191

Owner:
The National Trust

Open: Garden: Apr to Oct,
Sat to Wed 11–6; Park: Apr
to Oct, daily 11–6; Nov to
20 Dec, Sat, Sun 12–4. 7
acres of garden. House open

KEDLESTON is the grandest and possibly the prettiest of Robert Adam's houses, built for Nathaniel Curzon in the 1760s. Adam also had a hand in the park, scattered with splendid ornamental buildings, which forms a lovely approach for the house. To the north, a long serpentine lake is spanned by a three-arched bridge with a rocky cascade below it and nearby, on the banks, a charming Fishing Room with a Venetian window is flanked by a pair of pedimented boathouses. Behind the house, in the well wooded old pleasure grounds, a circular garden of beds of roses radiating from a central pool is hedged in laurel and overlooked by a domed hexagonal temple. Shrubberies of rhododendrons, dogwoods and roses are embellished by a fine stone urn and, round a corner, the Medicean Lion rises up with a roguish grin.

KIRBY HALL
Northamptonshire

4m NE of Corby by minor roads
Tel: 0536 203230

Owner: English Heritage

Open: Daily 10–6. 5 acres

THIS IS A GHOSTLY place on the edge of the industrial sprawl of Corby – the uninhabited remains of an exquisite late 16th-century palace built for one of Queen Elizabeth's favourite courtiers, Sir Christopher Hatton. In the late 17th century Charles Hatton made a great garden here, which was restored after excavations in the 1930s. But this was highly inauthentic and English Heritage are now in the process of redoing it and it will be fascinating to see what they achieve. Charles Hatton was a distinguished gentleman-botanist, corresponding with John Evelyn and other garden connoisseurs of the day. His garden is particularly well documented, including detailed lists of the plants he grew. If the garden that emerges is anything like as beautiful as the house it will be wonderful to see.

LEA GARDENS
Derbyshire

Lea, Matlock DE4 5GH
5m SE of Matlock by A6 and minor roads
Tel: 0629 534380

Owner: Mr and Mrs J. Tye

Open: Mid-Mar to Jun, daily 10–7. 4 acres

THIS GARDEN, inspired by Bodnant and Exbury, although quite small by comparison, was started in 1935 by John Marsden-Smedley. Lea possesses a marvellous site, high up on south-facing wooded slopes that run down to the valley of the River Derwent. Here is an excellent collection of rhododendrons in a setting ideally suited to them. New owners have developed the garden even further and added many new trees and herbaceous plants. A wide range of bulbous plants of an alpine kind are displayed in a large scree bed. They have also started a nursery which sells alpines, conifers and rhododendrons by post, of which a list is issued.

MELBOURNE HALL
Derbyshire

Melbourne DE7 1EN
9m S of Derby by A453
Tel: 0332 862502

Owner: Lord Ralph Kerr

Open: Apr to Sept, Wed, Sat, Sun and Bank Hol 2–6. 16 acres. House open

MANY HISTORICALLY famous gardens are not especially exciting for the garden visitor; Melbourne is full of history but it is also full of interest. The house, of grey stone, presents its most glamorous façade, of 1744 with an elegant pediment, to the garden which was laid out in the early 18th century. Giant steps of turf descend to the Great Basin, a curved pool that crisply reflects the house. On its eastern side is one of Melbourne's most famous features, the 'Birdcage', Robert Bakewell's airy arbour of wrought iron of exquisite delicacy. To the south lies a pattern of lime alleys, unchanged in almost 300 years, with grassy walks punctuated by urns and statues of marvellous quality, some of them by John Van Nost, the greatest maker of garden ornaments of the early 18th century. Of the same period, leading to the west, is an immense tunnel of yew between whose gnarled trunks the visitor may walk. On its south side are some very good new mixed borders, showing that the spirit of gardening at Melbourne is still alive and kicking.

201

MOSELEY OLD HALL
Staffordshire

Moseley Old Hall Lane,
Fordhouses,
Wolverhampton
WV10 7HY
3 1/2m N of
Wolverhampton, between
A460 and A449, S of M54
Tel: 0902 782808

Owner:
The National Trust

Open: Apr to Oct, Wed,
Sat, Sun and Bank Hol
2–5.30 (Bank Hol 11–5);
Jul to Aug, also Tue
2–5.30. 1 acre. House open

AROUND AN UNASSUMING Elizabethan and 17th-century house the National Trust has made a little formal garden rich in the garden features of that period. The old windows overlook a parterre with a geometric pattern of box hedges, coloured pebbles and lollipops of clipped box – all this was taken from a design of 1640. On one side a nut walk leads to a paved path flanked by pairs of medlars, mulberries and quinces. Running down one side of the parterre is a 'carpenter's work' tunnel, festooned with purple-leafed vines and Virgin's Bower clematis (*C. flammula*) and underplanted with aquilegias, geraniums and lavender. A wrought-iron gate leads into the enclosed front garden which has box topiary clipped into cones and spirals and lively borders. All the planting here and elsewhere in the garden is of plants known to have been in gardens before 1700.

NEWSTEAD ABBEY
Nottinghamshire

Linstead NG15 8GE
9m N of Nottingham by
A60
Tel: 0623 793557

Owner: Nottingham City
Council

Open: Daily 10–sunset. 25
acres. Abbey open

LORD BYRON'S family, the Gordons, acquired the Augustinian abbey at the Dissolution and the decaying monastic ruins were immensely attractive to Byron's romantic imagination, although the oak he planted in 1798, whose stump remains to this day, never grew well. Much of the romanticism survives, but although there are medieval touches such as the monks' stew pond, most of the garden is a 20th-century creation. In the heart of the abbey building, laid out in the former cloister yard, is a reconstructed, enclosed medieval 'Mary' garden. To the south-east of the abbey lawns are ornamented with fine trees, some of them unusual such as a variegated sweet chestnut. Beyond them an elaborate rock garden has a good collection of heathers, from which a Japanese garden is seen across a lake, with a curved pergola of roses and wisteria, rushing streams crossed by hump-backed bridges, snow lanterns and Japanese maples.

PACKWOOD HOUSE
Warwickshire

Lapworth, Solihull
B94 6AT
11m SE of Birmingham by
A34
Tel: 0564 782 024

Owner:
The National Trust

Open: Apr to Sept, Wed to
Sun and Bank Hol (closed
Good Fri) 2–6; Oct, Wed
to Sun 12.30–4. 5 acres.
House open

A SOLEMN GROUP of immensely tall clipped yews, known as the Multitude and the Apostles, surrounds a mount covered in box. A mysterious spiral path leads to the top which is crowned by a clipped parasol shape of yew. Some of these yews date back to the 17th century although the biblical references are a much later interpretation, of the 19th century. Whatever the truth of that, the giant topiary pieces have an unforgettable atmosphere. Towards the house, a stately gabled brick mansion of the late 16th century, there is a completely different mood with a pronounced Arts and Crafts feel. A fine wrought iron gate leads down into in a handsomely walled garden overlooked by a long terrace edged with floriferous borders and with a gazebo at each end. A decorative sunken garden with a pool is hedged in yew and has lively summer bedding schemes. To one side, running along a wall, beds of roses, alternately cream and scarlet, are enclosed by box hedges. By the house a further pair of elegant brick summer houses overlooks the garden.

ROSES DU TEMPS PASSÉ
Staffordshire

Woodland House, Stretton,
nr Stafford ST19 9LG
9m SW of Stafford by
A449; 2m from Jnct 12 of
M6
Tel: 0785 840217

Open: Daily 9–6

THERE IS NO mistaking what this seductively named nursery is up to: it sells old and wild roses of which it stocks an enormous selection. John Scarman, who runs it, knows an immense amount about his subject and has produced one of the best catalogues of roses ever assembled, beautifully illustrated in colour and with a great deal of background information about the plants and their cultivation. He describes it as a selective guide to the most interesting and reliable of the old roses. Many of the plants are available in containers for visitors at any time of year but the nursery also supplies bare-rooted plants by post for winter planting.

RYTON GARDENS
Warwickshire

Ryton-on-Dunsmore,
Coventry CV8 3LG
5m SE of Coventry by A45
Tel: 0203 303517

Owner: The Henry
Doubleday Research
Association

Open: Apr to Sept, daily
10–6; Oct to Mar, daily
(except Christmas holiday)
10–4. 10 acres

THIS IS the home of the National Centre for Organic Gardening; as well as being the leading research centre of its subject, it is a fascinating display garden, showing the techniques of ecologically-friendly gardening. Regarded by some until recently as the world of cranks, this is now seen to be the best way to garden, working with nature rather than zapping it with chemicals. At Ryton, demonstration areas show techniques of vegetable growing, how to make compost, how to control weeds and pests and many other things. This is not only muck and magic – there are also some attractively laid out pleasure gardens.

SHUGBOROUGH
Staffordshire

Milford, nr Stafford
ST17 0XB
6m E of Stafford by A513
Tel: 0889 88 1388

Owner:
The National Trust

Open: Apr to Oct, daily
11–5. 18 acres. House open

SHUGBOROUGH is a dream-like picturesque landscape garden in which marvellous ornaments and garden buildings float into view at every turn. From the house, largely built by Samuel Wyatt for Viscount Anson in the 1790s, a series of shallow terraces descend to the River Sow, decorated with golden yew topiary and rose beds. A wild picturesque ruin designed in 1750 by Thomas Wright crouches on the water's edge. To one side a rose garden with an Edwardian flavour has roses trained on arches and pillars. A path now winds away into the informal heart of the garden where an arched scarlet Chinoiserie bridge leads to the pagoda-like Chinese house (1747). In the woods there is a mysterious Cat's Monument; the riddling Shepherd's Monument; a dapper Doric temple; and, in front of the house, handsome parkland with James 'Athenian' Stuart's Temple of the Winds. Do not miss, on the way out, Brackenside Nurseries which has taken up residence in part of Wyatt's superb old walled kitchen gardens, complete with grandly classical Head Gardener's house which it is hoped to restore.

SULGRAVE MANOR
Northamptonshire

Sulgrave, nr Banbury
OX17 2SD
7m NE of Banbury by
B4525
Tel: 029 576 205

Owner: Colonial Dames of
America

Open: Mar, daily except
Wed 10.30–1, 2–4; Apr to
Sept, daily except Wed
10.30–5.30; Oct to Dec,
daily 10.30–4 (closed 25
and 26 Dec). 2 acres.
House open

GEORGE WASHINGTON'S ancestors lived here and the American connection is proudly emphasised, with the stars and stripes flying above the roof. The house is a 17th-century stone-tiled manor and the garden was designed by Sir Reginald Blomfield in 1927, who laid out a crisply formal entrance of yew hedges. The entrance to the house lies across an orchard with gravel walks and the forecourt has lawns decorated with topiary yew birds and herbaceous borders flanking the porch. A little herb parterre on a terrace above is shaded by an old walnut tree. To one side a rose garden is edged in box and a sundial stands in the middle, fringed with lavender. There is no attempt at historical planting here but the garden makes an attractive setting for the old house.

PHILIP TIVEY & SONS
Leicestershire

28 Wanlip Road, Syston,
nr Leicester LE7 8PA
6m NE of Leicester by
A607
Tel: 0533 692968

Open: Daily 10–3

Illustration: Dahlia 'Doris
Day'

PHILIP TIVEY specialises in dahlias and chrysanthemums, of which he produces a huge range which may be seen in season at his nursery. These are plants usually associated with flower shows and specialist fan clubs but, increasingly, their use in the border is coming back, bringing brilliant late season ornament. Philip Tivey has won R.H.S.

Gold Medals for his dahlias and this is one of the best sources for them in Britain. There is a mail order service and a catalogue is issued; tucked away at the back is a brilliant list of cultural hints which forms a perfect thumbnail guide to the subject.

UPTON HOUSE
Warwickshire

Banbury, Oxfordshire
OX15 6HT
7m NW of Banbury by
A422
Tel: 0295 87 266

Owner:
The National Trust

Open: Apr and Oct, Sat,
Sun and Bank Hol 2–6;
May to Sept, Sat to Wed
and bank Hol 2–6. 19
acres. House open

THE HOUSE, finished in 1695 and built of golden Hornton stone, lies on the edge of a steep combe; on its slopes the garden is spread like a patchwork quilt. Formal steps and a balustrade entwined with wisteria lead downwards towards areas enclosed in wavy old yew hedges. An impeccable kitchen garden, like a celestial vision of the perfect allotment, benefits from the southerly exposure. Sweeping down the hill are a pair of herbaceous borders with accents of hot red and a cool turf path running down between them to the pool at the bottom. A mile from the house is a delightful piece of landscape gardening dating from the 1760s – a lake and Doric temple (possibly by Robert Adam) deftly slipped into the countryside.

WARWICK CASTLE
Warwickshire

Warwick CV34 4QU
In the centre of Warwick
Tel: 0926 495421

Owner: Pearsons plc

Open: Mar to Oct, daily
10–5.30; Nov to Feb, daily
except Christmas Day
10–4.30. 50 acres. Castle
open

THE EARLS of Warwick lived in this spectacular
castle until quite recently, but since 1978 it has
been owned by Pearsons who have done an immense
amount to restore the gardens. In front of the
orangery there is a hexagonal parterre designed in
1869 by Robert Marnock with vivid contrasts of
golden and common yew and blood-red roses.
Peacocks preen themselves and fit well with the
mood of the place. From the parterre the land falls
away and, framed by 18th-century cedars of
Lebanon, there is one of the best garden views in
England – 'Capability' Brown's breathtaking park
sweeping down to a curve in the River Avon 200 feet
below. Robert Marnock also designed a great rose
garden which has very recently been beautifully
restored; old roses with irresistible names like
'Adélaïde d'Orléans' and 'Variegata di Bologna' are
draped in festoons, arched over tunnels and rise in
columns to produce unforgettably swoony scents in
late June and July.

WHICHFORD POTTERY
Warwickshire

Whichford, nr
Shipston-on-Stour
CV36 5PG
22m NW of Oxford E of
A34
Tel: 0608 84 416

Open: Mon to Fri 9–5; Sat
and occasional Suns in
season 10–4

JIM KEELING, trained in the traditional craft of hand-throwing terracotta pots, now leads a team of potters making a very wide range of different styles. From plain flower pots to giant Florentine vases dripping with swags and foliage, all are beautifully made in local clay and are guaranteed frostproof. There is nowhere in Britain quite like this and it is very well worth visiting. Outside the pottery are displayed immense numbers of pots and planters, some beautifully planted up to show their effectiveness in the garden. An excellent catalogue is produced and pots may be delivered by carrier.

WIGHTWICK MANOR
West Midlands

Wightwick Bank,
Wolverhampton WV6 8EE
3m W of Wolverhampton
by A454
Tel: 0902 761108

Owner:
The National Trust

Open: Mar to Dec, Thur
and Sat, Bank Hol and
preceding Sun 2–6 (closed
25, 26 Dec). 10 acres.
House open

WIGHTWICK MANOR is a piece of ripe High Victoriana – a decorative Pre-Raphaelite mansion made for a paint millionaire – with a garden in keeping. It was laid out in 1887, partly by the watercolourist Alfred Parsons and partly by the architect and garden designer T.H. Mawson who was responsible for the south terrace and the dramatic procession of great clipped drums of yew that marches purposefully away from it. On one side a 'writers' bed' is filled with plants from the gardens of Dickens, William Morris, Shelley and Tennyson. A formal garden of zig-zag yew hedges and yew topiary and rose beds leads to a walk of variegated holly.

WOLSELEY GARDEN PARK
Staffordshire

Wolseley Bridge, Stafford
ST17 0YT
8m SE of Stafford by A513
Tel: 0889 574888

Owner: Sir Charles and
Lady Wolseley

Open: Apr to Oct 10–6.30;
Nov to Mar, 10–dusk). 45
acres

WOLSELEY GARDEN is a new phenomenon – a garden designed specifically to open to the public. The site had advantages to start with – a winding stream, fine old beeches and an old walled kitchen garden. An immense amount of new planting had been done and there is much to admire: a very large rose garden in the kitchen garden; a shady woodland area with camellias, rhododendrons and lilies; a formal garden with an avenue of cypresses; a romantic dell. New additions are constantly being made and there is an air of horticultural bustle about the place. At the entrance there is a large branch of Cramphorns Garden Centre.

H. WOOLMAN LTD
West Midlands

Grange Road, Dorridge,
Solihull B93 8QB
3m SE of Solihull E of M42
Tel: 0564 776283

Open: Mon to Fri 7.30–4.15

JACK WOOLMAN specialises in chrysanthemums – hardy and non-hardy – which he sells in vast quantities. He is extremely knowledgeable about them and has written an excellent book on the subject. You can only buy by mail order and a very informative catalogue is produced which also lists a few other plants such as anemones, dahlias, freesias, begonias and cyclamen. But the nursery can be visited and you will see some eye-stopping blooms. With the increased interest in Victorian planting schemes the use of hardy chrysanthemums is becoming fashionable once again.

The East of England

⁂

Bedfordshire, Cambridgeshire, Essex, Hertfordshire,
Lincolnshire, Norfolk, Suffolk

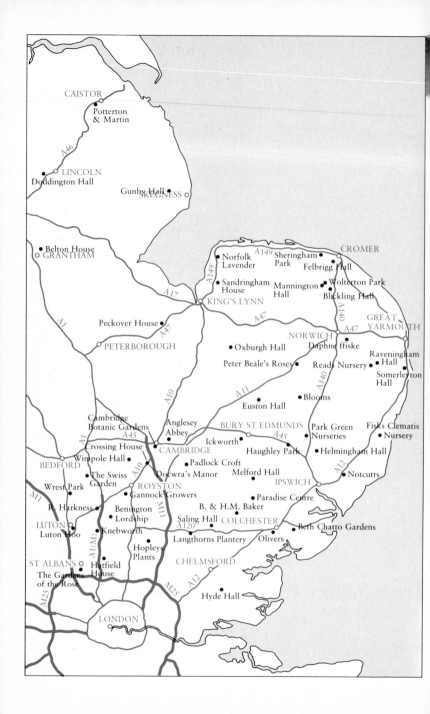

CAISTOR

Potterton
& Martin

LINCOLN
Doddington Hall

Gunby Hall
SKEGNESS

Belton House
GRANTHAM

CROMER
Norfolk   Sheringham
Lavender   Park   Felbrigg Hall
Sandringham   Wolterton Park
House   Mannington
KING'S LYNN   Hall   Blickling Hall

Peckover House   GREAT
                                       YARMOUTH
PETERBOROUGH   Oxburgh Hall   NORWICH
                                   Daphne ffiske
                   Peter Beale's Roses   Reads Nursery   Raveningham
                                                         Hall
                                                         Somerleyton
                                                         Hall
                        Euston Hall   Blooms

Cambridge   Fisks Clematis
Botanic Gardens   Anglesey   BURY ST EDMUNDS   Park Green   Nursery
                  Abbey   Nurseries
Crossing House   Ickworth   Helmingham Hall
Wimpole Hall CAMBRIDGE   Haughley Park
BEDFORD   Padlock Croft   Notcutts
The Swiss   Docwra's Manor   Melford Hall
Wrest Park   Garden   IPSWICH
              ROYSTON
R. Harkness   Gannock Growers
              Benington   Paradise Centre
LUTON   Lordship   B. & H.M. Baker
Luton Hoo   Knebworth   Saling Hall   COLCHESTER
                          Langthorns Plantery   Beth Chatto Gardens
ST ALBANS   Hopleys   Olivers
The Gardens   Plants   CHELMSFORD
of the Rose   Hatfield
              House
                          Hyde Hall

LONDON

ANGLESEY ABBEY
Cambridgeshire

Lode, Cambridge CB5 9EJ
In the village of Lode 6m
NE of Cambridge by B1102
Tel: 0223 811200

Owner:
The National Trust

Open: End Mar to mid-Jul,
Wed to Sun and Bank Hol
11–5.30; mid-Jul to early
Sept, daily 11–5.30; early
Sept to mid-Oct, Wed to
Sun 11–5.30. 100 acres.
House open

ANGLESEY ABBEY was an Augustinian priory and its buildings, with many additions, form an alluring ornament at the heart of gardens that Lord Fairhaven started to lay out in 1930. In this, one of the grandest and most complex of all 20th-century gardens, he successfully deployed a marvellous collection of statues and garden ornaments, giving them their full decorative presence in subtly contrived settings of alleys, vistas, hedged enclosures and distant prospects. Although the site was flat, Lord Fairhaven inherited handsome parkland and some exceptional old trees – particularly limes – which give his scheme a rich background. The statues and bold formal designs are what makes Anglesey famous, and walking among them is indeed an exciting experience. But contrasting with these grand formal schemes are more intimate areas – gardens devoted to dahlias and hyacinths, some exceptionally good borders in the herbaceous garden enclosed in a great horseshoe hedge of beech and a river walk with grassy banks and a mill-house of rural atmosphere.

B. & H.M. BAKER
Essex

Greenstead Green,
Halstead CO9 1RJ
6m NE of Braintree by
A131 and minor roads
Tel: 0787 472900

Open: Mon to Fri 8–4.30,
Sat to Sun 9–12, 2–4.30

THE BAKERS sell only fuchsias and their fuchsia-red list is a connoisseur's delight. There has been an explosion of new fuchsia cultivars in recent years and some of the best old varieties have been trampled to death in the rush to buy new ones. Baker's fascinating catalogue lists varieties going back to the early 19th century and gives the dates of introduction and the names of their breeders. Many of these represent the best varieties of the past – very few are the latest. Most of the list consists, of course, of tender varieties but there is also a section devoted to hardy kinds as well as a very unusual list of species. No mail order service is available.

PETER BEALE'S ROSES
Norfolk

London Road,
Attleborough NR17 1AY
15m SW of Norwich by
A11
Tel: 0953 454707

Open: Mon to Fri 9–5, Sat
9–4.30, Sun 10–4

Illustration: Rosa
'Zéphirine Drouhin'

PETER BEALES is the author of one of the best rose books of recent times, *Classic Roses*, and here at Attleborough may be seen one of the best rose nurseries in Britain. It sells all kinds of roses but the heart of the business is old-fashioned, species and modern shrubs, of which it sells a staggering range. If you are searching for an old rose this is probably the best nursery to start. It is essential for the keen rosarian but for the ordinary gardener a visit in late June will provide an unforgettable sight. A wonderful catalogue is produced, a model of such things, full of information about the history and cultivation of roses. Plants may be supplied by post.

BELTON HOUSE
Lincolnshire

Grantham NG32 2LS
3m NE of Grantham by
A607
Tel: 0476 66116

Owner:
The National Trust

Open: Apr to Oct, Wed to
Sun and Bank Hol 11–5.30.
100 acres. House open

BELTON HOUSE is an exquisite mansion dating from the 1690s. The park was landscaped in the late 18th century by William Emes in the style of 'Capability' Brown, but traces of an earlier formal garden survive – including a slender canal at the head of which is a pretty pedimented temple. Between the house and the church a grand conservatory designed by Sir Jeffry Wyatville in 1811 overlooks a formal garden with a circular pool and fountain surrounded by a low hedge of purple plum and pale pink roses. Columns of Irish yew, mounds of clipped box and stone urns give vertical emphasis. To the north of the house a walk of golden and common yew columns and mounds is backed by borders with a ghostly planting of white roses, cream petunias and lavender edging. This might have been a pompous and overwhelming setting for a very grand house but cheerfulness keeps breaking through.

215

BENINGTON LORDSHIP
Hertfordshire

Benington, nr Stevenage
4m E of Stevenage by
minor roads; signposted
from Watton-at-Stone
Tel: 043 885 668

Owner: Mr and Mrs
C.H.A. Bott

Open: Apr to Sept, Wed
12–5; Apr to Aug, also Sun
2–5; Easter, spring and
summer Bank Hol 12–5.
20 acres

AT BENINGTON the remains of a Norman castle, a gothic gatehouse and a 1700 brick mansion give character that is in every way matched by the garden. The house looks across a gentle valley to lakes below, fed by a stream edged with acanthus, astilbes, ferns, geraniums and primulas. Above it a curious figure of Shylock erupts from a thicket of 'Iceberg' roses in a circular, yew-hedged enclosure. To one side, descending the slope, a pair of dazzling herbaceous borders has a colour scheme of cream, white, yellow and blue with touches of orange and red. Beyond it, the walled kitchen garden has more borders and a small nursery with some of the best plants from the garden for sale. On the other side of the house a formal garden has pink and white roses underplanted with irises, aquilegias and catmint.

BLICKLING HALL
Norfolk

BLICKLING HALL, turreted, gabled and irresistible, was built in around 1620 by Robert Lyminge. The chief part of the garden lies to the east of the house where a parterre of four square herbaceous beds is brilliantly contrived: the planting rises towards the centre, giving, in late July, the shape of a pyramid.

Blickling, Norwich
NR11 6NF
15m N of Norwich
Tel: 0263 733084

Owner:
The National Trust

Open: Apr to Oct, daily
except Mon and Thur
(open Bank Hol and
preceding Sun 12–5; closed
Good Fri) 1–5; Jul and
Aug, also daily 1–5. 46
acres. House open

Colours are subtly graded – the beds near the house
in yellow and cream, those farther away in blue, pink
and red. Rounded cones and curious 'grand-piano'
shapes of clipped yew, fine urns and a central
fountain decorate the parterre. A pair of sphinxes
flank steps that lead up to a long gravel walk, backed
by azaleas and woodland, leading to a classical
temple, from which on either side oak avenues
plunge into the woods.

BLOOMS OF BRESSINGHAM
Norfolk

nr Diss IP22 2AB
3m W of Diss by A1066
Tel: 0379 88 386

Owner: Alan Bloom

Open: Daily 10–5.30.
Garden: Mar to Sept, Thur
and Sun; Aug, also Wed
10–5.30. 6 acres

FEW FAMILIES choose their occupation so happily as
the Blooms of Bressingham. Although best known
for a very wide range of herbaceous plants (more,
probably, than any other nursery in the country) they
also sell choice collections of alpines, bamboos,
hardy ferns, bamboos, conifers, grasses,
rhododendrons and heathers. Many varieties,
especially of herbaceous plants, bear the name
'Bressingham' and give some idea of the liveliness
and enterprise of this influential nursery. Although
the business done here is primarily wholesale there is
still plenty for individual gardeners to see, admire
and buy. A very well planned catalogue is produced
twice a year, packed with detailed information about
the cultivation of their plants. A Reserves List of
specially choice perennials is also published. Orders
may be supplied by mail.

BRESSINGHAM GARDENS
Norfolk

Bressingham, Diss
IP22 2AB
In the village of
Bressingham
Tel: 0379 88 243

Owner: Alan Bloom

Open: Easter to Nov, daily
10.30–5. 5 acres

ALAN BLOOM has, through his nursery and his books, had a great influence on garden taste. In his own garden, alongside the nursery, visitors may see these ideas put into practice. There is, of course, a huge range of herbaceous perennials grown in his famous sweeping island beds. Many conifers and heathers, offering especially striking contrasts of colour at times when the herbaceous plants are not performing, are grouped together. There are very few places where such a range of plants is displayed and there is the added interest that most of them may be ordered from the nursery next door.

CAMBRIDGE BOTANIC GARDENS
Cambridgeshire

Cambridge CB2 1JF
3/4m S of city centre by
Trumpington Road (A10)
Tel: 0223 336265

Owner: The University of
Cambridge

Open: Daily except Sun
8–6 (4 in winter); May to
Sept, also Sun 2.30–6.
35 acres

Illustration: Geranium
sanguineum striatum

ALTHOUGH the primary purpose of botanic gardens is to provide material for study, many of them are both beautiful and instructive places for gardeners to visit. This is no exception and at any time of the year there is much to be seen. Of special interest to gardeners is a particularly good rock garden in which plants are grouped according to country of origin; comprehensive collections of tulips and cranesbills; a huge collection of European species of saxifrage (of which the garden holds the National Collection); and glasshouses protecting different types of plant, from alpines to tropical food plants. There are several beds of herbaceous plants and of shrubs, and everywhere there are fine trees, many rare and all seen to advantage in the attractively laid out grounds.

BETH CHATTO GARDENS
Essex

Elmstead Market,
Colchester CO7 7DB
1/4 mile E of Elmstead
Market by A133
Tel: 0206 222007

Owner: Mrs Beth Chatto

Open: Mar to Oct, Mon to
Sat 9–5; Nov to Feb, Mon
to Fri 9–4

BETH CHATTO'S garden is next door to her nursery and the two together make one of the most attractive of places for gardeners to visit. Her nursery is particularly strong on herbaceous plants and she has a special interest in plants with ornamental foliage. She also fully recognises the importance of a plant's natural habitat, as she has shown in her excellent books on the dry and the damp garden; the nursery displays a comprehensive range of plants suitable for those conditions. In the garden a series of pools runs along a shallow hollow edged with moisture-loving plants. Farther up the slopes are sweeping beds containing a rich abundance of bulbs and herbaceous perennials backed with shrubs and trees. It is inconceivable that any gardener could come here and fail to discover something seductive and unfamiliar. A long and very informative catalogue is produced and plants are sold by mail.

219

CROSSING HOUSE
Cambridgeshire

78 Meldreth Road,
Shepreth, Royston SG8 6PS
In Shepreth village 8m S of
Cambridge off A10
Tel: 0763 261071

Owner: Mr and Mrs
Douglas Fuller

Open: Daily, dawn–dusk.
1/4 acre

Illustration opposite:
Crossing House garden

THE URGE to make a garden can often be so overwhelming that the small matter of a railway line running through one's plot may easily be brushed aside. Mr Fuller was in charge of the railway crossing and Mrs Fuller made a garden, at first immediately about the house but increasingly creeping along both sides of the railway line itself – this part is not open to visitors. It is an astonishingly exuberant place and, although in general appearance a cottage garden, signs of serious plant collecting are soon detected. Here is an immense range of plants, many exceedingly rare and beautifully grown. Alpines are grown on cunningly made raised beds and there are some excellent groups of particular plants – eighteen varieties of witch hazel, for example. Although the area is small, the winding paths and decorative interludes of ornaments and a yew arbour give the impression of something much bigger. The level of interest is unflagging and there are very many far bigger gardens in which there is much less to admire.

DOCWRA'S MANOR
Cambridgeshire

Shepreth SG8 6PS
In Shepreth village 8m S of
Cambridge off A10
Tel: 0763 60235

Owner: Mrs John Raven

Open: Mid-Mar to
mid-Oct, Sun, Mon, Wed
and Fri 10–5. 2 1/2 acres

COLLECTIONS OF PLANTS can be extremely boring to gardeners if they are not given a harmonious setting. Mrs Raven and her late husband collected plants in the wild, especially in the eastern Mediterranean, and gave them a home in this cold but very dry part of England. Many of them flourished and the Ravens designed a layout which would provide both a satisfactory habitat for the plants and make a satisfying garden for non-botanists. In this they were triumphantly successful. There is just enough formality, such as a decorative tunnel of pears and clematis, to prevent a mere jungle but there is no artificial regimentation of plants. Old outhouses and courtyards give protection from the wind on this flat and well-drained site. An excellent nursery sells plants propagated in the garden.

DODDINGTON HALL
Lincolnshire

Doddington,
nr Lincoln LN6 4RU
5m W of Lincoln by B1190;
signposted off A46 Lincoln
bypass
Tel: 0522 694308

Owner: Mr and Mrs A.G.
Jarvis

Open: May to Sept, Sun,
Wed and Bank Hol 2–6.
12 acres

ROBERT SMITHSON, the greatest Elizabethan architect, designed this lovely brick mansion which casts its spell over the gardens that surround it. Rare Elizabethan garden walls enclose the courts at back and front, making a wonderfully ornamental background to the varied planting that they enclose. To the front, with its simple pattern of lawns edged with box, ornament is added by cherry trees shaped into lollipops and mounds of clipped yew. In the courtyard on the west side ebullient box parterres make a brilliant display, in which crown imperials and many irises are followed by roses, and where deep herbaceous borders line the walls. Beyond this a wild garden has excellent old trees, including some superb ancient sweet chestnuts, and many decorative incidents – a new turf maze, an elegant Temple of the Winds and a water garden.

EUSTON HALL
Suffolk

Euston, Thetford IP24 2QP
3m S of Thetford by A1088
Tel: 0842 766366

Owner: The Duke and
Duchess of Grafton

Open: 4 Jun to 24 Sept,
Thur 2.30–5. 70 acres.
House open

EUSTON HALL was built by the Earl of Arlington in the 1670s and in the early 18th century a pioneer landscape garden was laid out by William Kent; later in the century 'Capability' Brown was consulted by the 3rd Duke of Grafton. South of the house a formal terraced garden is ornamented with summer planting in urns, and a balustrade. To one side, the King Charles Gate, a survival from the 17th century, leads out into the park, and in the far distance Kent's exquisite domed temple rises on an eminence. From the formal garden a beautiful wrought iron gate leads through a high wall with a very successful mixed border. Beyond, to the west, the remains of a great lime avenue stretches out towards Kent's arched lodge. The present Duke has added new borders to the east of the house and contrived a charming setting for a wooden William Kent summer house.

FELBRIGG HALL
Norfolk

Roughton, nr Norwich
NR11 8PR
2m SW of Cromer by A148
and B1436
Tel: 026 375 444

Owner:
The National Trust

Open: Apr to Oct, daily
except Tue and Fri
11–5.30. 6 1/2 acres. House
open

A WINDY PLAIN surrounds the mansion at Felbrigg with its curious contrasting Jacobean and mid-Georgian façades. Handsome parkland – dating from the 17th century and with some survivals from that time – is planted with beech, oak and sweet chestnut but the object of chief interest is the magnificent old walled kitchen garden at a distance from the house. Gravel paths and low box hedges divide the area in which productive plants – vines, figs, pears and plums – are trained against the walls. Borders line the walls – peonies and lilies under shrub roses. An orchard is underplanted with spring bulbs and there is a collection of thorns planted in formal rows in grass. An octagonal dovecote with white doves stands in the centre of the north wall, forming an eye-catcher at the end of the central path. Of particular interest is the collection of colchicums of which Felbrigg has the National Collection.

DAPHNE FFISKE HERBS
Norfolk

Rosemary Cottage,
Bramerton, Norwich
NR14 7DW
4m SE of Norwich by A146
Tel: 05088 8187

Open: Thur to Sun 10–4

ROSEMARY COTTAGE is well named and perfectly conjures up the character of the place. Herb gardens have become tremendously fashionable but here the plants are displayed in the attractive setting of an unpretentious garden of a pretty old brick cottage. Daphne ffiske cultivates, in charmingly rural surroundings, a wide range of culinary, aromatic and medicinal herbs with an especially good collection of thymes. She produces a list from which herbs may be ordered by post.

FISKS CLEMATIS NURSERY
Suffolk

Westleton, Saxmundham
IP17 3AJ
5m NE of Saxmundham by
A12 and minor roads
Tel: 072 873 263

Open: Mon to Fri 9–5;
summer only, also Sat and
Sun 10–1, 2–5

Illustration: Clematis
'Sealand Gem'

IT IS HARD to imagine any garden not possessing at least one or two clematises. Here at Jim Fisk's marvellous nursery, which has its own display garden, the visitor can see an immense range of varieties and get some idea of the great garden value of these plants. The large-flowered hybrids as well as the species and other small-flowered sorts are stocked in variety and many of them are rarely seen in gardens or nurseries – such as 'Louise Rowe' with frilly pink double and single flowers. There is always something of interest flowering from spring to late autumn. The nursery publishes a model catalogue, well illustrated in colour, and with much valuable information on cultivation. Fisks supply by mail order, and meticulous planting instructions are sent with each consignment.

GANNOCK GROWERS
Hertfordshire

Gannock Thatch, Sandon,
Buntingford SG9 0RH
3m SW of Royston by
minor roads
Tel: 076 387 386

Open: Mar to Oct, Tue to
Sun and Bank Hol 10–4;
also by appointment

Illustration: Campanula
takesimana

GANNOCK GROWERS specialises in unusual hardy herbaceous plants. The range is wide with many plants suitable for the border and some smaller items verging on alpines. The Pyles have several aquilegias, good campanulas, an unusual range of centaureas, species dianthus, eryngiums, a good range of geraniums, lychnis, several species penstemons and some decorative sedges and grasses. The owners' garden alongside the nursery, containing many fully-grown specimens of the plants they sell, together with a 5-acre meadow, are also open to visitors. A list is published and plants may be supplied by mail order.

THE GARDENS OF THE ROSE
Hertfordshire

Chiswell Green, St Albans
AL2 3NR
2m SW of St Albans by
B4630
Tel: 0727 50461

Owner: Royal National
Rose Society

Open: Mid-Jun to mid-Oct,
Mon to Sat 9–5, Sun and
Bank Hol 10–6.
25 acres

THOUSANDS OF ROSES, including well over 1,500 varieties, are displayed here, and although there is a strong emphasis on modern varieties there are also interesting reference collections of the main historic groups. The site is flat and windswept and some vertical emphasis is given by Irish yews and pergolas on which the climbing roses are trained. Modern roses are generally arranged in large beds, often with a single block of one variety making a vast splash of colour. The Royal National Rose Society, one of the leading specialist plant societies, publishes a journal and provides advice to members.

GUNBY HALL
Lincolnshire

nr Spilsby PE23 5SS
7m W of Skegness by A158

Owner:
The National Trust

Open: Apr to Sept, Wed
and Thur (also Tue and Fri
by written appointment)
2–6. 7 acres. House open

*Illustration opposite: The
walled garden at Gunby*

GUNBY PRESENTS an elegant pastoral scene – the
Georgian brick mansion looking out over serene
parkland. In the old walled kitchen garden there is
more excitement, with a rumpus of roses, burgeoning
herbaceous borders, apples trained over arches and
underplanted with irises, and a dinky domed gazebo
painted a celestial blue. A second walled garden has
beds of fruit and vegetables and old pear trees
growing out of herbaceous borders. There is a rose
walk, a bed of hydrangeas and, hidden behind a yew
hedge, a stately walk of Irish junipers along a canal.
On the far side of the house lawns are ornamented
with specimen trees and there is a wild-flower walk.

R. HARKNESS & CO LTD
Hertfordshire

The Rose Gardens,
Hitchin SG4 0JT
On A505 between Hitchin
and Letchworth
Tel: 0462 420402

Open: Mon to Sat 9–5, Sun
and Bank Hol 10–5

Illustration: Rosa '*Just Joey*'

HARKNESS SELL only roses. The emphasis is on
modern cultivars, of which they are constantly
making new introductions, but they also stock a
worthwhile selection of old varieties. Immense
numbers of all these are available in containers at the
nursery, but more energetic visitors are also allowed
to visit the growing fields nearby. An especially
informative and well produced catalogue is issued; it
includes, for example, detailed information about the
origin of every rose. A mail order service is provided
and orders are sent between November and March.

HATFIELD HOUSE
Hertfordshire

Hatfield AL9 5NQ
In the centre of Hatfield
village, 20m N of London
by A1 and A1(M) Jnct 3
Tel: 0707 262 823

Owner: The Marquess of
Salisbury

Open: Apr to mid-Oct,
daily except Good Fri
11–6; East Garden Mon
2–5. 30 acres. House open

HATFIELD HOUSE, a Jacobean extravaganza of pink brick, was started in 1607 by Robert Cecil and the family have owned it ever since. There has always been a notable garden here and the present Marchioness of Salisbury has brought dazzling new life to it over the last twenty years. Near the house there are formal gardens, most of which have ancient origins. By the Old Palace Lady Salisbury made a new knot garden with old varieties of plants, including many of those introduced by John Tradescant the Elder who worked for the Cecils when the garden was started. The privy garden and the scented garden to the west of the house have been replanted and in summer are very beautiful. The East Gardens are decorated with formal rows of clipped Holm oaks (*Quercus ilex*), Italian statues and brimming beds of shrubs, especially roses, underplanted with herbaceous plants. Beyond are avenues of apple trees, a Victorian yew maze (alas, not open) and the New Pond which is full of atmosphere. There are few great historic gardens that demonstrate so visibly the excitement of gardening.

HAUGHLEY PARK
Suffolk

nr Stowmarket IP14 3JY
4m NW of Stowmarket by
A45
Tel: 0359 40205

Owner: A.J. Williams

Open: May to Sept, Tue
3–6. 8 acres plus woodland

THE GABLED HOUSE was built in 1620, with a pretty gothic wing added in 1820 and the whole restored by the present owner after a fire in 1961. Handsome old woodland, with some exceptional individual specimens, makes a fine setting for the gardens which are almost entirely of the 20th century. North of the house a broad apron of grass opens out, edged with mixed borders and, to one side, an immense hollow oak which is at least 1,000 years old. The vista is continued by an old lime avenue stretching across fields into the distance. A dell has shady walks fringed with hostas and the woodland garden, ablaze with bluebells in spring, has many azaleas and rhododendrons planted among majestic beeches and Scots pines.

HELMINGHAM HALL
Suffolk

nr Stowmarket IP14 6EF
9m NE of Ipswich by
B1077
Tel: 0473 890217

Owner: Lord Tollemache

Open: May to Oct, Sun
2–6. 2 acres

HELMINGHAM is an exquisite place in which house, parkland and garden together create an exceptional work of art. The brick house, with its romantic moat and drawbridge, is of several periods, starting in 1500, and has always been owned by the Tollemaches. It overlooks a deer park with a double avenue of oaks and, to one side, also moated, a walled kitchen garden has been turned to ornamental purposes. At the entrance a box-edged parterre with summer bedding is surrounded on three sides by borders of old roses and hedges of lavender. Winged horses cap the piers of the gates into the walled garden, and this is divided into four parts by two superb double herbaceous borders running down and across. Leading off them are paths through tunnels of sweet peas, runner beans or marrows, and behind the ornamental borders fruit and vegetables grow in impeccable beds. On the banks of the moat a grassy walk with narrow borders encircles the walls.

HOPLEYS PLANTS
Hertfordshire

High Street, Much
Hadham SG10 6BU
5m SW of Bishop's
Stortford by B1004
Tel: 0279 84 2509

Open: Mon to Sat (closed
Tue) 9–5; Sun 2–5; closed
Jan and Aug

YOU WOULD HAVE to be a gardener of steely
resolve to avoid buying something at Hopleys.
The nursery was started in 1967 by David and
Barbara Barker who have now retired to Dorset,
leaving their son Aubrey in charge. They have
introduced into commerce some of the most
successful new garden plants of recent years –
including, for example, *Potentilla* 'Red Ace' and
Lavatera thuringiaca 'Barnsley Pink'. Their list ranges
widely and every year new and exciting plants –
hardy and non-hardy – are offered. Although there
are some groups that are especially well represented
(for example, salvias) the striking quality of Hopleys
is the very careful choice of particular cultivars of a
single species (e.g. 14 different varieties of
Argyranthemum frutescens). The Barkers' 4-acre
garden, alongside the nursery, is also open to visitors
and their style in planting is strikingly displayed. An
impeccable catalogue is produced and a mail order
service is provided.

HYDE HALL
Essex

Rettendon, nr Chelmsford
CM3 8ET
7m SE of Chelmsford by
A130
Tel: 0245 400256

Owner: Hyde Hall Garden
Trust

Open: Sun, Wed and Bank
Hol 11–6. 24 acres

WHEN THE ROBINSONS came here to farm in 1955
there was no garden, merely a handful of trees
on top of a famously windswept hill in one of the
driest parts of the country. The garden they made is
now enormous, full of wonderful plants in diverse

habitats – a brilliant tribute to their gardening skill. The layout is essentially informal with a lively pattern of secluded or more open settings. The overwhelming attraction of the place lies in the range of plants grown. Hyde Hall has two National Collections: of crab apples (*Malus*) and of viburnums. In addition to these there are immense numbers of daylilies, irises, peonies, roses, snowdrops and countless ornamental trees and shrubs. This is not merely a plant collection, for many parts of the garden have carefully worked out colour harmonies – e.g. a gold garden and a series of herbaceous borders with hot or cool schemes. A nursery sells excellent plants but there is no mail order. No gardener could come here without being informed and delighted.

ICKWORTH
Suffolk

Horringer, Bury St
Edmunds IP29 5QE
3m SW of Bury St
Edmunds by A143
Tel: 0284 735270

Owner:
The National Trust

Open: end Mar to Apr,
Sat, Sun and Bank Hol
1.30–5.30; May to Sept,
daily except Mon (open
Bank Hol) and Thur
1.30–5.30; Oct, Sat and Sun
1.30–5.30. 33 acres. House
open

THERE IS no house like Ickworth – a dumpy, domed cylinder with curving wings designed in the late 18th century by Francis Sandys with help from his patron, the Earl of Bristol, Bishop of Derry. The garden is influenced by the shape of the house. At the front a sweeping herbaceous border, echoing the wings, is well planted in blues and purples – acanthus, campanulas, geraniums and sage – with clumps of purple-leafed cotinus. Behind the house there is a more formal arrangement, again related to the shape of the house, with a curved terrace and box-hedged alleys. There is a marvellous walk about the estate of Ickworth, with splendid views back to the house and to the Earl's obelisk in the distance.

KNEBWORTH
Hertfordshire

Knebworth SG3 6PY
28m N of London by
AI(M) Jnct 7
Tel: 0438 812661

Owner: Lord Cobbold

Open: 4, 5 Apr, 11 to 27
Apr, 2 to 4 May, 9, 10
May, 23 May to 30 Jul, 4
Aug to 6 Sept, 12, 13 Sept,
4 Oct 12–5; closed Mon
except Bank Hol, 12–5. 25
acres. House open

THE LYTTONS have lived here since the Middle
Ages and the house, a wild and woolly gothic
fantasy, was partly designed by Bulwer Lytton, the
best-selling Victorian novelist. Edwin Lutyens married
a Lytton daughter and between 1907 and 1911 he
simplified the immensely complicated Victorian
garden. From the facade of the house a pair of cool
pleached lime walks leads towards a formal rose
garden flanked by herbaceous borders. Beyond a
screen of clipped yew, with statues half-embedded in
niches, a circular pool has gold borders on either side
and a path leads to a formal garden of old roses
underplanted with artemisias, catmint and lamb's
ears. To one side of the house an attractive little herb
garden has been recreated from a Gertrude Jekyll
design of interlocking circles.

LANGTHORNS PLANTERY
Essex

Little Canfield, Dunmow
CM6 1TD
2m W of Dunmow by
A120. Jnct 8 of M11
Tel: 0371 2611

Open: Daily 10–5 or dusk
if earlier; closed Christmas
fortnight

IF ALL NEIGHBOURHOODS had general nurseries as
good as this, gardening would be much easier.
Without rising to plants of dazzling rarity Langthorns
have desirable things in every department – alpines,
herbaceous perennials, shrubs, trees and climbers.
Within each of these there are some groups of plants
that are especially well represented – an excellent

selection of bamboos and grasses, berberis, clematises, euphorbias, honeysuckles, hostas, penstemons and potentillas. Although they produce a good catalogue there is no mail order service, so a visit is the only means of buying.

LUTON HOO
Bedfordshire

Luton LU1 3TQ
1 1/2m SE of Luton by
A6129
Tel: 0582 22955

Owner: The Wernher
Family

Open: 14 Apr to 18 Oct,
daily except Mon (open
Bank Hol) 12–5.45. 10
acres. House open

THE MANSION at Luton Hoo was designed by Robert Adam in 1764 and revised by Sir Robert Smirke in 1827. It is a palatial affair and the terraced gardens which lie below it to the south are appropriately glamorous. At the upper level lawns on either side of the path have fine stone urns which in summer are filled with pale pink petunias and helichrysum; behind them are mixed borders of pale colours. In the middle of the lower terrace, hedged in yew, a circular water-lily pool has a central fountain with a bronze boy and dolphin on a rock. Box-edged rose beds surround it, ornamented with box topiary cones and spirals. On either side domed temples mark the corners and splendid old cedars of Lebanon rise up behind. At some distance from the house a romantic rock garden has a series of pools overhung with fine old Japanese maples, planted round about with conifers and rhododendrons, and rocky walks lead up the slopes above. The superb park at Luton Hoo is the work of 'Capability' Brown who dammed the River Lea to make two lakes and planted countless trees, many of which are now at their peak.

MANNINGTON HALL
Norfolk

nr Saxthorpe NR11 7BB
18m NW of Norwich by
B1149 and minor roads
Tel: 026 387 284

Owner: The Hon. Robin
and Mrs Walpole

Open: Apr to Dec, Sun
12–5; Jun to Aug, also
Wed to Fri 11–6. 20 acres

Mannington hall, with its moat, towers and crenellations, has a wildly romantic air. It dates from the late 15th century but was much changed in the 19th century. The moat is splashed with water-lilies and walled with yew on the inner bank. Behind the hedges are beds of modern roses and stone busts on plinths surveying the scene. Lawns and specimen trees – some fine cedars of Lebanon – lie on the far side of the moat and a classical pavilion with a statue of Diana gives architectural contrast to beds of shrub roses. In a large walled garden a little distance from the house the Heritage Rose Garden has a very large collection of roses of all the representative types, trained on pergolas or walls and in beds. Part of the garden is laid out to show the use of roses in different period styles. A nursery sells a good selection of these roses.

MELFORD HALL
Suffolk

If it were not for the gazebo at Melford Hall the garden would only just be worth visiting – but what a gazebo! It is octagonal, built of brick, and it bristles with pediments and finials. Gertrude Jekyll visited it and, recognizing its architectural distinction,

Long Melford, Sudbury
CO10 9AH
In village of Long Melford
4m N of Sudbury by A131
Tel: 0787 880286

Owner:
The National Trust

Open: end Mar to Apr,
Sat, Sun and Bank Hol
2–5.30; May to Sept, Wed
to Sun (except Fri) and
Bank Hol 2–5.30; Oct, Sat
and Sun 2–5.30. 9 acres.
House open

criticised it for being smothered in ivy. Today it is
revealed in its full eccentric glory. Steep steps lead up
to it and from tall sash windows there are views on
one side over the dry moat and on the other of the
garden with its curving herbaceous borders, old
weeping ash and mulberry, and a pretty little herb
parterre planted with low hedges of yew and patches
of purple sage, germander, lavender and rue.

NORFOLK LAVENDER
Norfolk

Caley Mill, Heacham
PE31 7JE
13 1/2m N of King's Lynn
by A149
Tel: 0485 70384

Open: Daily 10–5

LAVENDER USED to be very widely grown on a
commercial scale in southern England but
Norfolk Lavender is the only remaining lavender
farm in England and it holds one of the National
Collections of lavender – with 55 different species
and varieties. There are display beds in which long
strips of different kinds are planted, showing vividly
the variations in foliage and flower, and in late
summer filling the air with their scent. There are also
rose and herb gardens but these are of less interest
than the splendid collection of lavenders. Many of
these, and a few other plants, are sold in a small
nursery and a mail order service is provided.

NOTCUTTS NURSERIES LTD
Suffolk

Ipswich Road,
Woodbridge IP12 4AF
Tel: 0394 33344

Open: Mon to Sat
8.45–5.30, Sun 10–5

Illustration: Cistus *x* cyprius

NOTCUTTS is an institution and carries an immense general stock. In every department gardeners will find excellent things. New introductions are constantly being made and medals relentlessly won at the best shows. A mail order service is provided and the oustanding catalogue is a valuable gardening tool. It is well over 300 pages long, very detailed, and the main section, called 'Plants for a Purpose', gives lists of plants grouped under every imaginable heading. Apart from the Woodbridge branch there are also centres in the east of England at Orton Waterville, nr Peterborough (0733 234600); Smallford, St Albans (0727 53224), Ardleigh, Colchester (0206 230271); and Daniel's Road, Norwich (0603 53155). All these have similar opening times to the main centre.

OLIVERS
Essex

Olivers Lane, Colchester
CO2 0HJ
3m SW of Colchester by
minor roads
Tel: 0206 330575

Owner: Mr and Mrs David
Edwards

Open: May to Jul, Wed
2–5. 10 acres

ALTHOUGH PERILOUSLY CLOSE to creeping Colchester, Olivers could be in the remotest countryside. The present owners came here ten years ago and found a solid and logical layout which they have immensely enriched. The decorative 18th-century brick house has a terrace on its south side where more tender plants relish the protection. A box-edged parterre is laid out on the stone paving and views give onto the main lawn with pools on one side and a deep, curved border on the other. On both sides woodland presses in. Beyond the border a

series of beds is enclosed in walls of yew in which mixed planting is given carefully controlled colour schemes with an emphasis on late season interest. Beyond the lawn woodland is pierced by a vista, interrupted by a gleaming marble figure of Bacchus. This area was devastated by the 1987 storms but many hundreds of new trees have been planted. It is fascinating to see an interesting garden evolving in the hands of skilled gardeners.

OXBURGH HALL
Norfolk

Oxborough, nr King's
Lynn PE33 9PS
In Oxborough 9m E of
Downham Market by
A1122 and A134
Tel: 036 621 258

Owner:
The National Trust

Open: Apr to Oct, daily
except Thur and Fri
12–5.30. 18 acres. House
open

RISING FROM its moat, the 15th-century manor house is wonderfully romantic. It was built by the Bedingfields who gave it to the National Trust in 1952. To the east of the hall a splendid Frenchified parterre was made in the 19th century after the Bedingfields saw a similar one on a visit to France in 1845. Against a background of gravel, swirling beds hedged in box are filled with a permanent planting of rue and santolina which is enlivened by summer bedding of ageratums, marigolds and pelargoniums. Parterres of this sort were intended to be viewed from above, as this one can be from the windows of the hall or from the terrace to one side. A yew hedge separates a handsome mixed border from the parterre. A 19th-century brick-walled kitchen garden has been planted with a formal orchard of medlars, mulberries and different varieties of plum, with clematis and roses trained on the walls.

PADLOCK CROFT
Cambridgeshire

19 Padlock Road, West
Wratting, nr Cambridge
CB1 5LS
14m SE of Cambridge by
A1307, A604 and minor
roads
Tel: 0223 290383

Open: Mar to Oct, Mon to
Sat except Wed 10–6. 1 acre

Illustration: Campanula
punctata '*Pallida*'

Susan and peter Lewis are famous for campanulas
of which their garden houses the National
Collection; their splendid list leads with no less than
fifteen pages of them and nearly 300 different kinds
may be seen growing in the garden. Garden and
nursery blend indistinguishably at Padlock Croft,
forming a maze of alpine troughs, glasshouses and
packed beds. Alpines and smaller border plants are
the speciality of the nursery and there are very good
collections. Well over 50 penstemons, mostly species,
are listed for sale but twice that figure may be seen
growing in the garden. In every part of the list there
are desirable things – a choice range, for example, of
species digitalis. A mail order service is provided but
a visit is especially rewarding to see the many
unlisted plants growing in the garden.

PARADISE CENTRE
Suffolk

The heart of this unusual nursery garden is its
collection of bulbs and herbaceous perennials.
Among the bulbs are exceptionally long lists of
alliums, crocuses, erythroniums, many fritillaries and
species narcissi and tulips. Among the herbaceous
plants are excellent groups of epimediums, a good
range of ferns, hardy geraniums, hostas, a wonderful

Twinstead Road, Lamarsh,
Bures CO8 5EX
In village of Lamarsh 4m S
of Sudbury by minor roads
Tel: 0787 269449

Open: Sat, Sun and Bank
Hol 8.30–5.30

Illustration: Alstroemeria
pulchella

list of primulas and several saxifrages. All the plants
are well chosen and are available by post from an
attractively produced and very informative catalogue.
Cees and Hedy Stapel-Valk exhibit widely at the
R.H.S. shows and elsewhere and plants may be
collected from shows by prior arrangement. But, as
with many small and interesting nurseries of this
kind, there are always excellent plants available at
the nursery which have not been listed.

PARK GREEN NURSERIES
Suffolk

Wetheringsett, Stowmarket
IP14 5QH
6m NE of Stowmarket
W of A140
Tel: 0728 860139

Open: Thur to Sun and
Bank Hol 10–5.30

THE RANGE of hostas sold by Richard and Mary
Ford shows the great garden value of these
plants. They grow well over 70 different species and
varieties and there are few garden sites for which an
appropriate and beautiful specimen cannot be found.
From spring to late summer one or another is
performing to great effect. Many of the hostas they
sell are hard to come by and a few are available only
from them. As well as their chief speciality, the Fords
also have a choice collection of astilbes of which they
have many named varieties of both tall and dwarf
kinds. Plants are sold by mail order and hostas are
despatched from October to March when dormant.
An informative catalogue is produced with excellent
descriptions of the plants. Packets of seeds are also
sold and, as hostas cross-pollinate with abandon, you
may well germinate something new and interesting.

PECKOVER HOUSE
Cambridgeshire

North Brink, Wisbech
PE13 1JR
In the centre of Wisbech
Tel: 0945 583463

Owner:
The National Trust

Open: End Mar to Oct,
Sun to Wed and Bank Hol
2–5.30. 2 acres. House open

WHEN YOU HAVE got over the surprise of finding a garden as big as this behind an elegant town house in the middle of Wisbech, you can get down to admiring its distinctive charms. Lawns slope away from the back of the house with many substantial specimen trees of a Victorian character, and a rustic summerhouse adds to the period flavour. To one side of the main lawn, hidden behind brick walls, a pair of mixed borders leads up to a pool and an elegant little gazebo. The borders are ornamented with slender metal pillars with roses and clematis, and a pair of topiary yew peacocks. In a separate part of the garden a conservatory houses oranges, daturas and other tender plants and there is an unusual 19th-century fern house.

POTTERTON & MARTIN
Lincolnshire

Moortown Road,
Nettleton, Caistor
LN7 6HX
12m SW of Grimsby by
A46
Tel: 0472 851792

Open: Daily 9–5

POTTERTON & MARTIN call themselves 'The Cottage Nursery' which is misleading. In fact they sell a wide range of alpine plants, dwarf bulbs, ferns and orchids, with interesting excursions into such oddities as carnivorous plants some of which are hardy and make good plants for the edges of ponds. There is generally a strong emphasis on species and forms, with an exceptionally good list of anemones, dozens of crocuses, virtually every single species of cyclamen that is hardy out-of-doors (and some that are not), a good collection of the smaller irises, an excellent range of primulas, a long and interesting selection of saxifrages and all sorts of other tempting things of the smaller kind. Catalogues are issued and a mail order service is provided.

RAVENINGHAM HALL
Norfolk

Raveningham, nr Norwich
NR14 6NS
14m SE of Norwich by
A146 and B1136
Tel: 050 846 206

Owner:
Sir Nicholas Bacon Bt

Open: Garden: Apr to
mid-Sept, Sun and Bank
Hol 2–5.30; Nursery,
conservatory, arboretum
and vegetable garden: Mon
to Fri 9–4; Mar to May
and Sept to Oct, also Sat
9–4, Sun 2–5.30

THE NURSERY attached to the garden is a full-scale commercial enterprise with an excellent general stock, very largely propagated from the plants in the garden. Many of these are unusual without being trendy and are of exactly the kind that give so many old-established country house gardens their distinctive character. There is a good range of agapanthus, several ceanothus, cistus, euphorbias, snowdrop cultivars, many penstemons and pulmonarias. A good catalogue is produced and there is a mail order service. The garden itself, lying mostly to the south of the gentlemanly 18th-century brick mansion, has many grey and tender things such as *Buddleja crispa* doing surprisingly well in this part of the world. A rose garden is enclosed in brick walls and hedges of yew, a long deep herbaceous border runs along the outside of the walled kitchen garden, and to the south views open out over parkland.

READS NURSERY

Norfolk

Hales Hall, near Loddon
NR14 6QW
10m SE of Norwich by
A146
Tel: 050 846 395

Open: Tue to Sat 10–1, 2–5
or dusk if earlier

THIS OLD-ESTABLISHED (1890) nursery specialises in fruit, especially citrus fruits of which the Reads have the largest selection commercially available in Britain – not just oranges and lemons but all sorts of exotics like mandarins and kumquats. They also sell a very large selection of desert and wine grapes, several different varieties of figs, mulberries and tender climbing plants. The nursery holds one of the most exotic of all National Collections – that of cultivars of the fig (*Ficus carica*). All this makes the nursery especially worth visiting, the more so because it occupies a particularly attractive group of buildings – the potting shed is housed in the largest medieval brick barn in England. There is also the beginnings of a collection of historic boats. A very informative catalogue is produced and plants are supplied by post.

SALING HALL

Essex

Great Saling, nr Braintree
CM7 5DT
6m NW of Braintree by
A120
Tel: 0371 850141

Owner: Mr and Mrs
Hugh Johnson

Open: May to Jul, Wed
2–5. 18 acres

SOME GOOD GARDENS fall too easily into genteel ossification but at Saling Hall there is a constant buzz of horticultural activity. The present owners came in 1971 and found an old garden already full of interest surrounding the long, low, gabled brick house of the early 17th century. They redefined the best parts (including a very pretty walled garden south of the house and a decaying water garden) and expanded boldly into the woodland with new ventures. Here is an excellent collection of trees, many rare, skilfully deployed with vistas and ornaments to animate an otherwise flat site, and a deft sketch of a Japanese garden with a stream, billowing mounds of clipped box and a snow-lantern. If you don't like what you see here you have probably lost interest in gardening.

SANDRINGHAM HOUSE
Norfolk

Sandringham, King's Lynn
PE35 6EN
9m NE of King's Lynn by
B1440
Tel: 0553 772675

Owner: H.M. The Queen

Open: May to Sept, Mon
to Thur 10.30–5, Sun
11.30–5. Closed when the
Royal Family is in
residence. House open

THERE ARE NOT many gardens belonging to the royal family that are regularly open to the public so this is one of the very few places where its taste in gardening may be seen. First, it is on a huge scale and the chief impression is one of immense and impeccable lawns punctuated with specimen trees, many of which are 19th-century plantings of conifers. On this sandy, acid soil rhododendrons do well and they flourish in the protection of the trees. Nearer the house there is an attractive formality with pleached lime walks, hedges of yew and a series of herbaceous beds enclosed in tall box hedges. On the other side of the house a stream feeds a lake whose fringes are richly planted with conifers, maples and other ornamental trees and shrubs. Plants throughout the garden are impeccably labelled – even a clump of *Alchemilla mollis*.

SHERINGHAM PARK
Norfolk

Upper Sheringham
NR26 8TB
2m SW of Sheringham by
A148
Tel: 0263 823778

Owner:
The National Trust

Open: Daily dawn–dusk.
90 acres

Humphry Repton was the genius behind this place of woods and rambling walks around a shallow combe by the sea. It was commissioned by Abbot Upcher's family, for whom Repton also built a new house between 1812 and 1819 in a more picturesque position embowered by trees – many of them marvellous 18th-century oaks – on one side of the valley. Open fields lie between belts of woodland and this was a deliberate part of Repton's scheme, retaining them in view to vary the scene. In the woods across fields to the south of the house is a collection of rare rhododendrons started by Abbot Upcher's son Henry who helped finance plant-hunting expeditions to the Himalayas. Many of these rhododendrons have grown to great size in the sheltered combe. In 1975 Thomas Upcher built an arcaded temple to Repton's design, on an eminence with lovely views to the house and the sea beyond.

SOMERLEYTON HALL
Suffolk

nr Lowestoft NR32 5QQ
5m NW of Lowestoft by
B1074
Tel: 0502 730224

Owner: Lord and Lady
Somerleyton

Open: Easter Sun to Sept,
Thur, Sun and Bank Hol
2–5.30; Jul to Aug, also
Tue and Wed 2–5.30. 12
acres. House open

*Illustration opposite: Statue
of milkmaid at Somerleyton*

Somerleyton has a big, bold Victorian house and a garden to suit. The garden entrance leads through the former kitchen garden which now has a spanking pair of herbaceous borders marching down the middle. The well maintained glasshouses were designed by Joseph Paxton, and on the outside south walls of the kitchen garden there are rare peach-cases awaiting restoration. Wellingtonias and monkey puzzles on the lawn beyond the kitchen garden were part of the 19th-century layout but among them are much older trees including some superb sweet chestnuts. From the Victorian parterres by the house, planted with roses and columns of clipped yew, there are views of the remains of an ancient avenue of limes disappearing towards the horizon. There is also a hedge maze of yew built in 1846 and a magnificent winter garden of the same date in which the tea-room is now housed.

THE SWISS GARDEN
Bedfordshire

Old Warden,
nr Biggleswade
2 1/2m W of Biggleswade
by minor roads
Tel: 0234 228330

Owner: Bedfordshire
County Council

Open: Apr to Oct, daily
except Tue and Sat 1.30–6.
9 acres

IN THE EARLY 19th century there was a fashion for everything Swiss, and here at Old Warden the Lord Ongley made an enchanting 'Swiss' garden full of rustic thatched houses, precipitous rocky descents and picturesque views. The site, well-wooded and gently undulating, has interconnected ponds with ornamental islands, and paths wind about, revealing views of garden houses, delicate iron-work arched bridges, a kiosk with stained glass, statues and urns, a grotto and a fernery. All around are excellent trees and the garden has been beautifully restored by the county council.

WIMPOLE HALL
Hertfordshire

Arrington, Royston
SG8 0BW
8m SW of Cambridge by
A603
Tel: 0223 207257

Owner:
The National Trust

Open: Apr to Oct, daily
except Mon and Fri 1–5
(open Bank Hol and
preceding Sun 11–5). 20
acres. House open

ON THIS WINDY, open site on the borders of Hertfordshire and Cambridgeshire the 18th-century house rises on a slight eminence commanding wide and distant views. In the very early 18th century there had been a great formal garden here and an immense avenue of elms, planted by Charles Bridgeman in the 1720s, survived until it was killed by the elm disease; it has now been replanted in limes. In the 1750s the formal garden began to be dismantled and later both 'Capability' Brown and Humphry Repton worked here, naturalising the landscape even further. In recent years the National Trust has restored some of the formality (including parterres on the north side) but has respected the different layers of garden style that give Wimpole its interest.

WOLTERTON PARK
Norfolk

nr Erpingham NR11 7LX
2m N of Aylsham by A140
Tel: 026 387 4175

Owner: Lord and Lady
Walpole

Open: 9–5 or dusk if earlier

WOLTERON has a handsome house of orange brick and stone built in the 1730s for Horatio Walpole. It has remained in the family but it was abandoned in the 19th century, lived in once again in the 20th century but badly damaged by fire in 1952. Now the present Lord Walpole has taken it in hand and a programme of restoration is under way. The visitor starts with a wonderful rural amble, skirting fields and woods, passing a romantically ruined church tower and eventually emerging in a vast open space dotted with exceptional oaks. The south front of the house is then revealed, embowered in trees, overlooking in the far distance a great lake. It was in this part of the park that Charles Bridgeman worked when the present house was being built. Hedges and trees are being replanted in the park and the formal gardens that spread out south of the house (which are open only on occasional Sundays at the moment) are to be restored.

WREST PARK
Bedfordshire

Silsoe MK40 1LT
3/4m E of Silsoe by A6
Tel: 0234 262151

Owner: English Heritage

Open: Apr to Sept, Sat,
Sun and Bank Hol, 10–6.
80 acres

THE GARDEN at Wrest Park has only fragments – but they are wonderfully attractive. The de Grey family had lived at Wrest since the 13th century but the present house was built for the 1st Earl de Grey in the 1830s by a French architect and is on a palatial scale. A French-style parterre south of the house dates from the same time and has bedding schemes and fine classical statues. There had been an elaborate formal garden at Wrest in the early 18th century and of this there remains a slender canal and a swagger domed classical pavilion designed by Thomas Archer in 1710 which sticks in the mind and makes others seem insipid. Between the pavilion and the canal is a lead figure of William III. A garden of woodland vistas and a serpentined pool has a pretty Chinese gazebo and traces of 'Capability' Brown who worked here from 1758 to 1760. One of the charms of the place is the mixture of his informal landscaping overlaid on the fine survivals of the earlier formal garden.

THE NORTH OF ENGLAND

Cumbria, County Durham, Humberside, Lancashire,
Northumberland, Yorkshire

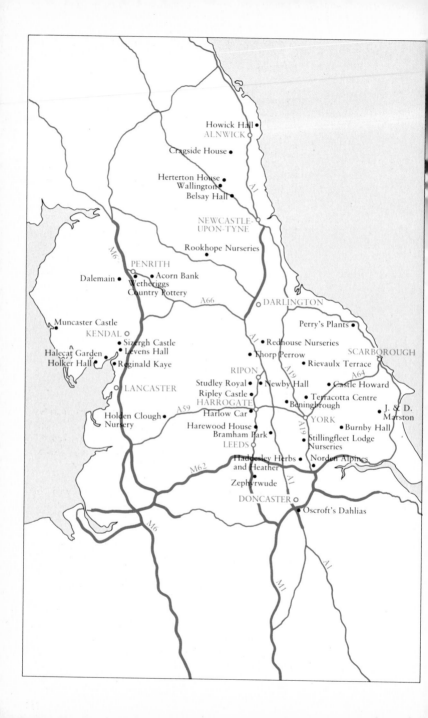

ACORN BANK GARDEN
Cumbria

Temple Sowerby,
nr Penrith CA10 1SP
6m E of Penrith by A66
Tel: 076 83 61893

Owner:
The National Trust

Open: Apr to Oct, daily
10–6. 2 1/2 acres

TO ONE SIDE of the brown stone 18th-century mansion a herb garden is beautifully laid out in the former kitchen garden, finely enclosed in 17th-century brick and sandstone walls. Three long borders run the length of the herb garden and, although this is primarily a reference collection – the largest in the north of England, with well over 200 species – it has been laid out in a very decorative fashion. A booklet describes the medicinal and culinary uses of the plants. Above the herb garden, in a further walled enclosure, a formal orchard is divided by a yew alley flanked by rows of cherry trees – the sour cherry (*Prunus cerasus* 'Rhexii') with lovely double white flowers. Narrow beds under the walls have mixed plantings of shrubs and perennials with clematis, roses and espaliered fruit trees.

BELSAY HALL
Northumberland

Belsay, nr
Newcastle-upon-Tyne
NE20 0DY
14m NW of Newcastle by
A696
Tel: 0661 81636

Owner: Sir Stephen
Middleton. In guardianship
of English Heritage

Open: Daily except Mon
10–6. House open

THE NEO-CLASSICAL brown stone mansion at Belsay was built to the design of its owner, Sir Charles Monck, in the early 19th century. The stone was quarried on the site and the resulting rocky hollows and ravines were made by Sir Charles into an unforgettable wild and romantic garden. The planting is boldly appropriate to the setting, with the striking foliage of Chusan palms, the larger-leafed rhododendrons, *Gunnera mannicata* and the handsome angelica tree (*Aralia elata*) looking wonderful against the cliffs and outcrops. A path winds gently upwards between the walls of stone fringed with ferns and emerges in meadows above the quarry. Here is a surprise – the substantial remains of 14th-century Belsay Castle rising up in the long grass. Near the house formal terraced gardens with yew hedges overlook woodland of conifers with a large collection of rhododendrons, and an unusual 'winter garden' is planted with different kinds of heathers for winter colour.

BENINGBROUGH HALL
North Yorkshire

Shipton-by-Beningbrough,
York YO6 1DD
8m NW of York by A19
and minor roads
Tel: 0904 470666

Owner:
The National Trust

Open: Apr to Jun, Sept to
Oct, daily except Mon and
Fri (open Bank Hol and
Good Fri) 11–5; Jul to
Aug, daily except Mon
11–5. 7 acres. House open

BENINGBROUGH HALL in flat country west of York is a very glamorous house built of fine brick and stone in the early 18th century for John Bourchier. The gardens are surrounded by water meadows and a hint of landscaping, although no known landscaper ever worked here. The chief garden interest now lies in the formal arrangements near the house. A long tunnel of pleached pears underplanted with herbs runs down the middle of the walled kitchen garden, now a picnic area. At the end of the walled garden a mixed double border is planned for all-season flowering. On either side of the house are elegant little formal gardens: to the west brick paths separate knots of box filled with apricot or red roses and pansies; to the east a rectangular lily pool is surrounded by clipped domes of box and lilies in pots, with clematis and roses scaling the walls behind.

BRAMHAM PARK
West Yorkshire

A GARDEN LIKE BRAMHAM is an exciting place, giving unique and special pleasure. There are borders and rose beds but the really wonderful thing here is the great formal garden of immense alleys of clipped beech, distant views of lonely statues, exquisite garden buildings commanding wide views, and refreshing vistas out into the surrounding countryside. It was designed in the very early 18th

Wetherby LS23 6ND
5m S of Wetherby by A1
Tel: 0937 844265

Owner: Mr and Mrs
George Lane Fox

Open: Easter weekend,
spring Bank Hol, May Day
1.15–5.30; mid-Jun to Aug,
Sun, Tue, Wed and Thur
and Bank Hol 1.15–5.30.
House open

century for Robert Benson, the 1st Lord Bingley, who probably masterminded the building of the beautiful house as well as the making of the garden. On the Grand Tour he had seen the latest French gardens and wanted to make something of the sort for himself. The garden he made has a definite French accent – but with an attractively playful English irregularity. Still owned by descendants of its maker, Bramham is maintained to wonderfully high standards and, of its kind, there is nothing in England to touch it.

BURNBY HALL
Humberside

Pocklington YO4 2QF
13m E of York by A1079
Tel: 0759 302068

Owner: Stewart's Burnby
Hall Gardens and Museum
Trust

Open: Easter to mid-Oct,
daily 10–6. 4 acres

WATER LILIES are the thing at Burnby Hall, with over 60 varieties of the hardy kind doing their stuff in two acres of pools edged with walks and shrubberies. They are displayed in bold clumps, clearly labelled – although you may need binoculars to read the more distant labels. There is little point in coming here before July but there is then a dazzling display which continues until very late in the season.

CASTLE HOWARD
North Yorkshire

nr York YO6 7DA
14m NE of York by A64
Tel: 065 384 333

Owner: The Hon. Simon
Howard

Open: End Mar to Oct,
daily 10–5. Castle open

Big is the word for Castle Howard but the garden gives pleasures that are both grand and intimate. Vanbrugh's gigantic early 18th-century palace is set in dramatic country that is very far from being overwhelmed by the house. To the south a vast formal arrangement of clipped yew hedges surrounds a pool with a figure of Atlas supported by Tritons, designed by W.A. Nesfield in 1850. To one side, in a secluded walled garden, yew hedges and screens of hornbeam divide rose beds edged in dwarf box, lavender, purple berberis or grey-leafed hebe. The very large collection of roses – old and new – is beautifully arranged, underplanted with grey and silver artemisias, phlomis, pinks and santolina. On the slopes far beyond the house a completely different atmosphere reigns. Ray Wood is an immense woodland garden with a marvellous collection of trees and shrubs – including very recent new introductions – in a naturalistic setting with colonies of cowslips, narcissus, and willow gentian.

CRAGSIDE HOUSE
Northumberland

Rothbury, Morpeth
NE65 7PX
13m SW of Alnwick by
B6341
Tel: 0669 20333

Owner:
The National Trust

Open: Apr to Oct, daily
except Mon (open Bank
Hol) 10.30–7; Nov to Dec,
Tue, Sat and Sun 10.30–4.
900 acres. House open

*Illustration opposite:
Cragside House from the
ravine*

Cragside was designed by Norman Shaw for the industrialist Lord Armstrong and built in 1870. The very name makes one think of a Grimm fairy tale and the appearance of the house rising high above a rocky bluff overlooking the Debdon Valley has more than a touch of Wagner. This is no place for genteel borders, and below the house a precipitous rockery cascades down the slopes. This has very recently been restored with plantings of heathers, rowans and the wilder kinds of rose. Farther down the slope giant steps lead to a sombre and beautiful pinetum; this spreads along the banks of the river below, which is spanned by an elegant steel bridge. On the way down there are views of marvellous trees, the fern-fringed stream below and the wild house rearing on the cliff above.

DALEMAIN
Cumbria

nr Penrith CA11 0HB
3m SW of Penrith by A66
and A592
Tel: 0768 486450

Owner: Mr and Mrs Bryce
McCosh

Open: Easter Sun to Sept,
daily except Fri and Sat
11.15–5. House open

ON ONE SIDE of the handsome 18th-century house
at Dalemain a broad gravelled terrace, fringed
with tumbling shrub roses, looks out over fields.
Behind the house a knot of box-edged compartments
is filled with artemisias, astilbes, campanulas,
penstemons and violas, and in summer pots of lilies
are arranged about a pool. A gravel walk with a
border of shrub roses leads under old fruit trees to a
door. Beyond this is Lobb's Wood where a wild
woodland walk is edged by the Dacre beck. On the
other side of the beck the wild garden is occasionally
revealed, with azaleas, rhododendrons and
ornamental trees. This is the kind of garden,
unpretentious and filled with good plants, that many
think of as the quintessential English garden.

HADDLESEY HERB AND
HEATHER CENTRE
North Yorkshire

West Haddlesey, nr Selby
YO8 8QA
4m SW of Selby by A19
Tel: 0757 228279

Open: Daily except Wed
and Christmas week
10–dusk

HERB GARDENS spring up all the time and vary
considerably in their interest. Carole Atkinson's
is a particularly good one and apart from herbs she
sells a wide range of heathers (over 150 varieties) and
a good collection of conifers. All her plants are raised
organically and most may be seen in the adjacent

display gardens which contain over 500 varieties of herbs and a National Collection of cotton lavender (*Santolina* species and cultivars). A list is issued and orders are supplied by mail order.

HALECAT GARDEN NURSERIES
Cumbria

Witherslack,
Grange-over-Sands
LA11 6RU
5m NE of
Grange-over-Sands by
B5277 and A590
Tel: 044 852 229

Open: Mon to Fri 9–4.30,
Sun 2–4

Illustration: Hydrangea
macrophylla '*Gênêrale
Vicomtesse de Vibraye*'

HALECAT HOUSE is an early 19th-century mansion looking south over terraced gardens and fields to exquisite, far-reaching views of Arnside Knott. This private garden is open to visitors, which gives an additional reason for coming to the very good nursery. Stone-paved terraces run along the south side of the house and a path skirts an unadorned lawn edged on two sides with generously planted mixed borders. A handsome gothic gazebo clings to the slope and provides an eye-catcher for a pair of borders with many shrub roses against a background of dark purple cotinus. In the nursery, to the far side of the house from the garden, an especially choice collection of over 60 varieties of hydrangea, chiefly *H. macrophylla* cultivars, is the star of the list but there are many good things, herbaceous and woody, in other departments. A well produced catalogue is issued but there is no mail order.

HAREWOOD HOUSE AND BIRD GARDEN
West Yorkshire

Harewood, Leeds
LS17 9LQ
7m S of Harrogate by A61
Tel: 0532 886225

Owner: The Earl of
Harewood

Open: Easter to Oct, daily
10–5. 36 acres. House open

HAREWOOD HOUSE is a palatial house designed by John Carr of York and Robert Adam and built in the 1760s. In the 19th century there were many changes by Sir Charles Barry who, with W.A. Nesfield, laid out the Italianate south terrace which survives today. A parterre with arabesques filled with sempervivums, stone urns and cones of clipped yew is embellished with a recent statue by Astrid Zydower – a nobly proportioned bronze figure of Orpheus with a lion draped over his shoulders and standing on a black marble plinth veiled with falling water. But the view from the terrace over 'Capability' Brown's landscape park is the most beautiful thing at Harewood. A lake is masked by trees and the land rises and falls with belts and clumps of trees alternating with meadows in which cattle graze. No building or ornament is visible and the simplicity of it is a splendid foil to the imposing house.

HARLOW CAR BOTANICAL GARDENS
North Yorkshire

Crag Lane, Beckwithshaw,
Harrogate HG3 1QB
1 1/2m W of Harrogate by
B6162
Tel: 0423 565418

Owner: The Northern
Horticultural Society

Open: Daily 9–7.30 or
sunset if earlier. 60 acres

THIS IS THE NORTHERN equivalent of Wisley Gardens and is crammed with the same sort of garden attractions. The site is a very handsome one, a shallow valley with a stream and well wooded on its south-western slopes. There are sections devoted to particular groups of plants – a rose garden, a bulb garden and an arboretum. Display areas have three different kinds of rockeries – peat, limestone and sandstone – and a winter garden. Much space is devoted to vegetables and a fruit cage. Something different is arranged for each season in the trial gardens with displays of new cultivars. A seasonal leaflet is produced, giving background information about what is going on in the season in question and about the plants displayed.

HERTERTON HOUSE GARDENS AND NURSERY
Northumberland

Hartington, nr Cambo
NE61 6BN
2m N of Cambo by B6342
Tel: 067 074 278

Owner: Frank and Marjorie Lawley

Open: Daily except Tue and Thur 1.30–5.30. 1 acre

FEW GARDENS so small give so much pleasure and interest as Herterton. Stone outhouses and beautifully made walls frame a series of enclosed gardens, each with distinctive character. A flower garden has hedges of box and yew and beds edged in stone which are filled with unstaked herbaceous plants, giving informality to the ordered design of the layout. A physic garden, overlooked by an arcaded loggia, has a great clipped drum of silver pear at the centre, surrounded by beds edged in London pride or thrift. On the road side of the house the formal garden has topiary of yew and of box, and square box-edged beds brim with different varieties of dicentra. The important thing throughout the garden is the strength and simplicity of the design. The nursery sells only herbaceous perennials and although the stock is not large the choice is fastidious.

HOLDEN CLOUGH NURSERY
Lancashire

Holden,
Bolton-by-Bowland,
Clitheroe BB7 4PF
7m NE of Clitheroe by
A671, A59 and minor roads
Tel: 020 07 615

Open: Mon to Thur 1–5,
Sat 9–5; Apr to May, also
Sun 2–5. Bank Hol 9–5;
closed Christmas to New
Year

Illustration: Gentiana saxosa

THIS IS an outstandingly good nursery, specialising in alpines above all but with many other worthwhile plants. The alpine department will excite even veteran fans with its splendid collections of, for example, gentians (over 20 species and cultivars), saxifrages (well over 100), dozens of sedums and so on. Apart from these there are some excellent ornamental grasses and a connoisseur's selection of ferns, heaths, shrubs and climbers. The elegant, very informative catalogue is a model of such things. A mail order service is provided.

HOLKER HALL
Cumbria

Cark-in-Cartmel, nr
Grange-over-Sands
LA11 7PL
4m W of
Grange-over-Sands
Tel: 053 95 58328; 24-hour
recorded information 0839
222011

Owner: The Lord
Cavendish of Furness and
Lady Cavendish

Open: Apr to Oct, daily
except Sat 10.30–6.
25 acres. House open

SOME OF THE most worthwhile gardens manage to juggle very different ingredients with complete success and Holker Hall is a prime example. The house, rebuilt in 1871 after a disastrous fire, is a splendid neo-Elizabethan creation by the firm of Paley and Austin of Lancaster. Inventive formal gardens near the house provide secluded sitting places and much to admire: an alley of glistening Portugal laurels, herbaceous borders with well judged colour harmonies, stately gravel walks, yew hedges and elegant thorns (*Crataegus orientalis*) set in squares of box hedging brimming with rows of ornamental cabbages. A gate pierces the wall and leads to a newly made meadow garden, a brilliant contrast to the formal enclosures by the house. To one side gardens of a

woodland character spread out; eucryphias, hoherias, magnolias, rhododendrons and stewartias ornament a background of venerable beeches and oaks. Among the trees a recently made ornamental staircase, with cascades of water either side, leads to a 17th-century Italian figure of Neptune. Everywhere there are distinguished plants and the garden will give great pleasure in any season.

HOWICK HALL
Northumberland

Alnwick NE66 3LB
6m NE of Alnwick by
B1340 and minor roads
Tel: 0665 577285

Owner: Howick Trustees
Ltd

Open: Apr to Sept, daily
1–6. 24 acres

Howick, very near the wild Northumbrian coast, has a secluded and romantic air. The grand late 18th-century house overlooks a series of balustraded terraces linked with steps. Thickets of *Choisya ternata* and *Carpenteria californica* flank the steps leading down from the uppermost terrace to a pool and to mixed borders rich with roses and lavender with, in late summer, great waves of blue agapanthus. Beyond the last terrace a meadow, brilliant in spring with narcissi and tulips, is planted with maples, birches and shrub roses. Although this is limestone country part of the garden at Howick has acid soil and here, between the wars, an excellent woodland garden was made with azaleas, camellias, outstanding magnolias and rhododendrons under a canopy of old oaks, beeches and sweet chestnuts. Later in the season eucryphias, hydrangeas and viburnums continue interest and in the autumn there is brilliant colour from cercidiphyllums and maples.

REGINALD KAYE LTD
Lancashire

Waithman Nurseries,
Silverdale,
Carnforth LA5 0TY
7m NW of Carnforth by
minor roads
Tel: 0524 701252

Open: Mar to Nov, Mon
to Sat 8–12.30, 2–5, Sun
2.30–5

PRACTICALLY ON THE SANDS overlooking
Morecambe Bay, Reginald Kaye is in a fairly
remote position but is well worth tracking down.
The nursery describes itself as possessing an
'old-fashioned' atmosphere and there is nothing
wrong with that at all. The speciality of the nursery
is rock and alpine plants of which it has specially
strong selections of campanulas, dianthus, primulas,
saxifrages and sedums. There is also a marvellous
range of hardy ferns, including some very rare
cultivars, and of ericaceous plants. A well produced
catalogue has valuable lists of plants for specific
situations. As a mail order service is no longer
provided a visit to this attractive nursery is the only
way to buy its plants; furthermore, what appear in
the catalogue merely as *Helleborus orientalis* 'Mixed
shades' may, on inspection, turn out to be something
absolutely wonderful.

LEVENS HALL
Cumbria

Kendal LA8 0PD
5m S of Kendal by A591
and A6
Tel: 0539 560321

Owner: C.H. Bagot

Open: Easter Sun to Sept,
daily except Fri and Sat
11–5. House open

*Illustration opposite: The
topiary garden at Levens
Hall*

A MYSTERIOUS FRENCHMAN, Guillaume Beaumont,
came to Levens Hall in 1690 and laid out an
exotic formal garden – a forest of topiary and cool
beech alleys – which still survives in splendid old age.
Fanciful shapes of yew, both golden and common,
and of box, many billowing and mishapen with age,
are scattered about. Among them beds are filled with
bedding plants making brilliant blocks of colour
whose boldness goes well with the monumental
topiary. Rising above all this is the grey stone house
with its great square pele tower. Although the
extraordinary topiary garden is the best-known
feature of Levens there is much more to see. On one
side, behind castellated yew hedges, are excellent new
borders, a herb garden and an ornamental *potager*.
Beaumont's extraordinary beech alley opens out into
a giant circle and a path leads to a field with a ha-ha
– the first in England – and an avenue of sycamores.

J. & D. MARSTON
North Yorkshire

Culag, Green Lane,
Nafferton, nr Driffield
YO25 0LF
2m NE of Great Driffield
off A166
Tel: 0377 44487

Open: Easter to mid-Sept,
Sat and Sun 1.30–5

Illustration: Polystichum
setiferum
plumoso-divisilobum

THE MARSTONS run the kind of specialist nursery that is one of the great glories of British horticulture. They specialise in ferns – hardy and tender – of which they sell a remarkable collection. These valuable garden plants, immensely fashionable in the 19th century, are now deservedly coming back into fashion and this is one of the best places to learn about them. J. K. Marston is an expert on the subject, about which he has written a very useful booklet. The nursery produces an excellent catalogue and orders will be fulfilled by post. The Marstons also produce containers and ornaments made of lead.

MUNCASTER CASTLE
Cumbria

Ravenglass CA18 1RQ
1m SE of Ravenglass by
A595
Tel: 0229 717614

Owner: Mrs P.
Gordon-Duff-Pennington

Open: Apr to Oct, daily
11–5. 77 acres. Castle open

MUNCASTER IS a wonderfully romantic place. Rising over ravines near the wild Cumbrian coast is a medieval granite castle, rebuilt by Anthony Salvin in 1862. From the entrance lodge the drive plunges down towards the castle and marvellous old rhododendrons line the way. Many of these were planted by Sir John Ramsden who financed some of Frank Kingdon-Ward's plant-hunting expeditions in the 1920s. Near the castle a grassy terrace walk snakes along the valley, giving unforgettable views of the Esk and the mountains beyond. The slopes above the terrace are richly planted with cherries, magnolias, maples, rhododendrons and other ornamental trees and shrubs. Along the other side of the walk a box hedge has regularly spaced topiary piers of golden and common yew and, on the

precipitous slopes below, are marvellous trees, including probably the biggest sweet chestnut you will ever look down on.

NEWBY HALL
North Yorkshire

Ripon, North Yorkshire
HG4 5AE
4m SE of Ripon by B6265
Tel: 0423 322583

Owner: R.J.E. Compton

Open: Apr to Sept, daily
except Mon (but open
Bank Hol); Oct, also
weekends 11–5.30. 25 acres.
House open

NEWBY HALL has one of the best private gardens in England, with outstanding collections of plants beautifully arranged and cared for. The gardens lie to the south of the house on a magnificent site that slopes gently down to the River Ure. Giant double herbaceous borders, hedged on either side in yew, sweep down to the river edge and paths lead off enticingly to other formal enclosures or into the surrounding woodland. Among the formal parts are a dramatic 19th-century statue walk, striking seasonal gardens designed specifically for spring and autumn, an excellent garden of old roses and Sylvia's Garden in which herbs and grey-leafed plants flourish round paved paths. In the woodland gardens are good collections of maples, birch and dogwoods and many other fine trees. Although full of rarities this is a garden that can be relished even by those who cannot tell a dandelion from a daffodil.

NORDEN ALPINES
Humberside

Hirst Road, Carlton, nr
Goole DN14 9PX
8m W of Goole by A614
and A1041
Tel: 0405 861348

Open: Mar to Sept, Sat,
Sun and Bank Hol 10–5

THIS NURSERY is, in the words of the owners, the result of a hobby that got out of hand. It sells only alpines of which it has a dazzling selection, over 2,500 varieties, with marvellous groups of campanulas, dianthus, gentians, irises, primulas, saxifrages (well over 70 varieties), sedums and violas. All these are propagated on the premises, often in quite small quantities, and new things are constantly appearing. The nursery, for the time being, does not issue a catalogue and cannot supply by mail order. Thus the only way to sample its delights is to pay a visit which will certainly be well rewarded.

OSCROFT'S DAHLIAS
South Yorkshire

Sprotborough Road,
Doncaster DN5 8BE
1m SW of city centre
near A1
Tel: 0302 785026

Open: Daily dawn–dusk

Illustration: Dahlia
'Hamari Bride'

THE NORTH of England is still the great place for nurseries specialising in plants for showing. Fred Oscroft, who has been growing dahlias for over sixty years, is the doyen of dahlia nurserymen and the winner of over 300 gold medals and 100 challenge trophies. What he does not know about dahlias is probably not worth knowing. He sells only dahlias and specialises in the real eye-stoppers – from the pom-poms to the cactus and Giant Decorative – the indication 'G.D.' in his list means flowers of over 10in in diameter if you grow them properly. His list is not long but it is very carefully chosen. Everything he sells is available either as a mini plant or as a ground tuber and there is a mail order service.

PERRY'S PLANTS
North Yorkshire

Sleights, Whitby
YO21 1RR
2 1/2m SW of Whitby by
B1410
Tel: 0947 810329

Open: Easter to Oct,
daily 10–5

Illustration: Geranium
himalayense *'Plenum'*

Patricia Perry specialises in herbaceous perennials
with a few woody plants and has charming
gardens on the River Esk – Victorian tea-gardens
with all sorts of amusements of the time: croquet,
boating and, of course, tea. The nursery has some
very good things: a fine selection of anthemis, good
hebes, excellent lavateras, mallows and a very choice
range of perennial wallflowers (erysimums). There is
an intriguing group of euphorbias including the
splendidly named *E. characias* 'Winter Blusher' which
sounds like a plant that all gardens should have. A
brief list is issued but there is no mail order service;
it is a charming place and a visit is a pleasure.

REDHOUSE NURSERIES
North Yorkshire

Woodside, High
Whinholme, Streetlam,
Northallerton DL7 0AS
N of village of Streetlam,
4m NW of Northallerton
by B6271
Tel: 0325 378721

Open: Sat and Sun, 10–dusk

This is a small nursery selling some specially
attractive plants: an exceptionally good selection
of auriculas; some charming old forms of double
primroses and good species primulas; many alpines
and rock plants (including several named varieties of
helianthemums) and dwarf shrubs suitable for
rockeries. A catalogue is produced and a mail order
service provided but a visit is always worthwhile as
there are many rarities available which exist in
numbers too small to be listed.

RIEVAULX TERRACE
North Yorkshire

Rievaulx, Helmsley
YO6 5LJ
2 1/2m NW of Helmsley by
B1257
Tel: 043 96 340

Owner:
The National Trust

Open: Apr to Oct, daily
10.30–6 or dusk if earlier.
15 acres

IT WAS ONE of the new ideas of 18th-century landscape gardening to make a terrace from which to admire fine views of the countryside and other beauties. At Rievaulx, high above the exquisite remains of the 12th-century abbey, a grassy terrace curves through woodland, giving wonderful views of the abbey, the valley and distant countryside. At each end of the terrace a little temple provides a punctuation mark: the plain round Tuscan temple has a simple interior but the Ionic temple is sumptuously furnished, with a table laid for a feast, and decorated with a noble painted ceiling. All this was made in the late 1750s by Thomas Duncombe, an early exercise in picturesque landscape design that still has the power to bowl you over.

RIPLEY CASTLE
North Yorkshire

Ripley, nr Harrogate
HG3 3AY
3 1/2m N of Harrogate by
A61
Tel: 0423 770152

Owner:
Sir Thomas Ingilby Bt

Open: Good Fri to Oct,
daily 11–5. 13 1/2 acres.
Castle open

RIPLEY CASTLE was built in the mid 16th century and rebuilt in the 18th century. Below the castle, beyond a serpentine lake made in 1842, fine parkland sweeps gently uphill. The walled formal gardens are behind the castle and there is much going on here. Ripley now houses the National Collection of hyacinths and has recently taken over the contents of Hull University's botanic garden which includes an excellent collection of ferns, many tropical and sub-tropical plants and a collection of 'economic' plants – yams, coffee, bananas and so forth. On either side of the conservatory in the walled garden there is a long, deep herbaceous border of a satisfyingly old-fashioned kind. Behind one of them, crinums and fuchsias line a secret walk. In a second walled garden borders of delphiniums, gladioli and peonies lie on either side of a rose pergola with brick barley-sugar columns.

ROOKHOPE NURSERIES
County Durham

Rookhope, Upper
Weardale DL13 2DD
22 1/2m NW of Bishop
Auckland by A68 and A689
Tel: 0388 517272

Open: Apr to Oct, daily
8.30–6; Nov to Mar, daily
10–5

Illustration: Dianthus *'Mrs Sinkins'*

KAREN AND ALAN Blackburn's nursery on the Upper Pennine moors is over 1,000 feet up and, among other things, provides a tough hardiness test-ground for garden plants. The most extensive part of the list is a representative collection of alpines with many good campanulas, erodiums, gentians, the smaller geraniums, helianthemums, saxifrages, thymes and violas. There are also departments devoted to dwarf conifers and heathers. In addition to these there are good ranges of herbaceous perennials (although some of these need winter protection in the Pennines – so don't fancy your chances of growing Rookhope's agapanthus on top of Ben Nevis) and of shrubs. The adjacent garden shows vividly what may be done in this cold, windy place which has regular heavy snowfalls. A useful catalogue is issued but there is no mail order service.

SIZERGH CASTLE
Cumbria

nr Kendal LA8 8AE
3 1/2m S of Kendal by
A591
Tel: 053 95 60070

Owner:
The National Trust

Open: Apr to Oct, Sun to
Thur 12.30–5.30. 14 acres.
House open

THE GREAT THING at Sizergh, in the shadow of the late medieval stone castle, is one of the best rock gardens in England. It was laid out in 1926 by a local firm, T.R. Hayes & Son of Ambleside, and is now a densely planted jungle of conifers and Japanese maples, laced with winding walks and a splashing stream and underplanted with a marvellous collection of hardy ferns – over 100 species and varieties. South of the castle steps lead down to an ornamental lake and to the west an avenue of rowans leads through a Rose Garden with species and shrub roses.

STILLINGFLEET LODGE NURSERIES
North Yorkshire

Stillingfleet, York
YO4 6HW
7m S of York by A19 and
B1222
Tel: 0904 87506

Open: Apr to mid-Oct,
daily except Thur and Sun
10–4

Illustration: Erigeron
karvinskianus

VANESSA COOK specialises in herbaceous perennials although she also sells some of the more decorative woody plants such as artemisias, cistus, hebes, lavenders and an unusual selection of Cape figwort (*Phygelius*). Mrs Cook's selection of herbaceous plants is particularly attractive, with good euphorbias, hardy geraniums, penstemons, primulas, pulmonarias (of which she holds a National Collection) and veronicas. There are also several interesting grasses, or grass-like plants. Vanessa Cook's list is specially rich in those smaller ornamental items which find a decorative home in odd corners of the garden and immensely add to its character. A catalogue is issued, from which plants may be supplied by post.

STUDLEY ROYAL
North Yorkshire

Fountains, Ripon
HG4 3DZ
4m W of Ripon by B6265
Tel: 0765 620333

Owner:
The National Trust

Open: Daily: Jan to Mar,
Nov to Dec 10–5 or dusk if
earlier (closed 24, 25 Dec);
Apr to Jun, Sept 10–7; Jul
to Aug 10–8; Oct 10–6 or
dusk if earlier

JOHN AISLABIE was Chancellor of the Exchequer at the time of the South Sea Bubble when it collapsed in 1720, and he retired to his Yorkshire estate to lick his wounds and make a garden. In the wooded valley of the River Skell he laid out a great water garden ornamented with statues of lead and stone and, in the woods above, built a banqueting house, an octagon tower, a Temple of Piety and a Temple of Fame. John Aislabie's son William later acquired the ruins of the neighbouring Cistercian Fountains Abbey and these were incorporated into the landscape scheme – suddenly revealed round a curve of the river, a gigantic and exquisite garden ornament to make all others seem trivial.

271

THE TERRACOTTA CENTRE
North Yorkshire

Plowman Trading, Broad
Oak Farm,
Sutton-on-Forest, nr York
YO6 1ER
5 1/2m N of York by
B1363
Tel: 0904 768230

Open: Daily dawn–dusk

THE OWNERS claim to stock in their cavernous
warehouse in a farmyard the largest range of
terracotta containers and ornaments, garden statues
and glazed pottery in the north of England – and it
would be a brave man who doubted them. The pots
– imported from several different countries – are
particularly good, with finely made, simple,
traditional terracotta pots as well as more exotic
glazed ware from the Far East. The ornaments –
which range freely from gnomes to goddesses – are
not quite so exciting.

THORPE PERROW
North Yorkshire

Bedale DL8 2PR
2m S of Bedale off B6268
Tel: 0677 453323

Owner: Sir John Ropner Bt

Open: Daily dawn–dusk.
80 acres

THERE IS SOMETHING particularly attractive about
private plant collections such as that at Thorpe
Perrow. This, chiefly the work of the father of the
present owner, Colonel Sir Leonard Ropner who died
in 1977, is one of the very best arboreta in the
country. Colonel Ropner started it in 1931, inheriting
some fine old trees, especially conifers planted in the
1840s, which provide both protection and a fine
sombre background to the more colourful ornamental
trees. To give a true idea of the range and depth of
the collection here would require a complete list.
There are great rarities and excellent specimens of
individual trees. From the gardener's point of view
there are in particular excellent collections of
flowering shrubs and these are not merely wild
species but garden cultivars as well – well over 50

cultivars of the common lilac, for example – and very large collections of the smaller ornamental trees such as cherries and crab-apples. The arboretum is handsomely laid out and there are many decorative touches – topiary and fine urns by a lake, a silver glade, statues rescued from the House of Commons and much else.

WALLINGTON
Northumberland

Cambo, Morpeth
NE61 4AR
12m W of Morpeth
Tel: 067 07 4283

Owner:
The National Trust

Open: Good Fri to Sept,
daily 10.30–7; Oct to Mar,
daily 10.30–4.30. 100 acres.
House open

THE HOUSE at Wallington looks out over a ha-ha and parkland with calm lawns and good trees on either side. This is as it should be but the real garden lies at some distance from the house on the other side of the road, hidden in woodland that sparkles with lakes – the remains of an early 18th-century garden. Overlooking one of the ponds there remains the handsome Portico House, a classical gardener's cottage, and one of the lakes is named the China Pond and was in the 18th century ornamented with 'a very expensive Chinese building'. In the heart of these woods an immense and eccentrically shaped walled garden bursts into view – long and narrow, irregularly shaped and built on a slope. Along one side a high terrace is planted with a long white and silver border and its retaining wall is crested with lead statues. From the gravelled terrace walk there are views over grassy paths sweeping between mixed borders in the lavishly planted gardens below.

WETHERIGGS COUNTRY POTTERY
Cumbria

Clifton Dykes, Penrith
CA10 2DH
1m SE of Penrith by minor
roads
Tel: 0768 62946

Open: Daily 9–5

WETHERIGGS is a rare thing these days – an old pottery still producing handmade earthenware in the traditional way. Everything it makes is guaranteed frost proof and the excellent catalogue is rich in terms like 'Long Toms' and 'Square Pans'. Bay tree pots, rhubarb blanchers, parsley and strawberry pots are made in quantity and pans made to Alpine Garden Society specification are sold. In addition to these garden practicalities they make a wide range of very decorative ornaments.

ZEPHYRWUDE
West Yorkshire

48 Blacker Lane,
Crigglestone, Wakefield
WF4 3EW
2 1/2m SW of Wakefield
by A636. Jnct 39 on M1
Tel: 0924 252101

Open: Display garden: May
to Jun, daily 9–dusk; also
other times, but telephone

Illustration: Iris *'Blue Icing'*

RICHARD BROOK sells only bearded irises, of which he has one of the best collections in the country. He offers for sale well over 400 varieties, very many of which may be bought in this country only from him. He produces a plain catalogue that is full of detail; it has exceptionally good notes on the planting and cultivation of irises, with a particularly good section on disease control. In addition to those for sale there are many more irises on trial and these may be seen when the display garden is open. A mail order service is provided.

SCOTLAND

————— ❧ —————

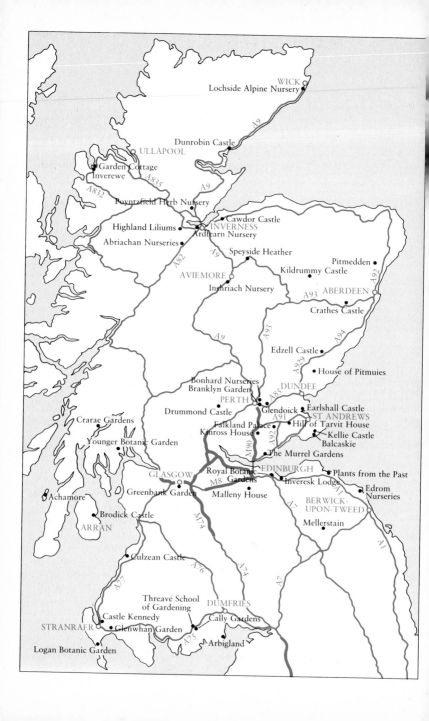

WICK
Lochside Alpine Nursery

Dunrobin Castle

ULLAPOOL

Garden Cottage
Inverewe

Poyntzfield Herb Nursery

Cawdor Castle
Highland Liliums
INVERNESS
Ardfearn Nursery
Abriachan Nurseries

Speyside Heather

Pitmedden

Kildrummy Castle

AVIEMORE

Inshriach Nursery

ABERDEEN

Crathes Castle

Edzell Castle

House of Pitmuies

Bonhard Nurseries
Branklyn Garden
DUNDEE
PERTH
Drummond Castle
Glendoick
Earlshall Castle
Falkland Palace
ST ANDREWS
Kinross House
Hill of Tarvit House
Kellie Castle
Balcaskie
The Murrel Gardens

Crarae Gardens

Younger Botanic Garden

GLASGOW
Greenbank Garden
Royal Botanic
Gardens
EDINBURGH
Plants from the Past
Inveresk Lodge
Edrom
Nurseries
Malleny House
BERWICK-
UPON-TWEED

Achamore

Brodick Castle

ARRAN

Mellerstain

Culzean Castle

Threave School
of Gardening
DUMFRIES
Castle Kennedy
Cally Gardens
STRANRAER
Glenwhan Garden
Arbigland

Logan Botanic Garden

ABRIACHAN NURSERIES
Highland

Loch Ness Side,
Inverness-shire IV3 6LA
9m SW of Inverness
on A82
Tel: 046 386 232

Open: Daily 9–7

O N THE VERY BANKS of Loch Ness Abriachan Nurseries has an enviable south-facing sloping site. Here are grown a good range of plants of which herbaceous perennials and alpines are the strongest suits. Among the herbaceous plants there are excellent aquilegias, with an emphasis on the species, a very good range of hardy geraniums and an immense collection of primulas. In the alpine department are gentians, helianthemums, lewisias, the smaller phlox and a large number of saxifrages. Well planted beds surround the nursery area and paths entice the visitor uphill to a further garden area. An attractive catalogue is produced and plants are supplied by mail order.

ACHAMORE
Strathclyde

Isle of Gigha, Argyllshire
PA41 7AD
Off Mull of Kintyre, ferry
from Tayinloan
Tel: 058 35 267

Owner: Mr Malcolm Potier

Open: Daily dawn–dusk.
50 acres

G IGHA IS a small island in the Inner Hebrides. Here Sir James Horlick came in 1944 and started to make a woodland garden, his new plantings protected by evergreens and old broad-leafed trees. Rhododendrons now reign supreme, constituting one of the best collections in Scotland, with the aristocratic, large-leafed species such as *R. falconeri* and *R. macabeanum* growing to exceptional size and beauty in this mild climate of high rainfall. Sir James was also adept at hybridising and there are several handsome cultivars that bear the name 'Gigha'. Apart from the rhododendrons there is much else to admire, not least the rich underplanting of herbaceous and bulbous plants and the very wide range of ornamental trees and shrubs with excellent camellias, magnolias, mahonias, many shrub roses, viburnums and rare, tender trees such as the New Zealand Christmas tree *Metrosideros umbellata* and other very unusual things from the Southern hemisphere. The wide range of plants growing in such a mild climate means that something interesting is happening in the garden on any day of the year.

ARBIGLAND
Dumfries & Galloway

Kirkbean, Dumfriess-shire
DG2 8BQ
14m SW of Dumfries by
A710
Tel: 038 788 283

Owner: Captain and Mrs
J.B. Blackett

Open: May to Sept, daily
except Mon (open Bank
Hol) 2–6. 20 acres

SOME GARDENS give the thrill of exploration and discovery, gradually unlocking their charms to the visitor. Arbigland, with its elegant mid-Georgian house handsomely framed in fine trees, does not at first reveal signs of any particular garden interest. But behind the house the Broad Walk plunges down through woodland towards the hidden sea. From this central axis enticing paths lead to Japan – a bosky water garden; to a hidden rose garden built on the site of old Arbigland hall; and to glades planted with ornamental trees and shrubs that flourish in this climate of high rainfall and mild winters. There are wonderful rhododendrons such as the tender, giant *R. sino-grande*; beautiful old maples; eucryphias grown to great size; and very fine conifers giving shelter from the coastal winds. The cry of seagulls and the sound of unseen waves provide a curious further dimension to the delights of this rare garden.

ARDFEARN NURSERY
Highland

Bunchrew, Inverness-shire
IV3 6RH
4m W of Inverness by A862
Tel: 0463 243250

Open: Mar to Nov, Mon
to Sat 9–5, Sun 1–5

JAMES SUTHERLAND has quickly established this relatively new nursery as one of the best sources of alpine plants. A courtyard surrounded by old cow byres makes an attractive setting for the plants, many of which are displayed in beautifully planted raised beds and troughs. Over 1,000 species and varieties are available and there is a constant stream of new introductions – some introduced from the wild by plant-hunting expeditions to which the nursery subscribes – and even expert alpinists will find unfamiliar things. The ordinary gardener will be bowled over by the range and quality of plants offered. A catalogue is produced in September and orders are fulfilled by post between October and March. There is still plenty for the visitor to buy but great rarities are snapped up quickly.

BALCASKIE
Fife

nr Pittenweem KY10 2RD
2m W of Anstruther by
A917
Tel: 0333 311202/330585

Owner: Sir Ralph
Anstruther of that Ilk Bt

Open: Jun to Aug, Wed to
Sun 2–6. 3 acres

THE CLASSICAL MANSION was built in the 1660s by the architect and garden designer Sir William Bruce who laid out the garden in a series of great terraces descending towards the Firth of Forth. Beyond the final terrace an avenue continues an axis centred on the house with, 13 miles away to the south, the hump of the Bass Rock forming an eye-catcher. William Sawrey Gilpin advised on the garden in the early 19th century and W.A. Nesfield made new parterres in 1848. Today it is a marvellous period piece with its spectacular views, old plantings of cedars and many tender plants such as hoherias, myrtles and sophoras flourishing in the protection of the old terrace walls.

BONHARD NURSERIES
Tayside

Scone, by Perth, Perthshire
PH2 7PQ
At Bonhard 2m N of Perth
by A94
Tel: 0738 52791

Open: Daily 10–6

IN A SPLENDID Victorian kitchen garden with fine brick walls and an elegant glasshouse of the period, Charles Hickman grows an attractive range of plants. The main collections are conifers, roses old and new (including a selection of David Austin's roses), ornamental trees, soft fruit and a good range of herbaceous plants in which astilbes, geraniums, hostas and phlox are prominent. This is not a huge collection but it is well chosen and displayed in an atmospheric setting which includes a very ornamental area of woodland. A catalogue is issued but there is no mail order.

BRANKLYN GARDEN
Tayside

Dundee Road, Perth,
Perthshire PH2 7BB
On the eastern edge of
Perth by A85
Tel: 0738 25535

Owner: National Trust for
Scotland

Open: Mar to Oct, daily
9.30–sunset. 1.7 acres

JOHN AND DOROTHY Renton started to make this garden in 1922. On a south-facing slope with acid soil they built up a wonderful collection of appropriate plants – smaller rhododendrons, maples, daphnes, magnolias and many alpine plants such as meconopsis, primulas and saxifrages. Their aim was to p.ovide 'a home from home for plants' but they also made a memorably original garden in which narrow paths of turf wind along the contours of the land, bringing the visitor nose-to-nose with countless plants of distinction beautifully grown. The combination of woody plants underplanted with spring bulbs and later herbaceous plants is executed with brilliant aplomb. There are excellent plants for sale, especially alpines, at modest prices.

BRODICK CASTLE
Strathclyde

Isle of Arran, Ayrshire
KA27 8HY
2m from Brodick Ferry
Tel: 0770 2202

Owner: National Trust for
Scotland

Open: Daily 10–sunset.
80 acres. Castle open

BRODICK CASTLE occupies a splendid position well protected from westerly winds and looking east across the Firth of Clyde. The castle with its castellated towers is partly medieval but rebuilt in the early 17th century and in 1844. The present garden dates from 1923 when the Duchess of Montrose started an ambitious woodland garden with a collection of rhododendrons, many of them recent introductions from the great plant-hunters, in particular George Forrest; among them the huge-leafed *R. macabeanum* and *R. sino-grande*. In spring the woodland, with meconopsis and primulas flourishing about the ornamental shrubs, is a brilliant sight. A walled garden, dated 1710, has been restored with Victorian style carpet-bedding and good mixed borders on three sides which prolong the flowering interest to the very end of the summer.

CALLY GARDENS
Dumfries & Galloway

Gatehouse-of-Fleet,
Castle Douglas,
Dumfriess-shire DG7
2DJ
E of Gatehouse on
Dumfries Road
Tel: None

Open: Apr to Sept, Sat
and Sun 10–5.30

AN OLD WALLED GARDEN of almost three acres, enclosed in splendid 15ft walls, is the setting for this treasure trove of plants. It is well protected by Forestry Commission woods and preserves some handsome old buildings – vineries and the gardener's bothy. Michael Wickenden has around 3,000 different species and varieties of which about 500 are in stock at any one time. The sources for these plants are exchanges from other collectors, seeds from botanic gardens and his own finds on plant-collecting trips. His catalogue, which provides a wealth of information about the plants, is therefore a moveable feast but you may be sure of finding something unfamiliar and extremely desirable. He also sells some beautiful terracotta pots from Crete. A mail order service is provided but a visit is particularly worthwhile to inspect the premises and the stock, much of which is handsomely displayed in deep, well-filled borders against the walls.

CASTLE KENNEDY
Dumfries & Galloway

Rephad, Stranraer,
Wigtownshire DG9 8BX
5m E of Stranraer by A75
Tel: 0776 2024

Owner: The Earl and
Countess of Stair

Open: Easter to Sept,
daily 10–5

MANY GARDENS seem interesting enough at the time but later fade in the memory to a blur of borders. Castle Kennedy is a vast place, a piece of heroic landscaping with intimate moments, that would be hard to forget. There are two castles here – the ruins of the 15th-century Castle Kennedy, and Lochinch Castle built in 1864. The bulk of the garden lies between the castles which make splendid eye-catchers to vistas through woods and up hills. All this is on a long spit of land between two lochs – the black and white lochs. North of the old castle are the rare remains of the 2nd Earl of Stair's early 18th-century formal gardens – extraordinary terraces and turf mounds sculpted in the ground. Open areas alternate with woodland embellished with an immense collection of distinguished trees and shrubs: many very large conifers, exceptional rhododendrons and flowering shrubs like eucryphias which grow to vast size. By the old castle a walled garden has excellent borders and, to its south, an avenue of eucryphias and embothriums plummets down to the shores of the white loch.

CAWDOR CASTLE
Highland

Cawdor, Nairnshire
IV12 5RD
11m NE of Inverness by
A96 and B9090
Tel: 066 77 615

Owner: The Earl of
Cawdor

Open: May to Sept,
daily 10–5.30

CAWDOR, with its outlook towers, crow-steps, drawbridge, dungeons and courtyards, is exactly what a Highland castle should be. To one side of the castle ancient stone walls enclose a flower garden in which a broad grass path runs down the middle between a pair of excellent herbaceous borders with old apple trees rising behind. A rose garden, its oval beds edged in lavender, is given height by soaring columns of common and golden yew. There are some beautiful pieces of formal planting: a long rose tunnel, a peony walk and, in late summer, a virtuoso pair of beds brimming with *Galtonia candicans* and pale orange lilies. On one side of the walled garden a gate leads to a wild woodland garden on the slopes

below, and, on the other side of the castle, a large
holly maze and herbaceous borders are laid out in the
old walled kitchen garden.

CRARAE GARDENS
Strathclyde

Crarae, by Inveraray,
Argyllshire PA32 8YA
10m S of Inveraray by A83
Tel: 0546 86614

Owner: The Crarae Garden
Charitable Trust

Open: Summer, daily 9–6;
winter, daily dawn–dusk.
50 acres

CRARAE GARDENS have a marvellous site in a
precipitous glen near Loch Fyne of which there
are handsome views from the very top of the
gardens. The garden was given to the trust that now
owns it by Sir Ilay Campbell Bt whose grandparents
had come to live here in 1904. It was his father, Sir
George, a cousin of the great plant-hunter Reginald
Farrer, who had the greatest influence on the garden.
The site was already well clothed with ancient Scots
pines and larch which gave shelter to the subsequent
immensely diverse plantings of rarer trees and shrubs.
The rainfall is very high but the effect of the Gulf
Stream drift is only modest; however, many tender
trees, especially those from the southern hemisphere
like the many eucalyptus, have done extremely well.
The great Asiatic flowering shrubs – azaleas,
camellias, magnolias and rhododendrons – are well
represented but there are choice collections of many
other groups: several species of the southern beech,
Nothofagus, excellent rowans, some lovely examples
of styrax and much else. Crarae is worth visiting in
any season, and there is always the piquant contrast
of exotic introductions in a natural Scottish setting of
special beauty.

283

CRATHES CASTLE

Grampian

nr Banchory,
Kincardineshire AB31 3QJ
3m E of Banchory and 15m
SW of Aberdeen by the
A93
Tel: 033 044 651

Owner: National Trust for
Scotland

Open: Daily 9.30–sunset.
92 acres. Castle open

ALTHOUGH THE BONES of this garden are old – the superb yew hedges were planted in about 1700 and the romantic tower house dates from the 16th century – the garden is almost entirely of the 20th century. Sir James Burnett of Leys inherited the estate in 1926 and he and his wife started a new garden much influenced by the Hidcote tradition of lavish plantings of often unusual plants within a firmly disciplined plan of enclosed areas. The Burnetts made a series of magnificent borders, some with single colour schemes, and one of the finest herbaceous borders in Britain. Gardeners from farther south will note that herbaceous plants, because of the much longer daylight hours at this northern latitude, grow exceptionally well. All this is maintained impeccably and visitors will both learn much about practical gardening as well as enjoying an exceptionally beautiful garden.

CULZEAN CASTLE, GARDEN AND COUNTRY PARK

Strathclyde

Maybole, Ayrshire
KA19 8LE
4m SW of Maybole and
12m S of Ayr by A719
Tel: 065 56 274

Owner: National Trust for
Scotland

Open: Daily 9–sunset.
120 acres

ROBERT ADAM'S towered and turreted gothic castle occupies a suitably dramatic site on the very brink of cliffs, looking west across the Firth of Clyde to the Isle of Arran. Formal gardens near the castle have terraces and a scalloped pool and fountain, and, in the former walled kitchen garden, fine old glasshouses and a peach-house. Fruit is still grown here and there are excellent borders of old roses and herbaceous perennials. The benign coastal climate allows many tender plants to flourish – cabbage palms (*Cordyline australis),* mimosa, myrtles, olearias and pittosporums. But the real excitement at Culzean is the woodland with its marvellous 19th-century conifers and, in spring, immense numbers of bluebells, narcissi and snowdrops. There is a selection of plants for sale in the walled garden.

DRUMMOND CASTLE

Tayside

Muthill, nr Crieff,
Perthshire PH7 4HZ
2m S of Crieff by A822
Tel: 076481 321

Owner: Grimsthorpe and
Drummond Castle Trust

Open: May to Aug, daily
2–6; Sept, Wed and Sun
2–6. 25 acres

THE CASTLE is composed of buildings of different periods – chiefly a late medieval keep and a fine 17th-century house. Backed by old woodland the castle sits at the top of of a slope below which spreads one of the most extraordinary formal gardens in Britain. Inspired by 17th-century garden taste it was laid out in the 1830s when garden makers looked to the past for inspiration. A huge rectangle is divided by paths forming a St Andrews cross, with a magnificent multi-facetted sundial at the centre, and within the areas formed by this division an intricate symmetrical pattern of ornament and planting is laid out. Box-edged parterres are filled with roses, bedding schemes or gravel, and height is given by stone urns, clipped cones of yew, Portugal laurels and purple Japanese maples. These varied ingredients are given order by the firm underlying pattern of the design and the place has an exuberant and festive air.

DUNROBIN CASTLE GARDENS
Highland

Golspie, Sutherland KW10
6RR
1m N of Golspie by A9
Tel: 0408 633177/633268

Owner: The Sutherland
Trust

Open: May to Oct, Mon to
Sat 10.30–5.30, Sun 1–5.30.
Castle open

DUNROBIN is the ancient estate of the earls and dukes of Sutherland and at its centre is a wonderful early 19th-century fantasy castle with a touch of the Loire and a dash of Bavaria, rising cheerfully on the slopes above the Dornoch Firth. Sir Charles Barry rebuilt the house in its present form and almost certainly laid out the formal gardens arranged on terraces that descend to the sea. The first terrace wall gives shelter to a long border with bold mixed plantings. Below this, a circular parterre in Barry's full-blown formal style, has box-edged compartments planted with red roses and clipped domes of yew rising above them.

EARLSHALL CASTLE
Fife

Leuchars KY16 0DP
1m E of the village of
Leuchars by minor road
Tel: 0334 839205

Owner: The Baron and
Baroness of Earlshall

Open: Easter weekend 2–6;
Apr, Sun 2–6; May to Sept,
daily 2–6. 4 acres. Castle
open

Illustration opposite: The
topiary garden at Earlshall

ROBERT LORIMER, who restored the castle and designed its garden at the turn of the century, wanted a 'garden that is in tune with the house'. Lorimer was an architect with a spritely interest in traditional styles of building and the gardens associated with them. Here at Earlshall he laid out between 1899 and 1901 a series of magical enclosures of stone walls and hedges of yew or holly at the foot of the romantic 15th-century towered and crow-stepped castle. These enclosures contain many different ingredients: a parade of giant yew topiary shapes; a sunken garden with lavish borders surrounding a bowling green; a formal orchard; a kitchen garden in which old espaliered fruit trees and vegetables mingle with flowering borders; and a secret garden of alpines and herbs scattered among paving stones. Everywhere there is the beautiful craftsmanship that one associates with the Arts and Crafts movement – fine ironwork, masonry and witty decoration: a row of cheeky monkeys carved in stone frolic along the gable of an outhouse. Lorimer was a brilliant designer of gardens and houses, and this is one of his most irresistible works.

EDROM NURSERIES
Borders

Coldingham, Eyemouth,
Berwickshire TD14 5TZ
12m NW of
Berwick-upon-Tweed by
A1 and A1107
Tel: 0890 771386

Open: Mar to Sept, Mon
to Sat 10–5, Sun 2–5

Illustration: Lewisia
'Sunset' strain

THIS IS NOT a large nursery but it has a very carefully chosen list of excellent plants, some of which are rarely found for sale. The great speciality is alpines but there are a few rhododendrons and various oddities that have caught the nursery's fancy (like *Zaluzianskya ovata* from Lesotho). In the alpine department there are androsaces, marvellous gentians, lewisias, several meconopsis and one of the most fastidiously selected collections of primulas you will find anywhere. The owners' woodland garden adjacent to the nursery is also open to visitors. The plants are described in valuable detail in the excellent catalogue from which mail orders are fulfilled. Occasional seasonal supplements, for example of spring bulbs, are also produced.

EDZELL CASTLE
Tayside

Edzell, nr Brechin, Angus
DD9 7TG
7m N of Brechin by A94
and B966
Tel: 0356 648631

Owner: Historic Scotland

Open: Apr to Sept, Mon to
Sat 9.30–6, Sun 2–6; Oct to
Mar, Mon to Sat 9.30–4,
Sun 2–4. 1 acre

IN THE EARLY 17th century the now ruined castle of the Lindsays had a fine ornamental garden, or 'pleasaunce', enclosed in walls carved with the Lindsay arms and all kinds of symbolic motifs representing virtues, the arts and planetary deities. To this rare and beautiful survival was added in the 1930s a box-edged parterre, of vaguely 17th-century character, and it is a pretty sight viewed from the upper rooms of the castle and corner towers of the garden walls.

FALKLAND PALACE
Fife

Falkland KY7 7BU
11m N of Kircaldy by A912
Tel: 0337 57397

Owner: National Trust for
Scotland

Open: Apr to Sept, Mon to
Sat 10–6, Sun 2–6; Oct,
Mon to Sat 10–5, Sun 2–5.
7 acres. Palace open

HIDDEN BEHIND stone walls in the centre of
Falkland the gardens still have the feeling of a
royal 'privy' garden. The 16th-century palace of the
Kings of Scotland, formerly a Stewart hunting lodge,
gives immense character to what is an almost entirely
20th-century garden. Large areas of lawn are broken
by island beds lavishly planted with shrubs and
ornamental trees – a scheme designed by Percy Cane
in the 1950s. These beds are straight where they run
along the perimeter walls but curved where they face
each other across the lawn, giving a lively, sinuous
walk between them. A giant mixed border almost 500
feet long faces west across the lawn to a blue and
white herbaceous border and a dazzling new border
of delphiniums. At the southern extremity of the
lawn monumental yew hedges shelter a lily pond and
at an upper level there is a formal arrangement of
yellow ('Allgold') and scarlet ('Frensham') roses – the
heraldic colours of the Stewarts – underplanted with
lavender and silver *Brachyglottis greyi* and given
emphasis with pyramids of golden yew.

GARDEN COTTAGE
Highland

Tournaig, Poolewe,
Achnasheen, Ross-shire
IV22 2LH
6m NE of Gairloch by
A832
Tel: 044 586 339

Open: Mar to Oct, daily
except Sun 12–7

Illustration: Tropaeolum
speciosum

THE RUSHBROOKES' NURSERY, just up the road from Inverewe, is a most attractive place; it is also one of the very few to offer midge-nets to visitors. A large number of plants is grown in their small and decorative garden which sprawls among mossy outcrops of rocks half shaded by old birches. There is an alpine emphasis but many other kinds of plants are sold, especially herbaceous perennials – an excellent range of geraniums, ornamental grasses and a huge selection of primulas, probably the best part of the list, with many species and unusual named varieties. Prices are very modest, a catalogue is issued and a mail order service provided.

GLENDOICK GARDENS
Tayside

Glendoick, Perth,
Perthshire PH2 7NS
6m E of Perth by A85
Tel: 0738 86205

Open: Daily 9–5; garden:
May, daily 2–5

AT FIRST GLANCE this looks like just another a big garden centre but although it carries a wide stock of plants and garden sundries, its overwhelming interest to gardeners lies in its outstanding collection of rhododendrons, one of the largest and most comprehensive stocks commercially available in Britain. Glendoick's proprietor, Peter Cox, is an authority on rhododendrons of which he has introduced many new species and hybrids. In the private garden adjoining the nursery the great collection, started by Peter Cox's father, may be visited at flowering time and it is well worth making a special visit to see it. But visitors to the nursery at other times will find much to interest and tempt them. Glendoick runs a mail order service for rhododendrons only and its catalogue is an amazing treasure trove.

GLENWHAN GARDEN
Dumfries & Galloway

Dunragit, by Stranraer,
Wigtownshire DG9 8PH
7m E of Stranraer by A75
Tel: 058 14 222

Owner: Mr and Mrs
William Knott

Open: Easter to Sept, daily
10–5. 7 acres

HIGH ABOVE the main road to Stranraer, Glenwhan Garden spreads out over a windy hilltop with marvellous views of Luce bay and the Mull of Galloway. Since 1979 the Knotts have made a very large, interesting and individual garden that is filled with good plants. At its heart is a large pool divided by a grassy causeway and fed by a tumbling stream. The slopes above are densely planted with trees and shrubs. Several different habitats are provided by the lie of the land and the wet, mild climate promotes luxuriant growth. There is no point in beginning to list plants – almost any gardener will find something unfamiliar here. But this is not just a plant collection for there are all sorts of well planned ornamental schemes and wonderful views over water and hills. There is a small nursery attached to the garden with a good collection of plants for sale, including an interesting selection of heathers.

GREENBANK GARDEN
Strathclyde

Flenders Road, Clarkston,
Glasgow G76 8RB
6m S of city centre
Tel: 041 639 3281

Owner: National Trust for
Scotland

Open: Daily 9.30–sunset.
16 acres

GREENBANK is an irresistibly decorative 18th-century Scottish house of stucco and stone with a pediment capped with urns. South of the house an old walled kitchen garden, of the same date as the house, is divided into several enclosures with, at its heart, a rondel of clipped yew hedges and a sundial. In other enclosed areas there is that beguiling mixture, so often found in Scottish gardens, of ornamental planting and fruit and vegetables. Old espaliered apple trees rise out of mixed borders which are particularly rich in shrub roses, and orderly vegetable beds spread beneath the walls. Beyond, a surrounding woodland garden provides further seclusion. At Greenbank the National Trust for Scotland runs a rare and worthwhile service – an advice centre specifically for owners of small gardens.

HIGHLAND LILIUMS
Highland

Kiltarlity, by Beauly,
Inverness-shire IV4 7JQ
12m SW of Inverness by
A862 and A833
Tel: 046 374 272

Open: Mon to Sat 9–5

Illustration: Alstroemeria
'Ligtu' hybrid

DESPITE ITS NAME this is a general nursery with a wide-ranging stock. Although there are no startling rarities here there are quite enough good plants to stock a very nice garden indeed. Alpine and rock plants are very well represented; among herbaceous perennials there are attractive collections of astilbes, hostas, irises, meconopsis, phlox, particularly good primulas and several forms of trollius; there is a specialist selection of grasses and a good range of flowering shrubs; and last of all, there *are* many lilies, all cultivars, sold conveniently in 3-litre pots. Many more plants are grown at the nursery than it is possible to list in the catalogue so a visit is all the more worthwhile. A mail order service is provided.

HILL OF TARVIT HOUSE
Fife

nr Cupar KY15 5PD
2 1/2m S of Cupar by A916
Tel: 0334 53127

Owner: National Trust for Scotland

Open: Daily 10–sunset. 10 acres. House open

Robert Lorimer rebuilt the 17th-century mansion at Hill of Tarvit in 1906 and gave it a new formal garden on the slopes below. Here an avenue of sentinel yews, blown sideways by the wind, links yew-hedged terraces which descend to the pastures below. A long border under the first terrace is planted with perennials and annuals and, specially planned for the blind and those with poor sight, has a section of aromatic plants with labels in braille. On one side a lead satyr pipes at the centre of a formal rose garden and, by the house, a well-head is decorated with a beautiful wrought-iron overthrow designed by Lorimer. Above the house, sweeping along a high wall interrupted by a grand iron gate, a deep border has repeated plantings of kolkwitzia, purple cotinus, philadelphus and *Rosa moyesii* underplanted with anemones, campanulas, geraniums and potentillas. The Edwardian potting shed, heady with compost, is also on view.

HOUSE OF PITMUIES
Tayside

Guthrie, by Forfar, Angus
DD8 2SN
8m E of Forfar by A932
Tel: 024 12 245

Owner: Mrs Farquhar
Ogilvie

Open: Apr to Oct, daily
10–5. 25 acres

To the front of the early Georgian house a gentlemanly atmosphere prevails – fine parkland beyond a ha-ha is framed by old trees, including an exceptional sweet chestnut. The flower garden is behind the house where, in an old walled garden, lavishly planted borders are planned to maintain their flowering interest over a very long season. Colour schemes are fastidiously chosen; a double border, for example, seen from the drawing-room window has a scheme of blue, cream, white and yellow to go with the colours of the room. Throughout this part of the garden use is made of shrub roses but abundant other planting, woody and herbaceous, extends the flowering period. The busy-ness of borders is alleviated by occasional simpler schemes – a collection of old delphinium cultivars, a stately walk of *Prunus serrula* with its glistening, peeling bark, hedges of coppiced *Prunus pissardii* and an airy arch of clipped silver pear. Beyond the walled garden a riverside walk leads past a castellated dovecote through old woodland of marvellous beeches and oaks underplanted with ornamental shrubs.

INSHRIACH NURSERY
Highland

Aviemore, Inverness-shire
PH22 1QS
2m SW of Aviemore by
B970
Tel: 054 04 287

Open: Mon to Fri 9–5, Sat
9–12.30

Illustration: Lewisia
cotyledon '*Inshriach*'

AMONG ALPINE plant enthusiasts this is one of the best-known nurseries in Britain. It was founded before World War II by Jack Drake, a former colleague of Will Ingwersen's. A very wide range is carried and rarities pop up all the time. A short list, in addition to the exceptionally informative main catalogue, describes rare and unusual plants in short supply. The main list, apart from plants for the rock garden, also includes plants suitable for wild and bog gardens. A mail order service is provided and, in addition to the two lists mentioned above, a special list of seeds of alpine plants is available every winter. The nursery lies in fine birch and juniper woodland and parts have been beautifully arranged to show the plants in action.

INVERESK LODGE
Lothian

nr Musselburgh, East
Lothian EH21 6BQ
6m E of Edinburgh
Tel: 031 226 5922

Owner: National Trust for
Scotland

Open: Mon to Fri 10–4.30,
Sun 2–5. 13 acres

INVERESK is a charming village rich in distinguished houses of the 17th and 18th centuries. Inveresk Lodge belongs to the earlier period and the unpretentious walled garden with its decorative central sundial complements it well. An excellent rose border was designed by Graham Stuart Thomas; a raised alpine bed is filled with ericaceous plants; good use is made of smaller flowering trees like cherries and the garden is a model of appropriate and floriferous planting in a modest space.

INVEREWE
Highland

Poolewe, Ross &
Cromarty, IV22 2LQ
6m NE of Gairloch by
A832
Tel: 044 586 356

Owner: National Trust for
Scotland

Open: Daily 9.30–sunset.
62 acres

FAMOUS GARDENS do not always live up to their reputations but it would be hard to imagine any gardener failing to be excited by Inverewe. In 1862 Osgood Mackenzie came to this very remote corner of the western Highlands – a windswept, bare rocky site at the very edge of a sea-loch. It was 15 years before he got much to grow, but once windbreaks began to be established, the high rainfall and balmy Gulf Stream Drift climate promoted luxuriant growth. Today it is a jungle of mature exotic trees and shrubs laced with winding walks, rising and falling, which give sudden glimpses of shimmering water through foliage. Spring is obviously the showiest season but flowering interest continues throughout the year; in any case, there is immense pleasure to be had at any time in admiring the exotic bark of giant eucalyptus, myrtles and rhododendrons and much strange and beautiful foliage.

KELLIE CASTLE
Fife

nr Pittenweem KY10 2RF
3m NW of Pittenweem by
B9171
Tel: 0333 8271

Owner: National Trust for
Scotland

Open: Daily 10–sunset.
1 1/3 acre. Castle open

ON SOUTH-FACING SLOPES to the sea Kellie Castle, with its crow-steps and turrets, is the perfect Scottish castle. It dates from the 16th to the 17th century but the little walled garden nestling against the castle walls was laid out in 1880 by Robert Lorimer, a great architect in the Arts and Crafts tradition, who was then a boy of 16. Here at Kellie, his family home, he made an appropriately romantic

garden of gravel paths, box-edged beds and rose arbours. His, too, is the gardener's house in the north-west corner with a jaunty carved stone bird on the ridge. Much replanting has recently been done, keeping to plants available when the garden was first laid out, and a recently appointed head gardener has introduced organic methods throughout the garden which looks in the pink of good health.

KILDRUMMY CASTLE

Grampian

nr Alford, Aberdeenshire
AB33 8RA
10m from Alford by A944
Tel: 09755 71264/71203

Owner: Kildrummy Castle
Garden Trust

Open: Apr to Oct, daily
10–5

KILDRUMMY is in the tradition of romantic Victorian gardens where the most important ingredient is the response to the site. Here, in a glen through which flows the burn of Backden, sandstone was quarried in the late middle ages to make Kildrummy Castle whose ruins rise above the old silver firs and beeches that clothe the glen. The estate was bought in 1898 by Colonel James Ogston, a soap tycoon, who developed the garden making excellent use of the old quarry, the linked pools of the burn and its wooded banks. He commissioned a rock garden from the famous Yorkshire firm of Backhouse, and this today has a good collection of alpine plants, in particular heathers. A copy of a bridge in Aberdeen – the Brig o' Balgownie – spans the burn and paths wind along its banks giving views of rhododendrons and other flowering shrubs.

KINROSS HOUSE
Tayside

Kinross, Kinross-shire
KY13 7ET
In the centre of Kinross

Owner: Sir David
Montgomery

Open: May to Sept, daily
10–7. 4 acres

DECORATIVE GATE-PIERS mark the entrance to
Kinross House and an avenue of limes leads
straight as an arrow to the house itself, long, low and
with a distinct whiff of something French. It was
designed by Sir William Bruce for his own use in the
1680s and he also designed the garden that goes with
it. The entrance avenue forms a central axis which
continues on the far side of the house to a gate with
a beautifully carved stone surround through which is
glimpsed the ruins of Loch Leven castle.
Romantically sited on an island, this is where Mary
Queen of Scots was imprisoned in 1567. The garden
between the house and the loch descends in gentle
terraces with grassy walks and herbaceous borders.
A deep border runs along the far wall which is finely
decorated with piers and heraldic animals.

LOCHSIDE ALPINE NURSERY
Highland

Ulbster, Caithness
KW2 6AA
7m S of Wick by A9
Tel: 095 585 320

Open: Mar to Oct, daily
10–6; also by appointment

TERRY AND JANE Clarke's nursery is almost
certainly the northernmost supplier of good
plants in Britain – and possibly in Europe. It is the
only nursery I know of that is so remote that it
offers its visitors bed and breakfast hospitality. The
Clarkes' list, brief but pithy, is full of good things at
exceptionally reasonable prices: campanulas in

variety, cyclamen, outstanding gentians, many phlox, a long list of primulas and wonderful saxifrages. It is never possible for them to list everything that is for sale at the nursery so a visit is to be recommended. Plants may be supplied by mail order but they prefer to limit despatch to the period between autumn and early spring when the nursery is closed to visitors.

LOGAN BOTANIC GARDEN
Dumfries & Galloway

Port Logan, Stranraer,
Wigtownshire DG9 9ND
12m S of Stranraer by A716
Tel: 07768 6231

Owner: Royal Botanic
Gardens, Edinburgh

Open: Mid-Mar to Oct,
daily 10–5. 10 1/2 acres

Illustration: Calceolaria *x*
banksii *and* Cuphea cyanea

PORT LOGAN lies in the middle of a narrow spit of land, the Mull of Galloway, which juts out into the sea in the extreme south-west of Scotland. A grove of Chusan palms immediately announces the character of this place – sub-tropical plants flourish here and provide some rare and beautiful sights. The garden was started by the McDouall family who lived here for 800 years, and since 1969 it has been in the care of the Royal Botanic Garden at Edinburgh. But this is not just a botanic garden, for it is beautifully laid out, particularly in the walled garden which has fine terraces and well planned borders under an avenue of cabbage palms (*Cordyline australis*). The climate is exceptionally mild and several different habitats provide conditions for a huge range of tender plants. A small selection of plants is offered for sale.

Malleny House
Lothian

Balerno, Midothian
EH14 7AF
In Balerno, 7m SW of
Edinburgh by A70
Tel: 031449 2283

Owner: National Trust for
Scotland

Open: Daily 10–dusk.
2 acres

THE HOUSE at Malleny is an ornamental riddle
with features of the 17th and 18th centuries and
hints of something much older. Its tower and conical
roof on the garden side contribute much to the
atmosphere of the place. A walled enclosure divided
by a yew hedge lies at the heart of the garden with a
splendid quartet of ancient yew trees clipped into the
shape of pointed mushrooms. Roses are everywhere
and Malleny has a National Collection of
19th-century shrub roses which are mingled with
other plants in handsome mixed borders on two sides
of the walled garden. There is, in addition, a separate
collection of modern roses. In a corner of the garden
behind the greenhouse is displayed a collection of
bonsai arranged by the Scottish Bonsai Society.
Despite being in the suburbs of Edinburgh, Malleny
has the remote and soothing athosphere of an
old-fashioned garden in the depths of the country.

Mellerstain
Borders

nr Gordon, Berwickshire
TD3 6LG
9m NW of Kelso by A6089
Tel: 057 381 292

Owner: The Earl of
Haddington

Open: Easter weekend
12.30–5; May to Sept, daily
except Sat 12.30–5. House
open

THE GREAT EARLY 18TH-CENTURY house at
Mellerstain, designed by William Adam and later
added to by his son Robert, originally had a formal
garden that was removed in the 18th-century
landscape gardening craze. In the early 20th century,
however, a version of it was reinstated by the

architect Sir Reginald Blomfield. A row of clipped cones of yew runs across the back of the house and terraces descend in stately progression – starting with a splendid double staircase – ornamented with parterres of modern roses, lavender, clipped shapes of box and generous lawns. All this provides a decorative foreground for the curvaceous lake set in woodland below – the last remains of William Adam's very early landscape scheme of the late 1720s with idyllic views of the Cheviot Hills in the distance.

THE MURREL GARDENS
Fife

Aberdour KY3 0RN
1m N of Aberdour by A987
Tel: 0383 860158

Owner: John Milne

Open: End Apr to
mid-Sept, Wed 10–5.
7 1/2 acres

HIDDEN IN A FOLD of land facing south towards the Firth of Forth, The Murrel has a rare site. Designed in 1908 by Frank Deas in the Arts and Crafts style the house and garden have been excellently restored since 1984 by a new owner. To one side of the house, on south-facing slopes, a walled garden gives protection to many tender plants rarely seen out-of-doors in these parts, such as *Buddleja crispa* and *Pittosporum tobira*. Below the walled garden a formal sunken garden with rose beds leads to a water garden overhung with old rhododendrons and ornamental trees. A ravine-like wild garden, still being replanted but already exquisitely beautiful, leads back up the hill where, to the west of the house, a large rock garden is laid out with scree beds. An excellent range of plants, some unusual and propagated in the garden, is for sale.

PITMEDDEN

Grampian

nr Pitmedden, Ellon,
Aberdeenshire AB4 0PD
14m N of Aberdeen by
A92(T) and B999
Tel: 065 13 2352

Owner: National Trust for
Scotland

Open: May to Sept, daily
10–6. 4 3/4 acres

IN THIS REMOTE CORNER of Aberdeenshire is one of the most beguiling gardens you could hope to see. History first: it was made by Sir Alexander Seton in 1675, influenced by fashionable French gardening ideas of the time. In 1818 the house was burnt down, the estate changed hands and the original garden disappeared. However, the garden walls, elegant pavilions, garden steps and gate-piers all survived and the National Trust for Scotland, starting in 1954, had the clever idea of planting immense formal parterres with a central avenue of clipped yew pyramids and a fountain. The patterns of some of the parterres were based on a 17th-century engraving. They are edged in intricately shaped box hedges with compartments filled with coloured chippings and arrangements of annuals, blocks of a single colour, different every year. One of the parterres has a characteristically Scottish multi-facetted sundial and another traces the Seton family arms and motto. None of this is historically authentic but, looking down from the surrounding terraces with their beautiful gazebos, the effect is marvellous and unforgettable. Running along the south- and east-facing walls are a pair of excellent borders designed by Lady Burnett of Leys who lived nearby at Crathes Castle. Up above the walled garden a tunnel of old varieties of apples leads to a formal herb garden.

PLANTS FROM THE PAST
Lothian

The Old House, 1 North Street, Belhaven, Dunbar, East Lothian EH42 1NU 27m E of Edinburgh by A1 in the W suburbs of Dunbar
Tel: 0368 63223

Open: Mar to Sept, daily except Tue 1–6

Illustration: Aquilegia 'Nora Barlow'

THIS VERY UNUSUAL and admirable nursery run by David Stuart and James Sutherland specialises in old varieties of chiefly herbaceous plants, about which David Stuart has written excellent books. Its owners are not interested in fashionable modern cultivars but in the older forms and species of garden plants which have been swept aside by changing tastes. Thus, while selling desirable and unusual plants, whose decorative charms will be a surprise to many visitors, they also help the cause of garden plant conservation. Aquilegias, campanulas, mints, pinks, violets and perennial wallflowers are stocked in variety. The nursery itself is in a charming walled garden with, at its heart, the elegant 18th-century stone summer house of the Lairds of Bielmouth. A new parterre has recently been laid out, based on a design from an 18th-century painting, with a pattern of box-edged beds densely planted with herbaceous perennials. A particularly informative catalogue is produced and plants may be ordered by post.

POYNTZFIELD HERB NURSERY
Highland

Poyntzfield, Black Isle, by
Dingwall, Ross &
Cromarty IV7 8LX
10m NE of Inverness by A9
and minor roads
Tel: None

Open: Mar to Oct, Mon to
Sat 1–5

THE BLACK ISLE is a romantic peninsula on the east coast well north of Inverness and this is one of the northernmost nurseries in Britain. Because of this it has special interest. It specialises in herbs and, over the years, a collection of clones has been built up that are hardy in this severe climate. Thus, anyone buying plants here may be confident that they are acquiring pretty tough customers. Over 300 varieties are stocked, all organically grown, and there is a particularly attractive collection of culinary plants native to Scotland. An extremely informative catalogue is produced which, as far as I know, is the only one that gives common names in Gaelic, where they exist. A mail order service is provided.

ROYAL BOTANIC GARDEN
Edinburgh

Inverleith Row, EH3 5LR
1m N of the centre of
Edinburgh
Tel: 031 552 7171

Owner: Department of
Agriculture and Fisheries
for Scotland

Open: Mon to Sat
9–sunset, Sun 11–sunset;
closed Jan 1. 75 acres

ONE OF THE OLDEST botanic gardens in Britain, it was founded in 1670 and moved to its present site in 1820. Today, from the gardener's point of view, it is an exciting place. There are areas of specific habitats – an unforgettable rock garden, a woodland garden and a peat garden; collections of rhododendrons, heaths and alpines; several magnificent glasshouses; marvellous trees everywhere; and excellent demonstration gardens. These are ingredients found in dozens of botanic gardens but at Edinburgh the beauty of the setting – high, undulating land with sweeping views of the city to the south and the glittering Firth of Forth to the north – the exemplary standards of upkeep, and the liveliness of it all make it exceptional. Also, unlike other botanic gardens, Edinburgh seems to have the interests of the ordinary gardener close to heart. For its size the Royal Botanic Garden has a remarkably diverse collection, so one plant or another will be flowering at any time of the year. Places like this set standards from which all gardeners may learn and which all should have a go at emulating.

SPEYSIDE HEATHER
Highland

Skye of Curr, Dulnain
Bridge, Inverness-shire
PH26 3PA
9m NE of Aviemore by
A95
Tel: 047 895 359

Open: Daily 9–5.30; Nov
to Mar, closed Sun

DAVID AND BETTY Lambie sell a very wide range of heathers and over 300 varieties are shown planted with appropriate conifers and shrubs in their display garden. A well produced booklet is published with an immense amount of valuable information: the different varieties are described, suggestions are made for garden designs and advice is given about cultivation. This is one of the best places in Britain to buy heathers and to see them in splendid colourful action. A mail order service is provided.

THREAVE SCHOOL OF GARDENING
Dumfries & Galloway

Stewartry, Castle Douglas,
Kircudbrightshire DG7 1RX
1m W of Castle Douglas by
A75
Tel: 0556 2575

Owner: National Trust for
Scotland

Open: Daily 9–sunset.
65 acres

THE NATIONAL TRUST FOR SCOTLAND has its own school of horticulture here and the gardens, largely created by the students since the school started in 1960, are of great interest. Mature woodland of beech, conifers and oak forms the background to a large collection of shrub roses, sweeping mixed borders, many dwarf heathers and conifers, peat and rock gardens, a collection of over 200 narcissi and a youthful arboretum that is already showing its paces. A walled kitchen garden has splendidly blowsy borders and superbly maintained glasshouses. Threave holds a National Collection of penstemons which, in high summer, may seen used in several borders throughout the garden.

YOUNGER BOTANIC GARDEN
Strathclyde

Benmore, Dunoon,
Argyllshire PA23 8QU
7m N of Dunoon by A815
Tel: 0369 6261

Owner: Department of
Agriculture and Fisheries
for Scotland

Open: Mid-Mar to Oct,
daily 10–6. 120 acres

Illustration: Rhododendron
morii

THE YOUNGER BOTANIC GARDEN is a country
annexe of the Royal Botanic Garden in
Edinburgh. Its history starts in the 1820s with the
first plantings of conifers and later in the century,
between 1870 and 1883, the owner, James Duncan,
planted well over 6,000,000 trees. Today, superb old
specimens of Douglas firs, larch, Scots pine and a
splendid avenue of Wellingtonias (*Sequioadendron
giganteum*) make a wonderful background to
subsequent collections of ornamental shrubs and
trees. The mild climate and very high rainfall
promotes spectacular growth in conifers and some of
the specimens here are among the largest in the
British Isles: examples of the Caucasian fir (*Abies
nordmanniana*) and the beautiful fir (*Abies amabilis*)
are the tallest in Britain. The climate also makes this
an ideal place for rhododendrons and large numbers
of those newly introduced from the Himalayas were
planted in the early part of the 20th century. Today
there are about 250 different species and cultivars,
including some natural hybrids that bear the name
'Benmore'. There are excellent specimens, too, of
deciduous trees such as southern beeches (*Nothofagus*
species), *Davidia involucrata* and tulip trees, and
autumn is brilliant with the foliage of azaleas,
cercidiphyllums and maples.

NORTHERN IRELAND

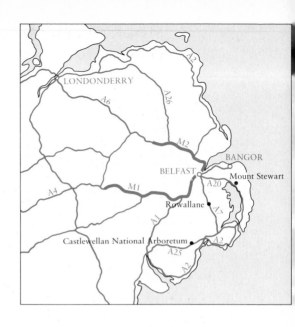

CASTLEWELLAN NATIONAL ARBORETUM

County Down

Castlewellan BT25 9KG
30m S of Belfast by A24
and minor roads
Tel: 03967 78664

Owner: Department of
Agriculture (Northern
Ireland)

Open: Daily, dawn–dusk.
108 acres

THE ANNESLEY FAMILY started this great arboretum and plant collection in the 1870s. It benefits from a fine site, with a curving lake, in the foothills of the Mourne Mountains near the coast of southern County Down. The original 12 1/2-acre walled arboretum, now called the Annesley Garden, has fine borders and exceptional flowering shrubs and ornamental trees, many of them rare and tender species from the southern hemisphere such as the evergreen *Carpodetus serratus* from New Zealand and *Pilgerodendron uviferum* from the Andes. North of the walled garden, azaleas, camellias and rhododendrons thrive under the canopy of beech and oak. An area of woodland by the lake is planted with deciduous trees chosen for especially brilliant autumn colouring. Throughout the arboretum there are outstanding specimens of trees, several of which date from the original 19th-century plantings.

MOUNT STEWART

County Down

Newtownards BT22 2AD
15m E of Belfast by A20
Tel: 024 774 387

Owner: The National
Trust

Open: Apr to Aug, daily
except Tue 12–6; Sept to
Oct, Sat and Sun 12–6. 78
acres. House open

GOOD GARDENS often bear the stamp of one exceptional creator, but few so firmly as Mount Stewart. Edith, Marchioness of Londonderry came to Mount Stewart as a young wife in 1921 and plunged into the making of the garden; today, restored by the National Trust, it is still very much as she made it. The climate at Mount Stewart is exceptionally mild with high humidity from the sea. This allows an exceptional range of tender plants: huge eucalyptus, an avenue of the New Zealand cabbage palm (*Cordyline australis*) and tender conifers such as *Cupressus cashmiriana*. To the west of the house a sunken garden is surrounded on three sides by a pergola with roses, vines and the rare *Billardiera longiflora* with brilliant blue berries in autumn. Beds in the centre are brilliant in spring with orange azaleas and in summer with a rich mixture of herbaceous plants. Behind the house the Italian garden is a giant parterre in which the beds – edged with purple berberis or golden thuya – have artful but ebullient colour schemes: grey, white and blue to the west and orange, yellow and scarlet to the east.

Curious statues of monkeys and other animals decorate the enclosing walls. On the far side of the house woodland, with many rhododendrons and ornamental trees, presses in on a lake whose banks are planted with drifts of iris, crocosmia or kniphofia. Mount Stewart is nothing if not bold, but Lady Londonderry's strong sense of design holds it brilliantly together and makes it one of the finest gardens in Britain.

ROWALLANE GARDEN
County Down

Saintfield, Ballynahinch
BT24 7LH
11m SE of Belfast by A7
Tel: 0238 510131

Owner: The National
Trust

Open: Nov to Mar, daily
except Sat and Sun 10.30–5
(closed 25, 26 Dec and
1 Jan); Apr to Oct daily
10.30–6 (weekends 2–6). 20
acres

Illustration: Penstemon
'George Home'

THE DRIVE leading up to Rowallane passes through dense woodland with mossy rocks pressing in on either side. The garden was chiefly made by Hugh Armytage Moore who came here in 1903. He was particularly interested in woody plants, especially rhododendrons which he planted in the handsomely undulating site in bold clumps and belts, as though they were the ingredients of a landscape garden. Many of his plantings were raised from seed collected by the great plant-hunters of the early 20th century – such as Wilson, Forrest and Kingdon-Ward. The microclimate is very benign, as the many species from the southern hemisphere show – olearias from Australia, the orange-flowered *Desfontainea spinosa* from Chile and *Pseudowintera colorata*, with curiously variegated foliage, from New Zealand. The character of the garden is essentially informal but in the walled garden beds have excellent shrub roses and flowering shrubs, and the National Collection of large-flowered penstemons.

TYPES OF GARDENS
AND GARDEN FEATURES

Arboreta
Batsford Arboretum
Bedgebury National Pinetum
Borde Hill
Castlewellan National Arboretum
Exbury Gardens
Hergest Croft
The Hillier Garden and Arboretum
Milton Lodge
Ness Garden
Royal Botanic Garden, Edinburgh
Royal Botanic Garden, Kew
Thorp Perrow
Wakehurst Place
Westonbirt
Winkworth

Especially Good Borders
Arley Hall
Barnsley House
Benington Lordship
Blickling Hall
Cottesbrooke Hall
Crathes Castle
Falkland Palace
Great Dixter
Hardwick Hall
Helmingham Hall
House of Pitmuies
Kellie Castle
Knightshayes Court
Mount Stewart
Parham House
Powis Castle
The Priory
Tintinhull House
Upton House

Botanic Gardens
Cambridge Botanic Gardens
Chelsea Physic Garden
Harlow Car Botanical Gardens
Logan Botanic Garden
Oxford Botanic Garden
Royal Botanic Garden, Edinburgh
Royal Botanic Garden, Kew
Younger Botanic Garden

Demonstration Gardens
Capel Manor

County Demonstration Garden
Harlow Car
Wisley Garden

Herb Gardens
Acorn Bank
Gunby Hall
Haddlesey Herb and Heather Centre
Hardwick Hall
Hollington Nurseries
Iden Croft
Leeds Castle
Lower Severalls Herb Nursery
Pitmedden
Poyntzfield Herb Nursery
Scotney Castle
Sissinghurst Castle

Japanese Gardens
Compton Acres
Heale House
Newstead Abbey
Saling Hall
Tatton Park

Kitchen Gardens
Barnsley House
Calke Abbey
Clumber Park
Earlshall Castle
Edmondsham House
Felbrigg Hall
Greys Court
Harlow Car
Gunby Hall
Helmingham Hall
Lackham College
Tintinhull House
Upton House
Wisley Garden

Landscape Gardens
Antony House
Blenheim Palace
Bowood
Claremont
Farnborough Hall
Mount Edgcumbe
Osterley Park
Painshill

Painswick Rococo Garden
Petworth
Rievaulx Terrace
Royal Botanic Garden, Kew
Scotney Castle
Sheffield Park
Sheringham Park
Shugborough
Stourhead
Stowe
Studley Royal
West Wycombe Park
Wolterton Park

Rock Gardens
Killerton House
Luton Hoo
Newby Hall
Royal Botanic Garden, Edinburgh
Sizergh Castle
Wisley Garden

Rose Gardens
Castle Howard
Cliveden
The Gardens of the Rose
Hyde Hall
Kiftsgate Court
Malleny House
Mannington Hall
Mottisfont Abbey
Polesden Lacy
Queen Mary's Garden
Sissinghurst Castle
Sudeley Castle
Warwick Castle

Water and Bog Gardens
Burnby Hall
Buscot Park
Beth Chatto Gardens
Coleton Fishacre
Docton Mill
Forde Abbey
Hodnet Hall
Marwood Hill Gardens
Sezincote
Stapeley Water Gardens
Westbury Court

Woodland Gardens
Abbotsbury Sub-tropical Gardens
Achamore

Antony Woodland Garden
Arbigland
Bodnant
Borde Hill
Brodick Castle
Caerhays Castle
The Dorothy Clive Garden
Castle Howard
Cotehele
Cragside
Crarae Garden
Exbury Gardens
Furzey Gardens
Glendurgan Garden
Gravetye Manor
Great Comp
Greencombe
Hare Hill
The High Beeches
Howick Hall
Inverewe
Killerton House
Knightshayes Court
Leonardslee
Muncaster Castle
Nymans
Rowallane
Saltram House
Savill Garden
Scotney Castle
Sheffield Park
Trebah
Telissick
Trengwainton
Trewithen

NURSERIES FOR SPECIFIC
KINDS OF PLANTS

Alpines
Abriachan Nurseries
Ardfearn Nursery
Edrom Nursery
Field House Nurseries
W. & L. Harley
Holden Clough Nursery
W.E.Th. Ingwersen
Inshriach Nursery
Reginald Kaye Ltd
Lochside Alpine Nursery
Norden Alpines
Old Court Nurseries

Padlock Croft
Perhill Nurseries
Potterton & Martin
Redhouse Nurseries
Rookhope Nurseries

Aquatic Plants
Rowden Gardens
Stapeley Water Gardens Ltd

Auriculas
Field House Nurseries

Bulbs
Jacques Amand
Avon Bulbs
Broadleigh Gardens
Paradise Centre

Camellias
Burncoose & Southdown
Coghurst
Marwood Hill Garden
Starborough
Jas. Trehane & Sons Ltd

Campanulas
Padlock Croft
W. E. Th. Ingwersen
Reginald Kaye Ltd
Norden Alpines
Plants from a Country Garden

Chrysanthemums
Philip Tivey & Sons
H.Woolman Ltd

Citrus Fruit
Reads Nursery

Clematis
John Beach Ltd
Caddick's Clematis Nursery
Fisk's Clematis Nursery
Great Dixter
Peveril Clematis Nursery
Treasures of Tenbury Ltd

Colchicums
Broadleigh Gardens
W.E.Th. Ingwersen
Conifers
Blooms of Bressingham

Hilliers Nurseries Ltd
Kenwith Nursery
Plaxtol

Cyclamen
Tile Barn Nursery

Dahlias
Philip Tivey & Sons
Oscroft's Dahlias

Daylilies
Apple Court

Delphiniums
Blackmore & Langdon Ltd

Ferns
J. & D. Marston

Fruit Trees
Deacons Nursery
Hilliers Nurseries Ltd
Reads Nursery
Scott's Nursery

Fuchsias
B. and H.M. Baker
Clapton Court
Oakleigh Nurseries

Geraniums
East Lambrook Manor
Glebe Cottage Plants
Plants from a Country Garden
Rushfields of Ledbury

Grasses
Apple Court
Hoecroft Plants
Rushfields of Ledbury

Heathers
Haddesley Herb and Heather Centre
Plaxtol
Speyside Heather

Hellebores
Avon Bulbs
Blackthorn Nursery
Fibrex Nurseries Ltd
Reginald Kaye Ltd

Herbaceous Perennials
Blackthorn Nursery
Blooms of Bressingham
Bosvigo House
Beth Chatto Garden
Cally Garden
Church Hill Cottage Garden
East Lambrook Manor
Eastgrove Cottage Gardens
Foxgrove Plants
Gannocks Growers
Garden Cottage
Green Farm Plants
Hadspen House
The Hannays of Bath
W. & L. Harley
Old Court Nurseries Ltd
Perhill Nurseries
Perry's Plants
Plants from a Country Garden
Plants from the Past
Rowden Gardens
Rushfields of Ledbury
Stillingfleet Lodge Nursery

Herbs
Daphne ffiske
Haddesley Herb and Heather Centre
Hollington Nurseries
Iden Croft
Lower Severalls Herb Nursery
Poyntzfield Herb Nursery

Hostas
Apple Court
Hadspen House
Park Green Nurseries

Irises
Zephyrwude

Ivy
Fibrex Nurseries Ltd

Magnolias
Burncoose & Southdown Nurseries
Pickards
Spinners
Starborough Nursery

Maples
Mallet Court Nursery
Spinners

Starborough Nursery

Peonies
Kelways Nurseries

Pelargoniums
Clapton Court
Denmead Geranium Nursery
Fibrex Nurseries Ltd
Oakleigh Nurseries

Pinks
Glebe Cottage Plants
Hayward's Carnations
W.E.Th. Ingwersen
Plants from a Country Garden

Primulas
Abriachan Nurseries
Edrom Nurseries
Garden Cottage
Glebe Cottage
W.E.Th. Ingwersen
Inshriach Nursery
Norden Alpines
Paradise Centre
Rowden Gardens

Rhododendrons
Burncoose and Southdown
Glendoick Gardens
Lea Gardens
G. Reuthe
Spinners
Starborough

Roses
David Austin
Peter Beale's Roses
Cranborne Manor
R. Harkness & Co Ltd
Mattock's Roses
Roses du Temps Passé
Scott's Nurseries Ltd
Sudeley Castle

Shrubs
Burncoose and Southdown
Hillier's Nurseries Ltd
Hopley's Plants
Notcutt's Nurseries Ltd
Spinners

Snowdrops
Avon Bulbs

Trees
Gardener's World
Hillier's Nurseries Ltd
Mallet Court
Notcutt's Nurseries Ltd
Scott's Nurseries Ltd
Spinners

Tulips
Jacques Amand
Broadleigh Gardens
W.E.Th. Ingwersen

Violas and Pansies
Hazeldene
W.E.Th. Ingwersen
Norden Alpines

Water Lilies
Stapeley Water Gardens Ltd

GARDENS BY FAMOUS DESIGNERS

Sir Reginald Blomfield (1856–1942)
Mellerstain
Sulgrave Manor

Charles Bridgeman (d.1738)
Claremont
Rousham Hall
Stowe
Wimpole Hall
Wolterton Park

Lancelot 'Capability' Brown (1716–83)
Blenheim Palace
Bowood
Chatsworth
Chilham Castle
Claremont
Clumber Park
Euston Hall
Harewood House
Luton Hoo
Petworth
Sheffield Park
Stowe
Warwick Castle
Wimpole Hall

Wrest Park

Percy Cane (1881–1976)
Dartington Hall
Falkland Palace

Dame Sylvia Crowe (1901–)
Cottesbrooke Hall

William Emes (1730–1803)
Belton House
Erddig

Beatrix Farrand (1872–1959)
Dartington Hall

W.S. Gilpin (1762–1843)
Balcaskie
Scotney Castle

Gertrude Jekyll (1843–1932)
Broughton Castle
Hatchlands
Hestercombe
Knebworth

Sir Geoffrey Jellicoe (1900–)
Cliveden
Cottesbrooke Hall
Mottisfont Abbey

William Kent (1685–1748)
Claremont
Euston Hall
Rousham House
Stowe

George London (d. 1714)
Petworth

Sir Robert Lorimer (1864–1929)
Earlshall
Hill of Tarvit
Kellie Castle

Sir Edwin Lutyens (1869–1944)
Castle Drogo
Hestercombe
Knebworth

Thomas Mawson (1861–1933)
Wightwick Manor

W.A. Nesfield (1793–1881)
Balcaskie
Castle Howard

Russell Page (1906–85)
Leeds Castle
Port Lympne

Sir Joseph Paxton (1803–65)
Chatsworth
Somerleyton
Tatton Park

Harold Peto (1854–1933)
Buscot Park
Heale House
Iford Manor
West Dean Gardens

Humphry Repton (1752–1818)
Antony House
Bowood
Clumber Park
Hatchlands
Plas Newydd
Sheffield Park
Sheringham Park
Tatton Park
Wimpole Hall

William Robinson (1838–1935)
Emmetts
Gravetye Manor
Killerton House
Nymans

Lanning Roper (1912–83)
Claverton Manor
Scotney Castle

Edward Weir Schultz (1860–1951)
Cottesbrooke Hall

F. Inigo Thomas (1866–1950)
Athelhampton

Sir John Vanbrugh (1644–1726)
Blenheim Palace
Claremont

NATIONAL COLLECTIONS
OF PLANTS
The National Council for the Protection
of Plants and Gardens (NCCPG) has set
up National Collections of groups of
plants, most of which are not normally
accessible to the public. However, some
of particular interest to gardeners are held
by gardens described in this book and
they are as follows:

astilbes: Marwood Hill Gardens
begonias: Stapeley Water Gardens
bromeliads: Stapeley Water Gardens
campanulas: Padlock Croft
cistus: Chelsea Physic Garden
clematises: Treasures of Tenbury Ltd
colchicums: Felbrigg Hall
crab-apples: Hyde Hall
crocosmias: Lanhydrock
daylilies: Antony House
dogwoods: Newby Hall
euphorbias: Abbey Dore Court
ferns (polystichum): Greencombe
figs: Reads Nursery
geraniums: East Lambrook Manor
hyacinth: Ripley Castle
ivy: Erddig
junipers: Bedgebury National Pinetum
kniphofias: Barton Manor
Lawson cypresses: Bedgebury National
    Pinetum
maples (excluding Acer japonicum
cultivars): Hergest Croft
Michaelmas daisies: Old Court Nurseries
oaks: The Hillier Garden and Arboretum
penstemons (large-flowered): Rowallane
pieris: The High Beeches
polygonums: Rowden Gardens
pulmonarias: Stillingfleet Lodge Nurseries
roses (pre 1900): Mottisfont Abbey
    "   (19th-century): Malleny House
saxifrages (European species): Cambridge
    Botanic Gardens
    "   (porphyrion): Waterperry
        Gardens
sedums: Abbey Dore Court
stewartias: The High Beeches
thymes: Iden Croft
viburnums: Hyde Hall

INDEX